Thinking about Friendship

Thinking about Friendship

Historical and Contemporary Philosophical Perspectives

Edited by

Damian Caluori
Trinity University, USA

palgrave
macmillan

First published 2013 by
PALGRAVE MACMILLAN

Palgrave Macmillan in the UK is an imprint of Macmillan Publishers Limited, registered in England, company number 785998, of Houndmills, Basingstoke, Hampshire RG21 6XS.

Palgrave Macmillan in the US is a division of St Martin's Press LLC, 175 Fifth Avenue, New York, NY 10010.

Palgrave Macmillan is the global academic imprint of the above companies and has companies and representatives throughout the world.

Palgrave® and Macmillan® are registered trademarks in the United States, the United Kingdom, Europe and other countries.

ISBN: 978–1–137–00398–0

This book is printed on paper suitable for recycling and made from fully managed and sustained forest sources. Logging, pulping and manufacturing processes are expected to conform to the environmental regulations of the country of origin.

A catalogue record for this book is available from the British Library.

A catalog record for this book is available from the Library of Congress.

10 9 8 7 6 5 4 3 2 1
22 21 20 19 18 17 16 15 14 13

Printed and bound in Great Britain by
CPI Antony Rowe, Chippenham and Eastbourne

To my friend K. D.

Contents

Part V Friendship in a Good Life

Acknowledgments

During the Spring Semester 2011 I organized a series of five lectures on the philosophy of friendship at Trinity University, San Antonio. I would like to thank the Martha, David and Bagby Lennox Foundation for their generous financial assistance. The lectures were accompanied by a seminar, and I am very grateful to the participating students whose enthusiasm encouraged me further to pursue the project of editing a book on this topic. I would also like to thank my colleagues at the philosophy department at Trinity University, in particular Steve Luper, for their support and advice throughout the process and Shirley Durst, our secretary, for her invaluable help in organizing the lectures and editing this volume. Finally, many thanks are due to all the contributors to this volume.

Contributors

Spyros Benetatos is teaching Ancient Philosophy at the Panteion University of Social and Political Sciences in Athens. He earned his PhD from the National University of Athens with a thesis on 'Friendship in Aristotle' and is participating in the International Research Program 'Ethics in Antiquity: The Quest for the Good Life' at the Centre for Advanced Study (CAS) at the Norwegian Academy of Science and Letters.

Curtis Brown is Professor of Philosophy at Trinity University. He has published articles on the philosophy of mind in such journals as *Philosophical Studies, Philosophy and Phenomenological Research,* and *Synthese*. He is the co-editor of an ethics text, *The Moral Life* (1999) and of a collection of essays, *Drugs, Morality, and the Law* (1994).

Damian Caluori is Assistant Professor of Philosophy at Trinity University. His research focuses on Ancient Philosophy, in particular Plato and late ancient Platonism. He has published articles on Plato, Aristotle, Plotinus, Damascius, and the Renaissance skeptic Franciscus Sanchez, whose main work, *That Nothing Is Known,* he co-translated from Latin into German.

Thomas Hurka is Chancellor Henry N. R. Jackman Distinguished Professor of Philosophical Studies at the University of Toronto. He is the author of *Perfectionism* (1993), *Virtue, Vice, and Value* (2001), *The Best Things in Life* (2011), and numerous articles in moral and political philosophy.

Ullrich Langer is Alfred Glauser Professor of French and Director of the Center for Early Modern Studies at the University of Wisconsin, Madison. His most recent book *Penser les formes du plaisir littéraire à la Renaissance* (2009) concerns philosophical definitions of pleasure and literary form. He is working on the concept of equity in early modern intellectual and literary culture.

Sheila Lintott is Associate Professor of Philosophy at Bucknell University with research interests in feminist philosophy, philosophical aesthetics, and environmental philosophy. Her work appears in journals such as *Hypatia, Environmental Ethics, Journal of Aesthetic Education,* and

British Journal of Aesthetics. She has also edited or co-edited three books and is presently working on a book-length manuscript on friendship.

John Lippitt is Professor of Ethics and Philosophy of Religion at the University of Hertfordshire. His interests include Kierkegaard, the philosophy of love and friendship, the virtues, the relationship between philosophy and theology, the relevance of philosophy to psychotherapy, and the philosophy of education. His publications include *Humour and Irony in Kierkegaard's Thought* (2000), the *Routledge Philosophy Guidebook to Kierkegaard and Fear and Trembling* (2003), and *Kierkegaard and the Problem of Self-love* (2013). He is co-editor of *The Oxford Handbook of Kierkegaard* (2013).

Anthony A. Long is Professor of Classics and Irving G. Stone Professor of Literature and Affiliated Professor of Philosophy and Rhetoric at the University of California at Berkeley. He is the author and editor of many books on ancient philosophy, including, *The Cambridge Companion to Early Greek Philosophy* (1999), *Epictetus: A Stoic and Socratic Guide to Life* (2002), and *From Epicurus to Epictetus. Studies in Hellenistic and Roman Philosophy* (2006). His most recent work, on Greek models of mind, soul, and human identity, has been presented as a series of lectures in 2012 at Renmin University, Beijing.

Alastair Norcross is Associate Professor of Philosophy at the University of Colorado, Boulder. He has co-edited *Killing and Letting Die* (1994) and written many articles on ethical theory. His overarching project is to make the world safe for consequentialist theories, in particular utilitarianism.

Jeffrey Seidman is Associate Professor of Philosophy at Vassar College. His research centers on the nature of caring and on the roles that caring plays in moral agency, rational agency, and autonomous agency.

Oliver Sensen is Associate Professor of Philosophy at Tulane University. He is the author of *Kant on Human Dignity* (2011), editor of *Kant on Moral Autonomy* (2012), and co-editor of *Kant's 'Tugendlehre'* (2012). In addition, he has published articles on Kant and autonomy, constructivism, dignity, the formula of humanity, freedom, political philosophy, the respect owed to others, and value.

Michael Slote is UST Professor of Ethics in the philosophy department at the University of Miami. He is a member of the Royal Irish Academy. He is also a past Tanner Lecturer and a past president of the American Society for Value Inquiry. His books include *From Morality to Virtue*

(1992), *Morals from Motives* (2001), *The Ethics of Care and Empathy* (2007), and *Moral Sentimentalism* (2010).

Laurence Thomas is Professor of Philosophy and Political Science at Syracuse University. He is well known for his work on moral theory. He is the author of *The Family and the Political Self* (2006) and editor of *Social Philosophy* (2007).

Introduction

Damian Caluori

Friendship plays an important role in our lives. We do things together with our friends and we enjoy being together. Friends are here for us when we need them. We feel with them when they are sad, and we share their happy times. The phenomenon of friendship, just as most important phenomena in human life, gives rise to a number of questions. Perhaps the first that occurs is this: what precisely is it that makes friendship so valuable that most of us think that a life without is seriously deficient? If it is possible at all to live a life that is strictly speaking solitary, friendship and other close relationships seem at least necessary for a *good* life. (Even a happy solitary contemplator of the divine appears to stand in some sort of close personal relationship to the divinity she contemplates.) Yet perhaps the importance of friendship goes deeper than that: it is conceivable that a life without friends not only fails to be a good life but is even deficient as a human life. In order to explore such issues we have to study more than the value of friendship (to which I will come back below) and turn to its very nature or essence. This is the topic of Part I, which consists of a new interpretation of Aristotle's notion of friendship by Spyros Benetatos and a discussion of the character of friendship by Laurence Thomas.

1 The nature of friendship

In order to understand the nature of friendship, it seems reasonable first to turn to Aristotle's famous treatise on friendship in books VIII and IX of the *Nicomachean Ethics* because this text set the stage for so many philosophical discussions of friendship throughout the centuries. Yet, as Benetatos shows, although we find in the *Nicomachean Ethics* a consideration of two essential elements of friendship (namely that of loving a friend and that of being a good for a friend), Aristotle, in this work, does not succeed in unifying these two elements into a single and coherent account. To find such an account, Benetatos argues, we have to turn to his other major ethical treatise, the *Eudemian Ethics* where the two essential elements are united in a coherent manner: a person is a friend of someone if she constitutes a good for her friend in virtue of her own loving agency towards him. This notion not only explains, as Benetatos demonstrates, how Aristotle's perfect friendship (that between virtuous persons) relates to the two imperfect kinds (those based on pleasure and utility) but also elucidates Aristotle's claim that friendship characterizes every human association.

Laurence Thomas develops a notion of companion friendship that is modelled against the background of Aristotle's perfect friendship. He compares and contrasts this sort of love with the love of romantic lovers and that between parents and children. According to Thomas, friendship is fundamentally characterized by mutual self-disclosing trust. Thomas explores in particular how a friendship begins: future friends realize that they understand one another, which gives them an initial motivation to mutual self-disclosing trust. Subsequent interactions deepen both mutual understanding and self-disclosing trust, and a friendship develops. This account shows how choice is involved in companion friendship and thus a feature that distinguishes it from parent-child-relations. Another characteristic aspect of friendship is expressed in the so-called 'mirror view' that Thomas defends: friends are reflections of one another in such a way that, in seeing themselves reflected in their friends, they can learn about themselves. This aspect is absent from romantic love as the latter, apart from being defined by an erotic component lacking in companion friendship, is also famously prone to blind people.

2 The unity of friendship

The fact that friends form some sort of unity is a striking feature of friendship. Our behaviour and our attitudes towards friends differ from those towards non-friends in crucial ways, and this seems to be grounded in whatever unites us with our friends as friends. Considering this unity sheds further light on friendship itself and gives us a foundation for exploring the distinctions between friends and others. In this chapter Ullrich Langer discusses Montaigne, and I consider Plato's view on the unity of friendship.

Following Aristotle, many philosophers have held that, for there to be a friendship, each friend must love their friends for the latter's sake in such a way that the beloved friends possess some property or properties in virtue of which the loving friend loves them. (Remember Aristotle's view that a friend constitutes a good for her friend.) In a classic paper, Gregory Vlastos has argued that (i) Plato has no room for this sort of love for persons and therefore (ii) cannot offer any substantial account of friendship. I agree with Vlastos on (i) but argue that (ii) does not follow. Considering the *Lysis*, the *Symposium* and the *Republic*, I try to show that Plato offers a substantial account of friendship that is based on a notion of unity distinct from that implicit in Aristotle. According to Plato, friends are not primarily directed to (and attracted by) one another as such but rather to a third thing, a project in which they are engaged together. The togetherness of this engagement must be understood, I argue, in terms of collective intentions and emotions.

Classical accounts of friendship were fundamental in the moral philosophy of the 16th century, and when Montaigne describes his friendship with La Boétie as a paradigm case of friendship, he first heavily relies on Aristotle as Langer shows: Montaigne, in keeping with Aristotle's notion of perfect friendship, praises La Boétie's virtue and emphasizes its fundamental importance to their friendship. However, Montaigne transcends the tradition and radicalizes another Aristotelian idea: that a friend is another self. According to Montaigne, in a perfect friendship, the souls mix and fuse completely so that the resulting unity no longer allows for any distinction between them. As a consequence, Montaigne believes, we can no longer explain why we love our friends: 'If you press me to tell why I loved him, I feel that it cannot be expressed, except by answering: Because it was he, because it was I.' Montaigne's account of the unity of friendship differs from Plato's in that friends are immediately directed towards one another (and not to a third thing). However, because of their complete fusion, they are no longer Aristotelian *other* selves either.

3 Friendship and reason

A consequence of the unity of friendship is the distinction between friends and non-friends whose most prominent expression is our being partial in favor of friends. Is this partiality justifiable? This question can be asked from at least two points of view. Since reason is impartial, we might ask whether the partiality of friendship is *rationally* justifiable.

This is the topic of Part III. But, as we shall see in Part IV, we may also ask whether it is *morally* justifiable.

Michael Slote maintains that there is indeed a tension between friendship and reason. He argues that love and friendship have to be understood against a developmental psychological background and explains how a child's need for parental love must be met for the child to develop its capacity for empathy. This capacity, Slote argues, is a (non-rational) precondition for friendship. Slote further argues that friendship and love compromise our epistemic rationality. He points out that we are more likely to take in attitudes and opinions of friends and loved ones than those of strangers but that we are not epistemically justified in doing so. Hence our epistemic partiality is irrational. Yet since such irrationality is a necessary consequence of friendship and love and since love and friendship are of great importance to us, this irrationality is an inevitable part of our lives.

Curtis Brown's chapter also deals with epistemic rationality. After a brief discussion of the epistemic benefits of friendship, he turns to its (apparent) epistemic dangers. He considers how we deal differently with the same sort of evidence when it concerns a friend and a stranger. For example, new negative evidence about a friend's character may influence our (positive) convictions about her less strongly than the same sort of evidence would in the case of a stranger. This is a clear case of epistemic partiality. Brown argues that, contrary to what one might think, epistemic partiality in this sense (as well as in a number of other senses he discusses) is not necessarily irrational. Because he believes that problems of epistemic partiality are best considered in terms of degrees of belief, Brown discusses them from the point of view of Bayesian epistemology, which focuses on subjective probabilities (or degrees of belief) instead of all-or-nothing-beliefs.

While Slote and Brown discuss *epistemic* rationality, Jeffrey Seidman's focus is on *practical* rationality and friendship. We do things for friends that we do not do for others; we feel differently when a friend lands a job and when a stranger lands a job. Moreover, we see ourselves as having *normative reasons* for such actions and emotions concerning friends, i.e. reasons that not only explain our behaviour or feeling but also make it appropriate. Finally, these reasons are specific to friendship: non-friends do not have the same normative reasons as friends. Seidman offers a principle whose function is to explain under what circumstances we indeed do have the reasons of friendship we see ourselves as having. Furthermore, he discusses what explains the fact that we have reasons of friendship at all and defends a non-reductionist account: there are, he argues, genuine, non-reducible normative reasons of friendship. If this account is correct, then there are reasons which make at least some of our friend-specific actions and feelings rational.

4 Friendship and morality

The partiality of friendship seems to clash with the demand for impartiality of such prominent moral theories as deontology and utilitarianism. This can bee seen from two problems: (i) From a moral point of view, it seems, I ought to treat my friend no different from anybody else, but friendship demands that I give preference to friends. (ii) A second problem concerns *motivation* and can be illustrated by an example: if I visit my friend in the hospital then my motivation to do so clearly should be that she is my friend and that I care for her. If obeying a Universal Law or maximizing welfare is part of my motivation then I seem to have, in Bernard Williams' famous phrase 'one thought too many'. Oliver Sensen discusses such problems within the framework of Kant's moral thought and Alastair Norcross from the point of view of utilitarianism. Interestingly, as John Lippitt shows, a version of problem (i) also occurs within the Christian tradition where the universal love of neighbor seems to conflict with the special love we reserve for friends.

Oliver Sensen considers the two problems in the context of Kant's account of friendship. The Categorical Imperative does not oblige us, he claims, to treat everyone, including our friends, equally. It rather only aims at testing whether one wants to make an exception for oneself to a rule that one wills to be a universal law. Sensen argues that the latter is compatible with many ways in which we give preference to friends. Addressing the second problem, he shows that Kant's moral theory does not demand that we are always motivated by morality. As long as it is the right thing to do, Kant does not object our visiting a friend in the hospital out of inclination. Morality is thus not necessarily in conflict with friendship in these two ways. However, as Sensen emphasizes, it restricts friendship according to Kant in that I am never allowed to act immorally in favor of friends. Sensen also discusses how Kant's notion of friendship is based on reason rather than the heart and explains why Kant is suspicious of friendship based on feeling.

Alastair Norcross considers the morality of friendship from a utilitarian point of view, but his arguments also apply to other forms of consequentialism. With reference to Sidgwick, he explains how the 'one thought too many' objection misses its target. Utilitarianism does not demand that people, to act rightly, must be motivated by utilitarian principles. Rather, if welfare is maximized if people act from other motives, then those other motives are preferable on utilitarian grounds. Opponents such as Williams or Michael Stocker have argued that if utilitarianism is true, it would be best if most people didn't believe it. Norcross rejects this but claims that even if it were true, it would not matter. What about the first problem mentioned above? Norcross argues that utilitarianism is not impartialist in a way that necessarily conflicts with the preference we give to friends. In his eyes, such allegations betray a simplistic view of consequentialist moral psychology. Friendship significantly contributes to happiness and this gives us consequentialist reasons to value friendship even though commitment to friends may bring it about that at times we miss opportunities to maximize welfare.

As John Lippitt shows, there is a strand within the Christian tradition, prominently exemplified by Kierkegaard, that is suspicious of friendship. Kierkegaard accepts Aristotle's claim that a friend is another self but sees it as revealing that friendship is a disguised form of self-love. But even for Christians who do not share this worry, there is no denying that friendship, by contrast to love of neighbor, is partial. If love of neighbor is commanded, is there still space for friendship? A second and related problem concerns the view – found already in Augustine – that the proper object of love must be God. Friends and neighbors seem ultimately only to be loved for the sake of God. The love of friendship thus appears purely instrumental. Against this Lippitt argues that Christians should see the love of God for God's sake as the foundation for our love of friends and neighbors and not as competing with it. Addressing the first problem, he suggests that love of friends may be the inspiration for love of neighbor and help us build a bridge from friend to neighbor.

5 Friendship in a good life

It is now time to come back to my initial question: what is it that makes friendship so valuable? Thomas Hurka explores three views on the value of friendship and other close relationships. According to the first view, friendship involves more generic values, such as pleasure, virtue, or knowledge. Even though such values can also be found elsewhere, they are realized in friendship to a particularly high degree. The second view focuses on the history that friends share. Hurka claims that a shared history makes for distinctive and better instances of generic goods. For example, knowing the personality of your friend is better than knowing the personality of a stranger because of the common history you have with your friend. The third view states with reference to G. E. Moore that there are distinctive goods specific to friendship and takes as its starting point that love in friendship is reciprocated. This mutuality in friendship, Hurka argues, possesses a value that goes beyond the sum of the value of your love for your friend and the friend's love for you. Hurka emphasizes that the three views discussed do not exclude one another and can be accepted collectively.

The ancient Stoics are famous for claiming that virtue, the excellence of one's character and mind-set, is the only intrinsic good, a view that Anthony A. Long in his chapter calls a 'monolithic theory of goodness'. Accordingly, friends may seem to be of no intrinsic value at all to a good Stoic life. However, as Long explains, this is not at all the case and the Stoics consider friends as (external) goods. Because of their monolithic theory of goodness, however, this means that a perfect friendship is only possible between perfectly virtuous persons. Yet we may still ask how a friend can be a good for me if all that matters for my happiness is the perfection of character? Answering this question, Long shows how the Stoics follow Aristotle in taking the friend to be another self and that, as they understand this notion, the love a perfect friend feels for her own virtuous character (which is a good) equally applies to the virtuous characters of their friends (which are goods). Long also discusses the value of friendship for imperfect human beings (such as ourselves) and explains how, according to the mirror view held by the Stoic Seneca, imperfect friendships possess epistemic value and help us on our way to ethical perfection.

In the final chapter of this volume, Sheila Lintott discusses how friendship enriches our lives in aesthetic ways. She considers a number of striking similarities between our attitudes towards art and friendship and shows how the openness and freedom required in art appreciation are also expressed in friendship. But friendship, like art, also offers us ways to escape alienation and gives rise to creativity and playfulness. Backed up with recent results from the social sciences, Lintott maintains that aesthetic similarities in terms of appearance and taste are key elements of how people choose their friends. While the dangers involved in distinguishing friends from non-friends on such grounds are not to be underestimated, neither should we ignore how valuable friendship is from an aesthetic point of view. Thanks in part to their aesthetic features, friends help us shape our lives and become the person we are.

Part I

The Nature of Friendship

1
Aristotle's Notion of Friendship

Spyros Benetatos

Philia, the Greek word for friendship, characterizes a wide field of human relationships (much broader than the field designated by the corresponding terms of modern European languages), including family bonds and even political relationships. In fact, Aristotle, whose inquiries into friendship are probably the best known in the history of Western philosophy, maintains that friendship characterizes every human association. In the two long essays dealing with friendship (*Nicomachean Ethics* Books VIII and IX and *Eudemian Ethics* Book VII), Aristotle attempts to support this thesis by claiming that, while there are various cases of friendship based on a variety of human relationships, all of them should still be understood in relation to a primary or central form of friendship: the intimate relationship between two (or very few) virtuous men, in which each one constitutes a good *per se* for the other – a case akin to our own current idea of friendship.[1] But what is the specific conception of friendship that supports this idea? Moreover, why does Aristotle decide that the study of an intimate personal relationship and the study of a feature which (in a variety of forms) characterizes every human association belong to the very same inquiry? It seems to me that an answer to these questions would also explain one further issue, namely that of the philosophical importance that Aristotle attributes to friendship. In what follows, I will deal with these questions, focusing mainly on the initial chapters of the two essays that present a general theory of friendship.[2]

As both the *Nicomachean* and the *Eudemian* essays attest, the issue of the nature of friendship is closely related to that of its scope. For Aristotle's conception is based on the claim that friendship is not of one form but that there are rather three forms of friendship that do not belong to a common genus. Instead, they are related to one another in a rather complicated way, which is why the investigation into the nature of friendship has to account for this diversity at a rather early stage.

In both writings, Aristotle deals with this complexity by proceeding in three steps:[3] In a first step (1) he claims that objects of love are goods in three different ways: an object of love is loved as a good *per se*, as useful or as pleasant. Subsequently, (2) he proposes a basic account of friendship and, claiming that this account holds for all three kinds of objects of love, (3) he concludes that there are three corresponding kinds of friendship. In a fourth step, (4) he distinguishes a primary[4] kind of friendship, where friends constitute goods *per se*, from imperfect kinds and focuses on its essential features. Finally, (5) he discusses the relation that links the three kinds of friendship to one another.

Although the same logical procedure is followed in both essays, the two expositions differ significantly in regard to three basic issues, namely the basic account of friendship (step 2), the theory of the primary kind of friendship (step 4) and the kind of link that relates the three kinds of friendship to one another (step 5). These are the three crucial issues on which I will focus in what follows.

1 The basic account of friendship

1.1 The Nicomachean approach

I shall first discuss the Nicomachean version of the basic account of friendship because I believe that the problems inherent in that version will help us realize the challenge that Aristotle's approach provides.

This account is preceded by a discussion of the three sorts of good (the good *per se*, the useful and the pleasant) (*EN* 1155b17–27). It consists of three features and is developed in a diaeretic way (*EN* 1155b27–56a5). The first feature is disinterested well-wishing: a friend wishes the other well for the other's sake and not for his own. Second, in friendship both persons involved have this attitude towards each other. Finally, among the relationships of mutual disinterested well-wishing, friendship is the one in which each person is aware of the other's disinterested attitude towards him. Thus, two persons are friends when they both express disinterested well-wishing towards each other and when they are aware of each other's attitude.

Since in the preceding discussion on the objects of love Aristotle repeatedly referred to the friend's 'loving' (*philein*), it has been correctly remarked that, according to Aristotle, disinterested well-wishing is the particular sort of loving that characterizes friendship (Cooper 1976/7, p. 621). This idea seems less striking if we consider the fact that *philein* is a loose term as compared to the English term 'loving'; very often it can be simply translated as 'liking'. It is important to observe that in this context Aristotle focuses on the friend as someone who loves: the essential property of the friend is thus his *attitude* and not, as at the beginning of the discussion, the fact that he constitutes some sort of good for his friend.

It is reasonable to expect that the two aspects of the friend, his loving attitude and the good that he constitutes for his friend, should be somehow related. Indeed, the presentation of this account is followed by the remark that the cause of the attitude of the friends towards each other is the sort of good that the friend constitutes as an object of love, whether he constitutes a good *per se*, or something pleasant or useful (*EN* 1156a4–5). Obviously, Aristotle aims at establishing a link between the account just presented and the initial step of the inquiry. However, his attempt to relate disinterested well-wishing to the good that the friend constitutes causes a serious difficulty, which is most evident in the secondary kinds of friendship: how can we claim that one's attitude towards someone else consists in disinterested well-wishing, while, at the same time, we claim that a friend of this sort has this attitude in view of the utility or the pleasure that he derives from the other?

It seems to me that the only possible way to avoid a contradiction is to adopt a well-known interpretation that has been proposed by John Cooper (Cooper 1976/7). According to Cooper, the goodness, the pleasantness or the usefulness of the friend should be understood simply as the psychological causes that create the positive disinterested attitude towards him and crucially not as a goal pursued. Thus, the three sorts of good that friends constitute function as efficient and not as final causes.[5]

Cooper's proposal avoids a contradiction and seems to me to be the only reasonable way to associate the above account of friendship with the three sorts of good that friends constitute for one another. However, this interpretation turns out to be quite alien to an Aristotelian understanding of the good. There are two reasons for this.

First, the interpretation of the good as an efficient cause contradicts not only basic tenets of Aristotle's practical philosophy, but also of his overall philosophic conception. For, according to Aristotle, the final cause is the only sort of cause that the good can constitute.[6]

Secondly, Aristotle believes that human activities must be understood as necessarily having some goal, which must be conceived of as some sort of good, as we already know from the initial lines of the *Nicomachean Ethics*.[7] Thus, once the good that the friend constitutes is interpreted not as a final but as an efficient cause, we still need to find the good that constitutes the goal of the friend's attitude. Although no alternative good is suggested in the text or by Cooper's interpretation, we may attempt to examine two possible candidates.

First, we could assume that the final cause of the disinterested attitude is its object, namely the friend. In this case the final good he constitutes should not be considered in the light of the threefold division of the good (the good *per se*, the pleasant and the useful) but rather as the object of disinterested well-wishing: one wishes good things for the other considering this person as a final end. But in an Aristotelian perspective, this can only mean that he is regarded as something good *per se*. Thus, in friendships based on utility or pleasantness, the friend would be appreciated not as useful or pleasant but as someone good in himself. This conclusion is quite paradoxical and in tension with both the overall spirit and several passages of the text.[8] Hence, it seems wise to abandon the attempt to relate the good to the object of love.

Second, we could try to dissociate the good pursued from the *object* of love and associate it with the *activity* of love. Thus, as in the cases of virtuous actions, we could assume that the activity of disinterested well-wishing is something good in itself, independently of the sort of good that the object of love constitutes. This, again, is a far-fetched assumption: there is not the slightest suggestion in that direction in the text; instead, there are a number of negative indications (see *EN* 1158a5–8; 1167a2–3). Thus, attempts to provide an alternative final cause for the friend's love have to be abandoned as unsustainable.

Summing up, if the three sorts of good that friends constitute are considered as final causes of the friend's attitude, the account of friendship given in *EN* 1155b27–56a5 is self-contradictory. If, instead, we consider them as efficient causes, we are in serious trouble both with the overall Aristotelian philosophical framework and with the initial presentation of the sorts of good that objects of love constitute (*EN* 1155b17–27), for they are clearly considered in terms of finality (*EN* 1155b20–21). Hence, this account of friendship fails to relate its basic notion, the loving attitude of the friend, with the good that a friend constitutes.

Moreover, there is a further problem with the above account: does the attitude of the friend, as presented in this account, differ in any significant way from the attitude of other disinterested well-wishers? In other words, is the attitude of the friend the same as the attitude in any other case of disinterested well-wishing?

Surprisingly, a careful look at the text reveals that the two features of friendship accompanying disinterested well-wishing (namely the requirement that both friends have this attitude and the awareness of each other's attitude) neither specify disinterested well-wishing nor, as we shall see, add some independent features of the friend's attitude. In the case of the requirement that both friends have this attitude, this is obvious, since here the initial attitude is attributed to the other friend. The second feature, the awareness of each other's attitude, does not in its own right constitute a further characteristic of the attitudes of the friends. My awareness of your attitude towards me may or may not affect my own attitude towards you. Of course, though it is not a characteristic of one's attitude, it could nonetheless cause a change of one's initial attitude. But if so, then this additional feature (the one that would be caused by the awareness of the other's similar attitude), which would differentiate the friend's attitude from all other cases of disinterested well-wishing, is the one that should be mentioned in the account of friendship. But it is not. Moreover, what would be the mark of such a differentiation? Our text does not offer any hint in that direction. In fact, it is quite difficult to imagine how disinterested well-wishing could be affected by the awareness that my friend has a similar attitude towards me.

Thus, we should conclude that, according to this account, the attitude of friends towards each other is not exclusive to friendship. Rather, it could as well be exhibited towards people who are not friends. Friendship thus amounts to nothing more than a coincidence of two cases of disinterested well-wishing – a coincidence of two cases of love. If so, then the reasonable object of our investigation should be disinterested well-wishing (i.e. love) and not friendship because friendship is nothing more than an accident occurring by the co-presence of two cases of love.

The above account of friendship covers only a very short part of the Nicomachean initial approach to friendship (about 10–11 lines). Its importance lies mainly in the fact that it is the only account of friendship presented more or less explicitly as such in the Nicomachean treatise. Most of the initial approach is based on the observation that the friend is an object of love (*philêton*) and that an object of love is necessarily recognized as some sort of good. This is the basis for the distinction between the three forms of friendship; indeed, it is the only basis on which the similarities, the differences and the overall relationship between the three forms are investigated in the concluding part of this initial approach.[9]

Thus, there is hardly any mention either of disinterested well-wishing or of any other notion of loving in friendship after their initial introduction.[10] Instead, the consideration of friendship is restricted to the good that friends constitute for one another. Accordingly, friends are conceived as 'those that constitute a good (of some sort) for each other'. This conception of the friend differs significantly from the one presented in the initial account; the basic notion that characterizes the friend is obviously a different one: now the basic feature is the good that the friend constitutes as an object of love, whereas, according to the initial account, the friend must be conceived of as such on the basis of his attitude, namely the specific kind of love (disinterested well-wishing) that he possesses towards his friend.

However, this alternative conception of the friend is equally problematic. First, according to this alternative approach, the friend is conceived of as such because he constitutes some sort of good, so in order to conceive of the friend as a friend, we should know, in each kind of friendship, what it is that distinguishes the good that a friend constitutes from other goods that are characterized in the same general way. In the case of pleasure-friendship, for example, the friend is conceived of as something pleasant; but since there are various other pleasant things, we should first know what the specific feature is that differentiates the pleasantness of the friend from the pleasantness of other pleasant objects. Yet our text does not provide us with any such explanation. As the text stands, the friend is simply presented (according to the corresponding kind of friendship) either as something good in itself or as something pleasant or useful. Never is the friend distinguished from other goods. For example, the pleasantness of a friend is not distinguishable from the pleasantness of honey and the usefulness of a friend is not differentiated from the usefulness of a hammer. Hence, this conception of the friend is clearly incomplete.

Moreover, since the good that the friend constitutes is considered independently of the relation between friends, this approach (similarly to the previous one) reduces the phenomenon of friendship itself to a mere coincidence of two relations of the same kind. Friendship merely becomes the coincidence of 'the usefulness of A for B' and 'the usefulness of B for A', which are in fact presented as two relations independent from one another.

In view of the above, let us make some elemental observations: the two Nicomachean approaches just discussed disclose two analytical features of the friend: the friend loves, and he constitutes an object of love. Once the object of love is conceived of as a good, these two features point to two notions: the notion of loving and the notion of the good. Thus, in the case of two friends, we can make four elemental observations:

1. A loves B.
2. B constitutes an object of love for A [= B constitutes a good of some sort for A].
3. B loves A.
4. A constitutes an object of love for B [= A constitutes a good of some sort for B].

The two alternative Nicomachean approaches of friendship that we have already considered are the following:

(a) A & B are friends on the basis of (1) & (3).
(b) A & B are friends on the basis of (2) & (4).

Both are adequate descriptions of friendship. But approach (a) considers friendship on the basis of just one feature, using only the notion of love. Approach (b) considers friendship also on the basis of just one feature, namely that of the object of love, and relies on only one notion, that of the good which the friend constitutes. Both approaches consider the notion used to be prior and more general than friendship, and both 1) fail to specify this notion adequately in order to propose an acceptable conception of the friend and 2) reduce friendship to a coincidence of two independent relationships.

Should we, in the light of these failures, abandon the analytical approach? This would be too hasty. Let us return to the four initial elements. Since (1) and (2) necessarily imply each other and the same applies to (3) and (4), we need a combination of just two elements, one element of each pair, in order to describe friendship adequately. Since we ruled out pairs (1) and (3) as well as (2) and (4), the remaining options are a combination of (2) and (3) or of (1) and (4). Because their notional content is the same, it makes no difference which pair we choose. Both pairs are crucially different from the pairs considered earlier: while the Nicomachean combinations used one feature (and, hence, one notion) twice, ascribing it to both friends, our new combinations ascribe both features (and both notions) to one of the friends. These alternative combinations, it seems to me, are explored in the Eudemian treatise on friendship to which I now shall turn.

1.2 The Eudemian approach

The Eudemian version of the basic account of friendship does not usually attract a lot of scholarly attention, presumably because it is much shorter than the Nicomachean one and seems to add nothing of significance to it. In fact, only one and a half Bekker lines are devoted to it (by contrast to the ten lines of the Nicomachean version):

> ... a man becomes a friend when he is loved and returns that love, and this is recognized by the two men in question.[11]

When confronted with these lines, a reader already acquainted with the Nicomachean version might get the impression that they simply repeat two of the three characteristics of friendship discussed in the Nicomachean account (the condition that both friends should love and the awareness of each other's love). At the same time, it omits the primary characteristic, namely the conception of the friend's love as disinterested well-wishing. The Greek phrase *hotan philoumenos antiphilei* (translated above as 'when he is loved and returns that love') is often translated as 'when he receives love and returns love',[12] alluding thus to the idea that the friend returns what he is given and thus implying that the feature presented in our account is that of love from both sides. However, studying the terms used and the context in which they appear in the Eudemian account will show that they do not allow for this interpretation.

The participle *philoumenos* is the term by which Aristotle denotes the object of love in the long discussion that precedes this account (*EE* 1235b18–36a14).[13] Hence, we should infer that this is the sense in which *philoumenos* should be interpreted here too. Since the quality of being an object of love was reduced to being some sort of good for someone, our account must consider as well the friend as someone who constitutes a sort of good for his friend. Further, it is obviously correct to translate the verb *antiphilein* as 'returning love', especially since the account does not make it explicit that both friends love. The symmetry of love is, of course, an obvious and necessary logical consequence of the return of love, but what matters in our account is not the fact that both friends love, but the fact that in friendship the object of love loves back.

Further observations can be drawn from the context: Aristotle argues (1) that *philoumena*, i.e. objects of love, should be conceived of as cases of good and insists on their threefold classification as good *per se*, pleasant and useful (*EE* 1235b18–36a14). Then he suggests (2) that the friend is a *philoumenon* that returns love (*EE* 1236a14–15) in order to proceed immediately afterwards to a further claim: it follows necessarily from (1) and (2) that there are three kinds of friendship (a15–16), corresponding to the three sorts of good that the objects of love constitute (cf. a30–2). Step (2), the account of the friend, is obviously not a parenthetical remark but part of the argument concluding that the three sorts of good that the objects of love constitute correspond to three different kinds of friendship. In view of this argument, we must infer that the account has a double function: first, it asserts that a friend may constitute any of the three different sorts of good and second, that the sort of good that he constitutes is essential with regard to the nature of the sort of friendship formed (otherwise, the difference of the sort of good wouldn't justify the claim that there are three kinds of friendship). The account can successfully fulfill this double task only if we interpret *philoumenos* as denoting the object of love, since we already know that the reduction to three cases of good concerns the different kinds of object of love and hence (up to this point, at least) the friend not in virtue of his loving attitude but in virtue of being an object of love.

Now what is the function of the features (the loving response and its recognition) that accompany *philoumenos* in our account? Since the conclusion states that there are three kinds of friendship, it must be shown that the essence of friendship is such as not to exclude any of the three sorts of good that a friend (qua object of love) may constitute. Hence, the features presented should (a) be those that matter in regard to the essence of friendship and should (b) restrict adequately the range of objects of love that count as friends. They must fulfill both these two conditions in order to lead to the conclusion that there is a friend in each of the three cases of good. Now since these features are not only essential to friendship but also restrict the range of *philoumena* that count as friends, the most reasonable way to interpret them is as further properties of those *philoumena* that count as friends. Thus, these features must specify the objects of love that friends are and distinguish them adequately from all other (non-friend) objects of love. Since the objects of love are conceived of as cases of some sort of good, these further features of the friend specify the sort of good that in each kind of friendship the friend constitutes.

This interpretation enables us to see the function that the last feature of friendship, the recognition of the friend's response, assumes in the account (a function that remains obscure in the Nicomachean version): an object of love is such by being recognized by the agent as some sort of good for him. Once a friend's loving response specifies the good that he constitutes, this particular feature (essential to the good that he constitutes) must also be recognized by his friend. This is necessary if he is to be recognized as the specific good that the friend is. In other words, the mere fact of the friend's loving response is not a feature of the object of love that he constitutes unless this fact is recognized by the other person. The friend's response (*antiphilein*) becomes an essential aspect of the object of love that he constitutes by being recognized as something that matters.

In fact, there is nothing far-fetched or sophisticated in this conception: a rich person, for example, is not *ipso facto*, on account of her wealth, useful to us. She could be useful in various ways (e.g., as a hostage taken for ransom), but she is useful qua friend only if she is responding to our interest in her by adopting a positive attitude towards us. And in this case, her liking us is a necessary and essential aspect of her usefulness. Similarly, the attractiveness of some person may be usually pleasant, but the pleasure this person provides us with is significantly different when he responds to our positive attitude towards him by being also attracted to us. It is in this last case that he is considered as a friend.[14]

Aristotle, in fact, simply brings forward two premises that we can easily detect if we reflect on our everyday experience: (1) a friend is someone who matters to us and (2) his attitude towards us constitutes an essential aspect of the way in which he matters to us. Aristotle rejoins these widely reputed opinions (*endoxa*) by bringing to the fore just two things: (a) the *par excellence* analytical features of the friend, loving and being loved; and (b) the conception of the object of love as some sort of good. In this way, the two analytical features of the friend bring to the fore two notions (the good that he constitutes and his loving response) which are the notions implicit in the above-mentioned reputed opinions.

Now, this basic account of friendship is not, in a strict sense, a general *definition* of friendship. Rather, as Aristotle warns us immediately after the presentation of the account (*EE* 1236a16*ff*), there is no such thing as a genus of friendship and hence no (Aristotelian) definition is possible. The main reason for this is already implicit in the account itself. For the friend is conceived of as a good that may be either good *per se*, useful or pleasant and, according to Aristotle, the various cases of good do not belong to one genus.[15] Thus, the account presents only a basic pattern which characterizes every form of friendship. But this does not mean that the relation between the three kinds of friendship is limited to a schematic similarity or to a structural analogy. Aristotle insists that one of these forms, the friendship in which the friends constitute goods *per se*, is in a crucial sense primary and the other two forms are in a crucial sense dependent on it. Thus, in order to better understand what unites all forms of friendship, according to this account, we should first focus on the primary form of friendship.

2 Primary friendship

The primary form of friendship is that in which friends constitute goods *per se*; it is a friendship between virtuous men. The idea of this kind of friendship poses a problem, which is absent in the secondary kinds of friendship: for if a friend is loved qua someone useful or pleasant to his friend, it is quite obvious that the friend constitutes some sort of good for his friend. But once the friend constitutes a good *per se* qua virtuous man, it is not at all obvious why he constitutes also a good for his friend: in what way does a virtuous man (qua virtuous) constitute a good for another virtuous man? The fact that he is good does not, *ipso facto*, imply that he is also a good for another good man. This problem has already been posed (and led to an impasse) in Plato's *Lysis* on the ground that a good man cannot be useful to another good man.[16] In fact, this conclusion is absolutely sound because, once we assume that the two men are perfectly good, the goodness of the one cannot add anything to the goodness of the other. They can only accidentally be useful to each other, for example, in virtue of their wealth or power, but not in virtue of their goodness. Now Aristotle's conception of primary friendship requires (and amounts to) the solution of this problem. It concerns not only the possibility but also the nature of this basic kind of friendship. For to be a friend to someone amounts to be some sort of good to him or her.

It is puzzling that there is no awareness of this problem in the relevant passages of the Nicomachean treatise on friendship, and accordingly, scholarly studies and commentaries on these passages do not address it. In fact, according to the Nicomachean version, the virtuous person is a good for his friend by being useful to him.[17] Although we would expect an argument given that, as we have seen, this statement has been refuted by Plato, Aristotle's claim is surprisingly not supported by any argumentation. But is usefuleness the only way in which something can be a good for someone?

There is a lengthy passage in the Eudemian essay (*EE* 1236b32–37b5) in which the theory of the primary kind of friendship is construed as an answer to the above problem (presented in *EE* 1236b32–38). In a first stage (*EE* 1236b38–1237a30), Aristotle attempts to establish a correspondence between the intrinsic goodness of the virtuous man and the good that he constitutes for his friend. The issue, as Aristotle conceives of it, is not that of usefulness but rather that of the way in which the good that the virtuous man constitutes for his friend corresponds to the good that characterizes the virtuous man in himself. Let us dwell briefly on this point, which scholars usually do not realize because of their belief that being good for someone amounts to being useful for someone. Contrary to this widely held assumption, however, there is another way in which x can be good for someone, quite distinct from the way in which x can be useful or pleasant for someone. To illustrate this, consider a great painting in a family living room. The father considers the painting as something useful for him because of its high market value; the mother finds it pleasant since it fits perfectly with the furniture of the living room. But let us also suppose the existence of a daughter who is a great fan and connoisseur of art and hence able to appreciate the painting as the great work of art it is. The painting is a good for her, too; she enjoys contemplating it. But, by contrast to her parents, what she enjoys is the very nature of this painting; what is good for her is the painting as it is in itself; her enjoyment is something intrinsically related to her understanding of what the object of her enjoyment really is; and she appreciates it as something which is good *per se* and not as a means to some further good. This is the sort of correspondence that Aristotle seeks between the intrinsic goodness of the virtuous man and the good that he constitutes for his friend.

The great work that the painting is becomes as such a good for the daughter by means of a certain activity, the activity of contemplating the painting. According to Aristotle, the contemplating person gains access to the nature of the object of contemplation in such an activity and enjoys what this object is in itself. Let us now apply this to the case of the friendship between virtuous men. The correspondence between the preciousness of the virtuous person and the good that he is for his friend consists in the particular activity by means of which another man may have access to the goodness of the virtuous man. According to Aristotle, this activity implies the acquaintance with the other (*EE* 1237a23–25; a31) and the pleasant recognition of his excellence, which is intrinsically pleasant. And this is nothing else but the activity of loving (*EE* 1237a23–30).

In primary friendship, 'active loving' (loving in its actuality) is, according to Aristotle, 'a response constituting a deliberate choice accompanied by pleasure, of another's acquaintance' (*EE* 1237a30–31). By 'response constituting a deliberate choice' I translate the Greek term *antiprohairesis*, which is a technical term, a neologism, probably devised by Aristotle. Similarly to *antiphilein,* it is a particular form of response: a response which constitutes a deliberate choice.[18] In fact, *antiprohairesis* designates the specific form of *antiphilein* that characterizes the primary form of friendship.

Aristotle's focus on the friend's choice shows that the activity of loving is conceived of by Aristotle as a practical activity, as an action. In this respect, two issues are crucial, both related to the fact that each friend's choice to know the other is a response to the choice of the other.

First, Aristotle considers the choice of each friend as a necessary condition for the choice of the other. If this is so, then it is quite justified – if we recall Aristotle's conception of choice. By contrast to the object of wish, the object of choice must be feasible; it must be within reach: we may *wish* to conquer Troy, but we cannot *choose* to do so. Thus, in the case of primary friendship, although it is quite natural to wish to have an intimate experience with a virtuous person and to enjoy his character, it is not feasible without his consent; and such consent would be odd, unless the other has a similar wish in regard to the first person. Thus, their friendship is formed when the mutual recognition of each other's wish makes it possible for both to choose one another. Their mutual choices are actualized simultaneously, each one being a necessary condition for the other.

Second, as far as the cognitive aspect of the activity of loving is concerned, the choice of each friend is also a manifestation of the final object of the action of the other: the knowledge of a fine man is above all knowledge of his virtue, and his virtue is manifested in his choice.[19] Thus, each friend's choice is enjoyed by the other as a manifestation of the fine being that his friend is. So each one's choice is itself a crucial aspect of the object of love that he constitutes for his friend.

Finally, by focusing on the friend's choice, Aristotle shows that in this form of friendship, each friend matters to the other as the distinct and self-sufficient agent that he essentially is. One's actions towards the other make no sense unless the other displays his own actuality as well and is actually present as an agent and appreciated as such. As we shall see in the next section, this is crucial for understanding how the other forms of friendship are related to the primary one.

3 The relation between the three kinds of friendship

On the basis of the above, we can finally consider the relation between the three kinds of friendship. In the Nicomachean essay, the way in which the forms of friendship are related to one another remains ambiguous since there is no discussion of whether there is an essential relation between them or whether they are all called 'friendship' homonymously (*EN* 1157a25–b5).[20]

In view of this, scholars often show some interest in the corresponding claim of the Eudemian essay, according to which the secondary cases constitute forms of friendship by being focally related to the primary form of friendship.[21] As a rule, this claim is understood on the basis of the focal reference of the pleasant and the useful to the good *per se*.[22] However, this interpretation is problematic: First of all, there is no evidence in Aristotle's ethical works or elsewhere in the corpus that Aristotle considers the useful and the pleasant as cases of good in virtue of a focal relation to the good *per se*.[23] Second, even if the different forms of *good* were focally related, we could not infer from this that the different forms of *friendship* are focally related. The focal (*pros hen*) relation, according to Aristotle,[24] is a relation by which various kinds that do not belong to the same genus, still form some sort of unity, analogous to but looser than that of a genus. They do so because these various kinds are essentially dependent on a primary kind. Hence their definition requires this primary kind and refers to it (*EE* 1236a20–21). So, more generally, their conception depends on the conception of the primary kind, and because of their reference to this kind, they all constitute one single 'general' object of knowledge.[25]

Let us return to the case of the kinds of friendship: What can we infer regarding their relationship by supposing that (1) the useful and the pleasant are focally related to the good *per se* and that (2) this is the crucial claim for the understanding of their relationship? Obviously, if we accept that the different kinds of *good* are focally related, then the definition of the useful friend entails the notion of the useful and, similarly, the definition of the pleasant friend that of the pleasant. If we suppose that the notions of the useful and the pleasant imply the notion of the good *per se*, the only thing that we can infer (relying just on this supposition) is that the useful friend and the pleasant one, ultimately, depend conceptually on the good *per se* (like all other pleasant and useful cases). The notions of the useful and the pleasant do not require any reference to the primary *friend*, so the useful friend and the pleasant friend do not necessarily depend conceptually on the primary one.

Thus, the supposition of a focal relation between all cases of the useful and the pleasant and the good *per se* fails to explain the focal relation between the kinds of friendship. This is due to the failure to discern a feature that is (1) proper to the primary form of friendship, which is not shared with any other entity, and (2) essential for the conception of the secondary forms. This failure, in turn, is due to the lack of focus on the crucial feature that differentiates the useful friend, the pleasant friend and the friend that constitutes a good *per se* from all other entities that are useful, pleasant or good *per se*, respectively.

Once we realize this, we do not need to search very far: the feature that distinguishes the virtuous friend from other goods *per se* is, as we saw, the appreciation of his loving response, which, in this kind of friendship, is a deliberate choice, *antiprohairesis*. Similarly, the feature that distinguishes the friend in the secondary kinds of friendship from other useful or pleasant things is his loving response (*antiphilein*). Thus, it is quite reasonable to interpret the focal relation proposed in the Eudemian essay as the focal reference of the ways in which the loving response of the friend matters in the secondary kinds of friendship to the specific good that the friend constitutes in primary friendship. Now, in primary friendship, the friend's loving response is recognized as a deliberate choice (*prohairesis*) and is appreciated as a manifestation of the excellent being he is. The different ways in which *antiphilein* specifies the good that the friend constitutes in the secondary kinds of friendship is to be conceived of by reference to *antiprohairesis*.

Though only in the primary form of friendship the friend matters for his friend in himself, as the human being he is, nonetheless in all three forms of friendship the friend is inconceivable unless some aspect of his own initiative, desires, wishes, intentions, decisions and choices is recognized as constitutive of the sort of good that he is for his friend. In this way, the usefulness or the pleasantness of a friend differs in a crucial way from the usefulness or the pleasantness of other goods, e.g., of an inanimate thing or of a slave. This difference remains crucial even in cases quite remote from what we usually consider as friendship, such as everyday commercial transactions: we cannot get beer from the brewer unless he decides to offer this good to us. We have access to his beer only on the basis of the consideration that, in the current state of things, when beer matters, then necessarily the intentions and the decision of the brewer matter too; evidently, this wouldn't be the case if the brewer were our slave. In all cases of friendship, however, the pleasantness or the usefulness of the friend implies the recognition of the friend's agency. His agency is constitutive of the good he is for his friend. Hence, the sort of good that he constitutes is to be understood by reference to the case in which the good that matters is the agent *per se*.

It appears that this conception of friendship can explain Aristotle's statement that friendship characterizes every human association. The explanation of this statement requires the solution of the three main issues that I discussed in the present chapter. The first one concerns the account of the friend that forms the basis for the whole discussion. I have argued that this account cannot rely exclusively on one notion, be it the notion of love or the notion of the good that the friend constitutes as an object of love. I have tried to show that in the Eudemian essay the friend is conceived of on the basis of a combination of both notions, where the friend's love specifies the good that he constitutes. Second, I have discussed the sort of good that a virtuous friend constitutes for his friend and shown that the idea that he should be considered a good to his friend by being useful to him proves to be problematic. Instead, I have focused on the Eudemian claim that a friend constitutes a good *per se* for his friend; this discussion revealed the friend's deliberate choice as a crucial aspect of his love and of the good that he constitutes for his friend. Finally, I turned to the Eudemian thesis that the secondary forms of friendship are focally related to the primary one. I rejected the usual explanation based on a focal reference of the useful and the pleasant to the good *per se* and argued instead that we should consider it in regard to the friend's loving response. In primary friendship, this loving response is appreciated as a deliberate choice, revealing the friend's excellence as an agent. Although in the secondary forms of friendship the friend is not appreciated as a good *per se* but as useful or pleasant, the appreciation of his agency is still an essential aspect of the good that he constitutes for his friend.

It seems to me that this interpretation enables us to see why Aristotle's theory of friendship is fundamental in his understanding of human associations. Human associations may differ in regard to the good that each person pursues, but whatever the aim and the nature of each association may be, in all of them each participant appreciates the others as distinct agents and not as instruments or extensions of his own agency.

Notes

I would like to thank Damian Caluori for his great editing work on my chapter.

1. One difference is that Aristotle only talks about friendships between men and does not consider women at all in this context. Giving an interpretation of Aristotle, I will use the masculine form only in what follows when talking about Aristotelian friends.
2. *EN* VIII.ii/2–iv/6, 1155b17–57b5; *EE* VII.2, 1235b18–37b7.
3. This is quite clear in the Nicomachean essay. But even in the *Eudemian Ethics*, where the text does not follow exactly this order, the logical order is the same.

4. In the *Nicomachean Ethics* this form of friendship is also characterized as 'perfect' (*EN* 1156b7, b34).
5. '[T]he "because"...expresses a consequence or result...rather than some purpose that the well-wisher has in wanting him to prosper' (Cooper 1976/7, p. 633); 'Aristotle will here be making, in effect, the psychological claim that those who have enjoyed one another's company or have been mutually benefited through their common association, will, as a result of the benefits or pleasures they receive, tend to wish for and be willing to act in the interest of the other person's good, independently of their own welfare or pleasure. A full-fledged friendship will exist, then, when such intentions are recognized by both parties as existing reciprocally' (ibid., pp. 633–4); '[h]ere pleasure or advantage serve as cause, *not as goal*, of the well-wishing.' (p. 634, n. 17, my emphasis. See also n. 16 for the distinction between 'an antecedent causal condition' and 'the well-wisher's purpose').
6. See, e.g., *Met A*, 988b6ff: Aristotle declares that, in some sense, he is not the first philosopher that conceived of the good as a cause, but, in a stricter sense, he is indeed the first because he conceived the kind of cause that the good constitutes, namely, the *final* cause.
7. 'Every art and every inquiry, and similarly every action and choice, is thought to aim at some good; and for this reason the good has rightly been declared to be that at which all things aim' (*NE* 1094a1–3, transl. Ross/Brown). See also the initial lines of the *Politics* (*Pol.* 1252a1–3).
8. This is most evident in the presentation of the secondary kinds of friendship (*EN* 1156a17–1156b6).
9. *EN* 1156b35–57b5. The perspective adopted here is already prepared in the previous chapter on virtue friendship, which focuses mainly on the idea that the virtuous friend is also useful and pleasant (*EN* 1156b12–24).
10. Well-wishing is mentioned only once (*EN* 1156b8–10), at the presentation of the primary kind of friendship, and it has no functional role in the discussion.
11. EE VII.2 1236a14–15: φίλος δὴ γίνεται ὅταν φιλούμενος ἀντιφιλῇ, καὶ τοῦτο μὴ λανθάνῃ πως αὐτούς. (Solomon's translation.)
12. Kenny (2011, p. 115). See also Rackham (1952): '...while receiving attention he returns it.' (p. 369).
13. The corresponding Nicomachean term is *φιλητόν*. Both terms refer to the same concept, the object of love.
14. The idea is clearly present in Xenophon's *Hiero*, I.35–36, where one of the rare pre-Aristotelian appearances of the term *antiphilein* is attested. See Marchant (1968²).
15. See the discussion of the good both in *NE* I.4/vi (1096a11*ff*) and in *EE* I.8 (1217b*ff*).
16. Plato, *Lysis*, 214e–215a and Burnet (1963²).
17. 'And each is good without qualification and to his friend, for the good are both good without qualification and useful to each other.' *NE* 1156b12–14 – Ross's translation.
18. On the parallel between the two terms, see also *EE* 1236b2–3. In both *EE* 1237a30–31 and *EE* 1236b2–3 the usual translation of *antiprohairesis* as 'mutual' or 'reciprocal' choice (Solomon, Rackham, Kenny) is unfortunate since it renders these passages excessively redundant. (See Dirlmeier's comments: Dirlmeier [1969], com. *ad. loc.*)

19. See *EE* 1228a20, 1228a11–13, *NE* 1105a31*ff*, 1144a18–20, 1111b5–6, *Rhet.* 1374b14*ff.*
20. The crucial passages are the following: 'For men apply the name of friends even to those whose motive is utility, ... and to those who love each other for the sake of pleasure ... Therefore, we too ought perhaps to call such people friends, and say that there are several kinds of friendship – firstly and in the proper sense that of good men *qua* good, and by resemblance the other kinds' (*EN* 1157a25–32). 'Good men are friends without qualification; the others are friends incidentally and through a resemblance to these' (*EN* 1157b4–5).
21. Aspasius (Heylbut, 1889), CAG XIX 161.10–17, 164.1–11; Michael of Ephesus (Heylbut, 1882), CAG XX, 461.21; Th. Aquinas (Litzinger, 1993), pp. 483–4; Fritzsche (1847, p. 27); Gauthier & Jolif (1958/9), II, p. 686; Joachim (1955, p. 245).
22. Price (1989), pp. 132–4; Fortenbaugh (1975), pp. 57–62.
23. See the general approach on the good in *EE* I.8, 1217b*ff*, and in *EN* I.4/vi, 1096a11*ff.*
24. The main presentation of the notion of focal reference in Aristotle's writings is *Metaphysics Γ* (1003a33*ff*), where it is presented as a basic notion in regard to *being.*
25. Aristotle's favorite examples are those of the 'healthy' and the 'medical': the word 'medical' may denote different properties, such as the property of possessing the medical science – the doctor's case – or the property of being an instrument of the medical science – e.g. a surgical knife, but all these properties are what they are because they all refer to and depend on the medical science (*Met Γ*, 1003a34–b3; see also *EE* VII, 1236a20–22).

References

J. Burnet (1963[2]) *Platonis Opera*, Vol. III, O.C.T. (Oxford: Oxford University Press).

L. Bywater (1894) *Aristotelis Ethica Nicomachea*, O.C.T. (Oxford: Oxford University Press).

J. M. Cooper (1976/7) 'Aristotle on the Forms of Friendship', *Review of Metaphysics* 30, 619–48. [Repr. in J. M. Cooper (1999) *Reason and Emotion: Essays on Ancient Moral Psychology and Ethical Theory* (Princeton: Princeton University Press), 312–335].

F. Dirlmeier (1969) *Aristoteles, Eudemische Ethik, übersetzt und kommentiert* (Berlin: Akademie Verlag).

W. W. Fortenbaugh (1975) 'Aristotle's Analysis of Friendship: Function and Analogy, Resemblance and Focal Meaning', *Phronesis* 20, 51–62.

A. T. H. Fritzsche (1847) *Ἀριστοτέλης περὶ φιλίας. Aristotelis Ethicorum Nicomacheorum Liber Octavus et Novus* (London /Amsterdam /Paris: Gissae. Sumptibus Librariae Academicae Ferberianae).

R. A. Gauthier and J. Y. Jolif (1958/9) *Aristote: L' Éthique à Nicomaque* (Louvain: Publications Universitaires de Louvain).

G. Heylbut (1882) 'Eustratii et Michaelis et Anonyma in Ethica Nicomachea Commentaria', *Commentaria in Aristotelem Graeca* (CAG) xx, (Berlin: Reimer).

—— (1889) 'Aspassii in Ethica Nicomachea quae Supersunt Commentaria', *Commentaria in Aristotelem Graeca* (CAG) xix (Berlin: Reimer).

H. H. Joachim (1955) *Aristotle: The Nicomachean Ethics* (Oxford: Oxford University Press).

A. Kenny (2011) *Aristotle: The Eudemian Ethics* (Oxford: Oxford University Press).

C. I. Litzinger (1993) (transl.) *St. Thomas Aquinas: Commentary on Aristotle's* Nicomachean Ethics (Notre Dame: Dumb Ox Books).

Marchant (1968^2) *Xenophon VII. Scripta Minora*, Loeb Classical Library (Cambridge-Mass/London: Harvard University Press).

A. W. Price (1989) *Love and Friendship in Plato and Aristotle* (Oxford: Oxford University Press).

H. Rackham (1952) (transl.) *Aristotle: The Athenian Constitution; The Eudemian Ethics; On Virtues and Vices*, Loeb Classical Library (Cambridge, Mass /London: Harvard University Press).

D. Ross (2009) (transl. revised by L. Brown) *Aristotle: The Nicomachean Ethics* (Oxford: Oxford University Press).

J. Solomon (transl.) (1915) *Ethica Eudemia* in D. Ross (ed.) *The Works of Aristotle*, ix (Oxford: Oxford University Press).

R. R. Walzer and J. M.Mingay (1991) *Aristotelis Ethica Eudemia*, O.C.T. (Oxford: Oxford University Press).

2
The Character of Friendship

Laurence Thomas

For all the ways in which human beings differ with respect to objectives, practices, and preferences, a striking commonality among human beings is the considerable value that is placed upon friendship. There is every indication that what counts as a good friendship is the same across the globe, even when there are differences owing to societal practices. For example, whether they are female or male, it is commonplace for good friends in France to *faire la bise* (the kiss on each cheek) as a form of greeting; whereas in other parts of the world, for example, North America, women may greet one another with a 'peck' on the cheek but not men.

If two people are walking down the street together, it is often easy to tell that they are good friends just by the non-verbal behavior that they exhibit in interacting with one another while walking and talking. From their non-verbal behavior, what is clear is not just that each knows who the other is, since acquaintance is possible without there being a deep friendship between the individuals at all. Rather, it is quite apparent that they are manifestly at-ease with one another and, moreover, that they are taking considerable delight in one another's company, as is evident from their smiles, glances, and bodily gestures. In the language of Aristotle, good friends love one another.[1]

Now, two people can love one another and not be friends at all. The most obvious example of this is the parent–child relationship. Can parents and children turn out to be the best of friends? No doubt that is possible. But surely it is rare. Or so I shall argue. Now with respect to love and friendship, romantic love presents an interesting case. It is not all that uncommon these days to hear people say that their romantic partner is their best friend. Yet, romantic love tends not to be what we first think of when we think of friendship at its best. And it seems unlikely that romantic love at its best and friendship at its best will ever be simply two ways of saying the same thing.

My aim in this essay is to offer an account of the character of friendship. The focus shall be what Aristotle calls perfect friendship, but which I shall refer to as companion friendship.

1 First things first: mutual affirming trust

Children do not ask to be born and they enter the world entirely dependent upon their parents for survival. Moreover, newborn children have no abilities that would warrant their being trusted by their parents. With respect to trust, then, the parent–child relationship is constitutionally asymmetrical at the outset. In a word, then, trust is not the beginning of the parent–child relationship. Interestingly, there is a very significant respect in which this point also holds for romantic relationships. This is because the initial impetus in a romantic relationship is not trust but erotic attraction; precisely what we know is that erotic attraction for another can render the person thus attracted 'blind' to the deficiencies of the erotically desired individual in the realm of trustworthiness or moral character generally. With companion friendship, however, the issue of the trustworthiness of each is front and center for both quite early on, if not at the very outset. To be sure, there is the issue of overlapping mutual interests.[2] But two people can easily have overlapping mutual interest and yet the issue of friendship between them is entirely out of the question. After all, most people who attend regularly the home games of their sports team have at least significant overlapping interest, namely the sport and the team in question. But few would suppose that this commonality is sufficient to make a friendship. As true as it is that friends like doing things together, common interests as such hardly suffice to make a good friendship.

Finally, there is the obvious fact that the trust of friendship is not about basic trust but self-disclosing trust. To be sure, each person asks whether they both share the same basic ideals and moral values. However, two people can have this much in common and yet be quite some distance from one another in a multitude of ways. In particular, they would never think to share anything personal with one another. They would not want a bond of revealing trust between one another. Presumably, in a just world this would be common enough. At the very center of self-disclosing trust is the issue of whether a person can trust another to understand her or him about quite personal matters and do so across the board. The very majesty of friendship is due in large part to the fact that each can count on the other to understand what she or he says in just the way that the person meant to say it, no matter how unexpected the remark might be. This is so whether the conversation pertains to a very serious matter or there is a wonderful moment of teasing between them. And on any given occasion with two companion friends, the direction of the conversation could pertain to a very serious matter or strike a very humorous chord; and with extraordinarily rare exception both friends respond as they should without any difficulty whatsoever. The following is an actual phone conversation between two close friends that took place:

> *Josh*: My father is in the hospital.
> *Neil*: Oh my, I must go and see him.
> *Josh*: But I should tell you that my father no longer likes black people.
> *Neil*: No problem. I am no longer black.

What followed was sheer laughter between Josh and Neil. Of course, Josh never expected Neil to take seriously that second claim about his father. And Neil spent not so much as a nanosecond taking that claim seriously. What is more, that simple and humorous exchange between the two served to marvelously underwrite the majesty of their friendship.

The preceding example helps us to see why it is that in terms of its initial formation companion friendship can resemble something akin to spontaneous combustion. First of it all, we really do not expect deep, deep understanding to occur between ourselves and most people. This is part of the explanation for maintaining a measure of privacy in our lives. While we can certainly be private about things that are shameful or embarrassing, there are lots of things about which privacy is warranted that do not at all merit that characterization. An obvious example is that a person can be rightly private about how much money she or he has in the bank although there is nothing at all inappropriate that is applicable to that reality. Second, there is no way to know in advance whether the person with whom we are socially interacting for the first time will exhibit such understanding. The third and last point is that it very rarely takes more than a few seconds here and there to see that during a conversation with another person one is being marvelously understood by that person in just the way that one was aiming to be understood; and when that perception is mutual, an initial chord for mutual trust of the self-disclosing kind has thereby been struck.[3] In some way or the other, person A offered a glimpse into her or his very soul; and by the very content of person B's comments it is clear that person B got the 'picture' precisely the way in which A meant to reveal it. And that, needless to say, tells person A something considerable about person B. Both individuals are aware of what has happened so unexpectedly.

To be sure, such enormous understanding could be a fluke. That is rare, though. In any case, two individuals who have had the initial interaction described in the preceding paragraph get to put their assessment of one another to the test through subsequent interactions and the conversations to which these interactions give rise. It does not take long for each to realize that indeed they can mightily trust one another to understand what she or he says. This consideration points to why friends so very much enjoy doing things together. On the one hand, there is the delight that comes with being in one another's company and participating together in activities that both like. This enjoyment is marvelously underwritten by the depth of self-disclosing trust between them. On the other, there is the reality that being in one another's company allows for either to display other instances of self-disclosing trust in the other, where this unfolds in quite an unscripted manner. Of course, companion friends can meet on this or that occasion precisely because one very much needs the advice of the other about some important issue. What will typically be the case, however, is that through any given routine conversation between them their self-disclosing trust in one another will manifest itself in some way or the other. After all, we can reveal much about ourselves without talking about ourselves but by commenting upon (making observations about) the things that go on around us. Likewise, there can be much room for misunderstanding if what is said is not taken in precisely the right way. Accordingly, companion friends can feel comfortable discussing matters with one another that neither would feel comfortable discussing with others, even though they are not disclosing to one another any personal information about themselves.

Owing to the very depth of their trust that has been tremendously underwritten over time, companion friends can be warranted in asking a quite searching question of one another. And, of course, what is of the utmost importance is that the friend asks the question in just the right way. For instance, suppose that we have companion friends Adrian and Leslie, each of whom is in a marital relationship. While they certainly do not talk about their sex life with their spouse, each makes a comment here and there that makes it manifestly clear to the other that things are going quite well in that domain. Given the appropriate context such a comment might be 'We got so busy while watching that movie that neither of us has clue as to how it ended'. Now, imagine that weeks go by, perhaps even a month or two, and no such comment is forthcoming from, say, Leslie. It could be perfectly appropriate for Adrian to inquire whether everything is all right on the home front, pointing out that it has been quite some time since Leslie has made one of those comments that indicate how marvelously things are going in terms of sexual intimacy. Notice that Leslie can hardly criticize Adrian for noticing the silence in that regard. Indeed, precisely because they are companion friends it would be rather natural for Leslie to say to Adrian 'I was wondering when you might say something'. Leslie can proffer an explanation or simply note that the time is not yet right to talk about the matter. Needless to say, Adrian will respect that decision and then add something like the following remark: 'You know that I will be there for you when you need me'.

It should be manifestly clear that one does not have to devalue romantic love at all in order to appreciate how absolutely wonderful and marvelous it is for mutual self-disclosing trust to be the fundamental bond between two individuals. A more forceful way of putting the point is that companion friendship is not some sort of romantic love manqué—a bond between two people that somehow falls short of romantic love thereby not reaching its full potential.

In simply spending time together, in order just to be together because they take such delight in one another's company, there is always a measure of self-disclosure between companion friends. Each new meeting either reinforces some important insight or adds a new insight (or both). This permits extraordinary refinement on the part of each friend with respect to the character, personality, and views of each other. When two people know one another well enough, a simple hesitation on the part of one friend can be revealing; and the friend who hesitated in the slightest before the other friend will not be at all surprised that the other friend noticed it. The other friend might make an inquiry right then and there, or raise the issue at a later date. In any event, the inquiry will be made at the appropriate time.

In order to understand the richness of companion friendship, learning to speak a foreign language proves to be rather instructive. No matter how much a person studies a foreign language, the person can have no better evidence that she or he speaks that language well than that native speakers of that language communicate with the person just as they would communicate with other native speakers of the language. They provide the person who has learnt the language with an insight into her or his command of the foreign language that the individual simply could not otherwise attain. One reason for this is that discussions between people who know one another are replete with quick digressions of one sort or another, either as a means of humor or in order to call attention to something that caught everyone by surprise. And so on.

Companion friends are very much a reflection to one another's life. The depth of their familiarity with one another's life and their purity of heart with respect to one another enables each friend to have a glimpse of himself or herself that self-reflection alone could not yield. For no matter how honest a person is in terms of the self-reflection that she or he does, that self-reflection will never be the equivalent of being witnessed by another person, just as practicing a foreign language in the classroom will never be equivalent of being engaged in a conservation with native speakers who, owing to one's command of the language, take it as a given that one understands all that is said.

The above consideration suggests that companion friendship plays a fundamental and equal role in the life of each friend. Interestingly this brings us to an important reason why companion friendship is not replaceable by romantic love.

As noticed above, a defining aspect of romantic love is its erotic component. When things go well, romantic love is unsurpassable in its majesty. However, we all know that erotic passion can 'blind' people to lots and lots of things. Indeed, it can get in the way of common sense itself. There are countless instances where out of feelings of deep erotic attachment people have stayed in a relationship that was obviously quite detrimental to them. In some cases, even physical abuse is involved. Thus, in ways that are truly astounding, erotic passion can override even self-interest.

Companion friendship is entirely without that kind of liability. Although companion friends care deeply about one another and are eager to spend time together, what is also true is that they stand entirely as equals with respect to one another. And the absence of eroticism in their relationship contributes mightily to that very reality. It is no doubt fair to say that even with the most admirable romantic relationship there is an interdependence forged through the erotic bond that does not take place between friends. This, in turn, further contributes to companion friends genuinely being a mirror to one another's soul. Their deep love for one another is not a threat to their independence.

The last observation brings us to one more consideration regarding companion friendship that needs to be brought out, namely that it is rare for companion friendships to be between the young and the elderly. I explain why in what follows.

A substantial difference in age between two people typically marks a significant difference in experiences, self-development, and perspectives regarding life, which in turn typically bears mightily upon what a person finds novel or enjoyable or worth exploring or most disgusting. One does not expect a 50-something person to be exploring the same issues and facing the same challenges as a 20-something individual. In the other direction, one does not expect a 20-something person to know either the successes or the failures of a 50-something individual. Then, of course, there are the typical differences with regard to sheer physical fortitude, health, and agility, with the 20-something individual far surpassing the 50-something individual in those respects. Lastly, there are the normal differences in the self-presentation and sheer tastes between a 20-something person and a 50-something person. Behavior that would be deemed immature for the latter can be quite appropriate or at least not inappropriate for the former. This applies also to language and attire. As for tastes, it is well known that, for instance, 20-year olds and 50-year olds tend to have quite different tastes in music. Nowadays, rap and hip-hop tend to be the music du jour among the 20-something, but not so among the 50-something. What is more, a 50-something moving her or his head while listening to music in that manner that a 20-year old does nowadays would tend to look rather silly.

Taken together, the above considerations simply make it rather unlikely that a companion friendship would take place between two individuals where there is a significant age difference between the two of them. But, of course, there can be exceptions here. A young person can be particularly mature and have a set of interests that set her or him apart from most people in the same age group. By contrast, an older person could share precisely those interests and also have a natural demeanor and measure of physical agility whereby the person's age does not readily call attention to itself. What is more, it turns out that the two individuals have no difficulty at all in communicating with one another in a way that is entirely natural for both and thus renders both quite at-ease with one another. Moreover, there is no respect in which either the older person is seeking to have authority over the younger person or the younger person is looking to have an authority figure in her or his life. Last but not least, it is clear to both that they both wondrously benefit from their interaction.

I noted earlier how quickly two individuals can sense that they identify with one another. That point holds no less so when there is a significant age difference between two individuals. Indeed, it would be ever so clear to both from the very outset that the other got her or his remarks just as they were intended. Perhaps the older person was trying to convey an experience without in the least being authoritative, and the younger person understood it in just that way. Or, from the other direction, the younger person had a quite novel insight to share with the older person, and it was manifestly obvious that the older person had no difficulty whatsoever in seeing the insight in just the way that it was intended and did not come across as patronizing in any way.

To state the obvious, a 50-something individual could be the parent of a 20-something person. Still, a friendship can happen. Yet, I suggest that it is far more rare for parents and children to become companion friends. I turn now to explain why.

2 Can parents and children be companion friends?

When a child enters into the world, the child's parents quite literally know more about the child than the child knows about her or himself, since a newborn child is entirely without a sense of self. Of course, the child comes to have a sense of self quite rapidly. Still, it remains true for a significant period of time that the parents know more about the child than the child knows about herself or himself. Good parents, then, are parents who do what is good for their child although the child is without a conception of the good. Indeed, part of being a good parent is fundamentally tied to helping the child to formulate a proper conception of the good, so that the child can make good decisions, and so live a good life, even in the absence of the parents.

If all goes well, the child fully realizes this; accordingly, it is perfectly natural for the child to talk to her or his parents concerning just about everything that takes place in her or his life: feelings, hopes, disagreements, and so on. Notoriously, without at all being malicious, children can ask questions and make comments that are quite embarrassing. This is because they do not yet have a developed sense of either propriety or privacy.

Needless to say, that changes with age. At the age of 6, a child might very well ask: 'Mommy, why were you and dad making so much noise last night in the bedroom?' No child at 13 will ever ask that question precisely because a 13 year old already knows the answer. The child is also respecting the privacy of her or his parents. Similarly, out of a sense of privacy and appropriateness, a 13 year old child would not take a shower with the parent of the opposite sex—probably not even with a parent of the same sex either, except in such public places as the gym. By the age of 13, a child grasps what it is for parents to have their own private conversation. Likewise, good parents give their child a measure of 'space', as the saying goes. Needless to say, their doing so constitutes none other than the recognition on their part that their child is entitled to a measure of privacy. Finally, I should point out that a 13 year old has friends of her or his age, and this is seen as wonderful sign of social development on the part of the child. Indeed, parents who did not encourage their child to have friends would be parents who are unsatisfactory in a fundamental way.

Now, there are four salient differences between the parental bond and the bond of friendship that is forged, including such a bond forged by the children of parents. (1) There is a complete absence of any antecedent obligation on the part of either individual to the friendship to the other. By contrast, parents have a fundamental obligation to care for their child thereby ensuring the child's proper development. In turn, the child rightly has an enormous debt of gratitude towards the parents who are good parents in that regard. (2) The formation of companion friendship is entirely an expression of the mutual wishes of both parties. There is no antecedent obligation for them to become friends with one another. By hypothesis, the parent–child relationship begins entirely without the permission of the child. (3) There is no antecedent sense in which friends have any entitlement to know anything about the other. By contrast, parents are clearly entitled to know all that there is to know about their child's wants, tastes, behaviors, psychology, and so on. 4) Companion friends do not have authority over one another. By contrast, parents have authority over their child.[4]

The foregoing points hold whether we are talking about friendships between young people who are still under the authority of their parents or individuals who have the complete moral and social standing of an adult. The significant difference between these two cases is that with young people who are still under the authority of their parents, a friendship which a young person wishes to forge may meet with the disapproval of the young person's parents. Strictly speaking, that could also happen with an individual who has the complete moral and social standing of an adult. The difference of course is that in the latter case the mere disapproval of the person's parents would presumably have no bearing on the individual pursuing the friendship in question, whereas in the former case, parental disapproval would typically mean that the friendship could not proceed.

Points (1) through (4) above make it clear that companion friendship is a fundamental expression of personal choice on the part of each individual to a companion friendship. And this consideration rebounds with an explanation for why it is ever so rare for there to be a companion friendship between a child and her or his parents, especially when the child is an adult but yet relatively young. On the one hand, there are simply too many moral debts that a child owes her or his parents for the salubrious role that they have played in the child's life. This consideration is related to the idea of a child having honor for her or his parents, where this constitutes the child's having a measure of moral deference with regard to them. There is also the issue of parental authority or, in any case, the residue of parental authority even when the child is an adult, whereas there is no sense in which the child even has a semblance of authority over the parents. This difference is a serious impediment to having companion friendship between equals with a parent and a child. Last, but certainly not least, there is way too much information that the parent knows about their child that precludes forging a relationship of genuine equality between the parents and child with respect to self-disclosure. Two individuals who have been companion friends can indeed say to one another 'I know you'. Alas, that truth is owing to mutual self-disclosure from the very start of their friendship, something that is not possible between parents and their child. Finally, in this regard, there is the idea of the sanctity of parenthood. It might be impossible to maintain that conception of a parent and, at the same time, have a companion friendship with a parent. For instance, while companion friends might be mindful of the ways in which each other has a rich sexual life and occasionally tease one another in that regard, people are less inclined to do that with their parents precisely because this is typically seen as being out of step with interacting with parents in a manner that is in keeping with the sanctity of parenthood, which is not altogether unrelated to the reality that there is a residue of parental authority and also to the idea of honoring parents. There is no need to insist that it is impossible for there to be a companion friendship between parents and a child. Enough has been said, though, to explain why it would be extremely rare for that to happen. Indeed, the considerations proffered suggest that such a rapport is perhaps even more rare than is a companion friendship between two people with a 30 year age difference between them.

A most interesting way of lending credence to the final point of the preceding paragraph is by noting that companion friendships can end. It does not take much imagination at all to see that if a companion friendship between parents and a child ends, this has all sorts of untoward and undesirable consequences for the parent–child relationship. In the typical case of the dissolution of a companion friendship each can go their separate ways. And there will effectively be no reason for them to interact with one another again with the same degree of trust and concomitant self-disclosure. This they could do even if they work in the same building, for they could manage to be agreeable and polite to one another. By contrast, if the companion friendship between parents and a child were to end, it is not at all clear how they could simply roll their relationship back to no more than the salubrious parent–child bond that they once had. In this regard, the principle of better-safe-than-sorry might be most applicable. It is perhaps better never to have a companion friendship with loving parents than to have one that dissolves.

3 Companion friendship: the beginning and the end

There is a very straightforward sense in which companion friendship has a remarkable parallel to parental love.[5] As noted earlier, parental love is surely an everlasting reminder that a most meaningful and salubrious bond need not in any way involve an ounce of eroticism. Companion friends delight in one another's company, spend enormous amounts of time together, and share significant details about their lives with one another without ever supposing that a romantic relationship would somehow make their relationship better. Nor, again, does anyone suppose that this is all in preparation for a romantic relationship.

A far from trivial difference between parental love and the love of companion friendship is that with the latter each has chosen the other from the very start. Thus, companion friendship is a profound way of sanctifying the wherewithal of both parties to the friendship to choose wisely, in exercising both their autonomy and their judgment of good character. Each is a living reminder to the other of that sublime reality. Yet, an inescapable truth would seem to be that parental love serves as the backdrop for that choice; for when parental love is as it should be, that child comes to have a deep sense of worth that is entirely independent of merely fulfilling the wishes of another, namely the parents in this case.

If I may invoke and extend the use of Kantian language, when parental love is as it should be, the child profoundly experiences being valued as an end and not as a means. The child is emotionally configured in that way when parental love is as it should be. That emotional configuration is entirely shorn of eroticism. The love of companion friendship

majestically moves the experience of being thus valued beyond the parents. In effect, I have suggested that in general we would expect the best companion friendships to be between individuals who have enjoyed parental upbringing at its best.

Needless to say, not even companion friendships always last. In the absence of simply having made a tremendous error of judgment at the outset which is quickly recognized, there are typically two possibilities. One is that the two individuals drift apart. Perhaps they come to be separated by a vast geographical distance that simply precludes spontaneous interaction. Or their interests pull them radically apart. Or, they come to differ markedly with respect to the values that animate each of their lives. What I want to draw attention to, however, is the case of betrayal, and my contention is that the betrayal in companion friendship is rather akin to betrayal in romantic love. Here is why. Romantic love involves two people in the endeavor to realize a shared ideal. Likewise, companion friendship involves two people in the endeavor to realize a shared ideal. In either case, to betray another is to give the person in question good reason to believe that one fully embraces and is committed to the continued realization of that shared ideal and then to turn around and do with unquestionable deliberateness and intentionality that which is unequivocally contrary to the realization of that very goal. With romance, the most well-defined and most decisive case of betrayal is typically sexual infidelity. With companion friendship, there is no well-defined act that is the parallel to sexual infidelity. It will be remembered, though, that sexual infidelity is none other than a particular form of the betrayal of trust. Alas, with companion friendship it is manifestly clear that there can be ever so disconcerting and pugnacious instances of the betrayal of trust.

Here is an example. Imagine that Leslie, who is a stunningly handsome man, is absolutely devastated over what he has done. Here is what happened. Having just been fired from Major Company, he goes back to his hotel (for he is on the other side of the country) and orders one drink after another at the bar. An hour later, he is completely inebriated. He is then approached by a woman and they have a sexual tryst. He is pained beyond measure over what he has done; and calls up his best friend Adrian, his buddy of 15 years, to talk about it. Needless to say, this is a conversation in confidence if ever there was one.

Now, Adrian does not doubt for a moment that Leslie is tremendously sorry for and pained by that unintended act of infidelity in which he (Leslie) engaged. Indeed, Adrian has never seen Leslie so pained. In fact, Leslie even considered committing suicide. In any event, it turns out that Adrian goes on to commit a tremendous indiscretion, for a week later, Adrian tells Leslie's wife about the affair. Adrian claims that he did so in order to help Leslie's wife understand Leslie's rather strange and stand-offish behavior around the house. Clearly, Adrian has betrayed Leslie's trust; and it is arguable on several accounts that Adrian's betrayal is worse than Leslie's untoward moment of infidelity, since there is a very straightforward respect in which Leslie's infidelity was not at all intentional. What is more, Adrian most certainly did not need to disclose that infidelity in order to make sense of Leslie's unusual behavior to Leslie's wife. One can debate whether the wife needed to be informed at all about this tremendously unintended transgression on Leslie's part. However, it is clear that Adrian should have given Leslie some time to make this confession. In fact, it is not at all clear that Adrian should ever have informed Leslie's wife about Leslie's unintended transgression. And if Adrian saw that Leslie was not going to do so, that could be a reason for Adrian to re-evaluate their friendship. However, that is another matter entirely.

Understandably, Leslie is simply furious with Adrian and has doubts about whether their friendship can continue precisely because Adrian's action has a level of intentionality to it that is entirely at odds with his respect for Leslie. Indeed, Adrian's action has all the air of utter indifference or callousness to it. Needless to say, Leslie's reaction is not at all unlike the kind of reaction that a person has when it is discovered that her or his romantic partner has been intentionally unfaithful. This, of course, tells us what we already know, namely that a violation of trust that tears at the very core of our being need not involve marital infidelity or physical violence. And the point that I am making here is that although romantic love differs from companion friendship in that sexual eroticism has an absolutely central place in romantic love but not friendship, it nonetheless turns out that romantic love and companion friendship are more alike than not with regard to the issue of betrayal.

Can parents betray their children or the other way around? Absolutely. However, it is manifestly clear that betrayal in either direction simply does not suffice to vitiate the parent–child ties. For one thing, there is simply no sense in which a child can say 'I made a mistake in my choice of parents. I should never have chosen you'. Of course, parents can perhaps make that claim, but short of putting their child up for adoption, nothing absolves them from their obligation to be good parents. And in looking back, a child can rightly ask whether her or his parents measured up in that regard.

This last observation provides us with a most fitting way to end this essay. When there can be no doubt whatsoever that in a companion friendship one of the friends has changed in negative ways that no one could have foreseen, there is a question that forcefully presents itself no less so in companion friendships than in romantic ties, namely the following: 'Did I choose well?'

An observation from Philippa Foot's profound essay 'Moral Beliefs' is most relevant here (Foot 1958–9). Acknowledging that even a just person makes mistakes, she makes the quite profound observation that a person cannot be just if she or he is prepared to do certain things, and if an individual is too easily tempted to do those things, then the individual was prepared after all. This insight applies equally to love for another, and we may refer to it as the preventive character of love.

If we respect and love another as a companion friend, then precisely what follows is that the very idea of harming that friend is repulsive to us. For example, the very idea of a sexual tryst with our companion friend's spouse would simply be repulsive to us. For anything like that to occur we would already have to be completely inebriated and the spouse would have to look for all the world like an entirely different person. Or, suppose that a companion friend has shared a most intimate detail about her or his life, such as the friend had been sexually abused by a sibling or parent. Again, the friend to whom this has been told would be so respectful of the friend's trust and the friend's privacy that it would take something akin to a lobotomy before the friend would ever reveal what has been shared with her or him.

In the language of Bernard Williams,[6] it takes a long and unobvious argument to excuse the absence of the preventive character of love. It is very rare that anyone has a good excuse in that regard; and no one should ignore that reality. Being guided by the preventive character of love is one of the immutable aspects of a friendship (or a romantic relationship). When that preventive character turns out to be absent on a particular occasion, the friend who has been wronged has a most important decision to make and the alternatives are simply the following: (a) Should I forgive the friend and maintain the companion friendship? (b) Should I end the friendship? Whatever else is true, the answer to that question cannot always be (a). Indeed, it is perhaps rarely (a). This speaks to a courage with regard to friendship (as well as romantic love), namely the courage to move on, that is rarely considered. Defending these last two points, however, would be an entirely different essay.[7]

Notes

1. The classic account of friendship is to be found in Aristotle's *Nicomachean Ethics*, books 8 and 9. While my intellectual debt to Aristotle should be apparent, the views concerning friendship developed in this essay go substantially beyond anything that Aristotle says.
2. For a most sophisticated and informed philosophical account of trust, see Baier (1991).
3. A lot concerning non-verbal behavior is presupposed in these remarks. Non-verbal behavior includes voice tonality, facial expressions, and body posture. For an important and classic discussion of facial expressions, see Darwin (1989). See also Barrier (2008).
4. The above four points owe much to the following individuals: O'Neill (1988), Schoeman (1980), and Schrag (1975).
5. I am relying upon the account of parental love developed in Thomas (2005). See also 'Friendship,' in the *Encyclopedia of Applied Ethics* (2011), where I briefly discuss the role of parental love in the development of friendship.
6. Williams (1973).
7. In writing this essay, I am particularly grateful to Helm (2010). I have also benefited enormously from the comments of Tarik Yildiz and two students: Jesse Feitel and Andrew Riess. A special word of thanks goes to the Rougemont family who has brilliantly modeled the ideal of familial love.

References

A. C. Baier (1991) *Trust. Tanner Lectures on Human Values* (Salt Lake City: University of Utah Press).

G. Barrier (2008) La Communication Non-Verbal. Comprendre les Gestes, Perception et Signification (Paris: ESF Éditeur).

C. Darwin (1989) *The Expression of Emotions in Man and Animals,* edited by Paul Ekman and Phillip Rodger (New York: Oxford University Press).

P. Foot (1958–9) 'Moral Beliefs', *Proceedings of the Aristotelian Society* N.S., 59, 83–104.

B. Helm (2010) *Love, Friendship, and the Self* (New York: Oxford University Press).

O. O'Neill (1988) 'Children's Rights and Children's Lives', *Ethics* 98, 445–63.

F. Schoeman (1980) 'Rights of Children, Rights of Parents and the Moral Basis of the Family', *Ethics* 91, 6–19.

F. Schrag (1975) 'The Child's Status in the Democratic State,' *Political Theory* 3, 441–457.

L. Thomas (2005) *The Family and the Political Self* (New York: Cambridge University Press).

L. Thomas (2011) 'Friendship,' in R. Chadwick, *Encyclopedia of Applied Ethics.* 2nd edition (Amsterdam: Elsevier).

B. Williams (1973) 'A Critique of Utilitarianism,' in J.J.C. Smart and Bernard Williams (eds), *Utilitarianism: For and Against,* (Cambridge [Eng.]: Cambridge University Press).

Part II

The Unity of Friendship

3
Friendship in Kallipolis

Damian Caluori

That friends form some sort of unity is one of the remarkable facts about friendship. We identify with our friends in a way in which we do not identify with non-friends. This identification forms the foundation for the distinction that we make between friends and non-friends. Many other facts about friendship are grounded in it – such as the fact that we are willing to help friends in a way that goes beyond what is otherwise demanded by morality or custom. When our friends need someone to help them move to a new apartment, for example, we will help them without demanding anything in return; we would be rather reluctant to do the same for a stranger. So it is important to ask what sort of unity friendship possesses. In what follows, I shall argue that we find an interesting conception of this unity in Plato.

The scope of this chapter is restricted in at least two ways. First, I shall exclusively be concerned with the unity of friendship and leave open the question whether there are other essential elements constituting friendship. A second restriction is its exclusive focus on Plato's *Lysis*, *Symposium* and *Republic*. I think the discussions of friendship and love in these three dialogues are importantly connected in such a way that we find in the *Republic* answers to problems arising in the *Lysis* and the *Symposium*. The notions of friendship (or, to use the Greek word usually rendered as friendship: *philia*) in the *Phaedrus* and the *Laws* will not be discussed.[1]

According to one reading of Plato, the claim that we find an interesting notion of friendship in his dialogues might seem surprising. For when reading Plato one might get the impression that, given his notion of *philia*, there is no room for friendship at all in his thought. In a classic paper Vlastos argues that Plato does not have the notion of *philia* as loving another person for his or her own sake and concludes from this that, according to Plato, our interest in friends is only instrumental (Vlastos 1981). It is easy to see how one might arrive at such a conclusion. The claim that friendship must consist in loving a friend for his or her own sake (and being loved equally in return) is almost universally accepted. Now Vlastos shows that Plato does not allow for such a notion of friendship because he denies that we can or should love another person for her own sake. But if so, we might feel the necessity to conclude that we are only interested in our friends for some selfish reason. He or she might be useful or pleasant to us, for example, and we love them for that reason alone. Most people find this latter notion of friendship unappealing, and we might well be reluctant to call such a relationship a form of friendship at all. For this reason, we might have doubts as to whether Plato has room for friendship in his thought.

Let us, for the sake of the following discussion, call such an account – according to which friends love one another, not for their respective other's sake, but for some selfish reason – an *instrumental account of friendship*. Let us call an account according to which one loves one's friend for their own sake (and is equally loved in return) a *per se ipsum account of friendship*. Using this distinction, I shall agree with Vlastos that Plato rejects a *per se ipsum* account of friendship and that he does so roughly for the reasons outlined by Vlastos. However, I shall argue that this does not imply that we are necessarily only left with an instrumental account. The reason is that the two sorts of account do not exhaust the realm of possibilities; there is at least a third option, and I shall argue that Plato presents this third option in the *Republic*.

My chapter has three sections. I first introduce the *per se ipsum* account of friendship. I then consider why Plato, in the *Lysis* and in the *Symposium*, rejects this account. Finally, I discuss Plato's third option, which is based on an interesting notion of the *unity* of friendship as it is developed in the *Republic*.

1 The *per se ipsum* account of friendship

Perhaps the most famous proponent of a *per se ipsum* account of friendship is Aristotle. As is well known, he distinguishes three kinds of friendship in his long treatise on friendship in the *Nicomachean Ethics* (*EN* VIII–IX): that based on virtue, on pleasure, and on usefulness respectively (*EN* VIII.3). It is important for our purposes to note that this distinction is based on three distinct sorts of object of love (*EN* VIII.2): goodness *per se*, pleasure and usefulness. Thus, in each form of friendship the friend represents a distinct sort of good on the basis of which we love them; we love friends because they are virtuous (virtue is the good *per se* for human beings), because they are pleasant (to us) or because they are useful (to us). Hence, friendship is grounded in some good which the friend represents (for us). Now there is scholarly debate as to whether in all three forms friends love their friends for the latter's sake or whether this is only the case in what Aristotle calls perfect friendship, i.e. the one based on virtue, the imperfect kinds being merely instrumental.[2] Since this is unclear, it will be prudent for our purposes to focus on the perfect form of friendship which undoubtedly is of the *per se ipsum* type. In a perfect friendship, a friend's virtue is what we find attractive about them, what gives us a reason to be friends with them and in virtue of which we love them. Perfect friendship is thus grounded in the characters of the respective other friend, or more precisely in the perfection of their characters.

These considerations show that a *per se ipsum* account of friendship is not only the negation of an instrumental account of friendship – it is stronger than that. For it presupposes that friends possess some property or properties in virtue of which we love them and on the basis of which our friendship is constituted. Moreover, these properties must be such as to make the friend what she is in herself. In Aristotle, this characteristic is virtue and thus some sort of perfection, but this need not be the case for every *per se ipsum* account. Other such accounts may provide some other property or properties on the basis of which we love our friends. Perhaps, in some such account, these properties need not even be the same in all friendships so that it is possible to love friend A because she possesses property x and friend B because she possesses a different property y (as long as those properties are such as to make the friend what she is in herself). It might even be, as it is perhaps the case in Montaigne, that we do not know at all what it is about a friend that makes us love him or her.[3] But in all cases, for it to count as a *per se ipsum* friendship, there must be, for each friend, some characteristic that makes him what he is in himself and on the basis of which he is loved.

Let us now turn to Plato. It seems to me that we find one version of a *per se ipsum* account in the Aristophanic myth in the *Symposium* (which is likely to have inspired Montaigne). In a preliminary way, let me note that the topic of the *Symposium* is erotic love (or *eros*) and not friendship (or *philia*) and that, accordingly, the *per se ipsum* account presented by the comic poet Aristophanes is one of *eros,* not of *philia*. However, as we shall see in the next section, the difference between *eros* and *philia* in this context can be neglected. For Plato is dissatisfied with the *per se ipsum* account of *philiatic* love for the same reason as he is dissatisfied with the *per se ipsum* account of erotic love.

According to Aristophanes' myth, human beings were originally completely round and each endowed with two sets of sexual organs; each of these beings was cut into two by Zeus and ever since each (half) human being longs for his or her other half. This longing is the desire of erotic love:

> And so, when a person meets the half that is his very own, whatever his orientation, whether it's to young men or not, then something wonderful happens: the two are struck from their senses of love, by a sense of belonging to one another (*philiai te kai oikeiotêti*), and by desire, and they don't want to be separated from one another, not even for a moment. There are the people who finish out their lives together and still cannot say what it is they want from one another. No one would think it is the intimacy of sex ... It's obvious that the soul of every lover longs for something else; his soul cannot say what it is, but like an oracle it has a sense of what it wants, and like an oracle it hides behind a riddle. (*Smp.* 192BC)[4]

The lover's soul cannot tell what it is about the beloved that makes him or her love the beloved. Thus, there is no specifiable property of the sort of Aristotle's virtue that would ground erotic love. However, there is a different sort of property: the beloved must be this particular person who once together with the lover constituted the original whole. Hence, there is some property that the beloved possesses (namely her being the lover's other half) which is grounded in the history of the two and that is the reason why the lover loves him or her. This is sufficient for it to count as *per se ipsum* erotic love: the lover's love is directed towards the beloved due to some property that makes the beloved what she is.

Now when thinking about erotic love, we might perhaps want to replace the strong notion of loving the beloved *per se ipsum* by a looser notion according to which the beloved is loved because of some non-relational lovable quality that she possesses (be this quality constitutive of what the beloved is in herself or not). Call this the quality theory.[5] Both the *per se ipsum* account and the quality theory agree with our common conception that erotic lovers are directed towards one another and that the respective other (or more precisely something about the respective other) is the ground for their erotic love. Plato disagrees with both the *per se ipsum* account and the quality theory because he thinks that the proper object of erotic love cannot be a person.

In the next section I will first briefly show why Plato is dissatisfied with Aristophanes' *per se ipsum* account of erotic love and why he would, for the same reason, reject a *per se ipsum* account of *philiatic* love. For the latter I will turn to the *Lysis*.

2 *Eros* and *philia* as kinds of desire

The main Platonic reason why we cannot erotically love other persons for their own sake is this. If x erotically loves y because of z then what x truly erotically loves is actually z and not y. For example, if Sue erotically loves Pete because of his being virtuous then what Sue really erotically loves is not Pete but his being virtuous. Moreover, what she loves must be virtue quite generally and not just Pete's virtue in particular because there is nothing in Pete's virtue in particular that makes it more loveable than any other person's virtue (if those people are virtuous to the same degree, etc.). Thus, the proper object of Sue's love is virtue quite generally.

This is one of the lessons we learn from Diotima, who, in the *Symposium*, describes the ascent of the lover from his infatuation with the beauty of an individual body to the proper love of Beauty itself:[6]

> A lover who goes about this matter correctly must begin in his youth to devote himself to beautiful bodies. First, if the leader leads aright, he should love one body and beget beautiful ideas there; then he should realize that the beauty of any one body is brother to the beauty of any other and that if he is to pursue beauty of form he'd be very foolish not to think that the beauty of all bodies is one and the same. (*Smp.* 210AB)

After having seen beauties of higher order than that of bodies, the ascending lover will finally arrive at the ultimate object of erotic love: Beauty itself. This is the only object, or sort of object, that one properly erotically loves because one loves it for its own sake. Generalizing this claim, we can say that only Forms are in themselves objects of proper erotic love. Every other object of love is only worthy of love in so far as it imperfectly manifests, or is an image of, the primary object or in so far as it is instrumental to climbing the ladder of love. But there is no other sort of object that could be a proper object of erotic love for its own sake. Most importantly, as opposed to what Aristophanes' myth suggests, persons are not erotically loved for their own sake. Vlastos calls this 'the cardinal flaw in Plato's theory' (Vlastos 1981, p. 31).

I shall now argue that the same applies to *philiatic* love in the *Lysis* – a dialogue that, since antiquity, has had the alternative title *On philia* and is thus often taken to be a dialogue about friendship.[7] However, it becomes less clear whether the dialogue really is about friendship if we consider how closely related its *philiatic* love is to the *Symposium*'s erotic love. Look at the very first scene of the *Lysis*: Socrates, on his way from the Academy to the Lyceum, encounters a young man, Hippothales, who is deeply in love with a boy called Lysis. The fact that Hippothales' erotic love stands at the opening of the *Lysis* ought to be taken seriously.[8] For although the dialogue as a whole focuses on a discussion of *philia* (and not primarily of *eros*), there is no doubt that the notion of *philia* that Plato here is interested in is closely related to that of *eros*. *Philia*, as it is understood in the *Lysis*, is, just as *eros*, a form of desire. In order to substantiate this point, let me briefly consider two passages.

The first passage is Socrates' discussion with Menexenus, which focuses on the question of who is *philos* (friend) of whom in a *philia* between two *philoi*. The idea behind Socrates' question is to establish which one of the two *philoi* is the one in which *philia* is grounded. This might strike us as a strange problem. It becomes somewhat clearer, I think, if we consider the Greek where we can replace the word *philos* by using either the active or the passive participles of the verb *philein* (to love). The idea of this move is to bring out the fact that *philein*, loving, has a direction. It goes from the *philôn*, (the loving friend) to the beloved friend (the *philoumenos*). So the question is whether a *philia* occurs because the loving friend loves the beloved friend or whether this is insufficient because we need reciprocity in addition. Clearly, if we translate *philoi* in this context as 'friends' then reciprocity is indeed necessary because friendship is essentially reciprocal: I cannot be friends with you unless you are also friends with me.

However, Socrates does not talk here about *philia* in the sense of friendship (at least not primarily).[9] For he claims in the immediately following lines that we are also *philoi* of objects, not only of persons, and that objects, of course, cannot reciprocate our love. Neither is a wine-lover loved by her wine nor a philosopher by wisdom. These considerations lead me to the final part of the dialogue and thus to the second passage I want to discuss:

> But now it looks like some other cause of loving and being loved has appeared. – It does look like it.
>
> Then can it really be, as we were just saying, that desire is the cause of *philia*, and that what desires is *philos* to that which it desires, and is so whenever it does so? ... – There's a good chance, he said.

> But still, I said, a thing desires what it is deficient in. Right? – Yes.
>
> And the deficient is *philos* to that in which it is deficient. – I think so.
>
> And it becomes deficient where something is taken away from it. – How couldn't it?
>
> Then it is what belongs to oneself, it seems, that erotic love and *philia* and desire are directed towards, Menexenus and Lysis (*Ly.* 221D–222B).

In this passage, Socrates refers to erotic love and *philia* and desire. They all are said to share the same structure: they are desires for something that we lack.[10] Now not every desire for what we lack is a case of *philia*. So we need to know what object or what kind of object is the object of this specific desire. Unfortunately, Plato remains rather vague about this ultimate object of *philiatic* desire, but we do learn that it is directed towards a first beloved, a *prôton philon*. This is important because the first beloved is, according to the account of the *Lysis*, the thing that we love for its own sake. Now the primary object of *philiatic* desire cannot be a friend: First, because Plato uses the neuter and not a masculine or feminine form of *philon*. Second, because it would be rather unclear what a first friend should be and how other friends would be related to the first friend and why other friends would not be objects of *philiatic* desire (would they be friends at all?). It rather seems that *philia* in the *Lysis* is quite similar to *eros* in the *Symposium*: a desire (or an attitude grounded in a desire) for what we lack even though it belongs to us and that is ultimately identified as the first beloved. If this is correct, then *philia* in the *Lysis* is a form of love but this form should not be identified with friendship.

This does not necessarily exclude that we can construct a notion of friendship on the basis of this primary function of *philia*. But even if it is possible to do this, it will not be a *per se ipsum* account of friendship because of the structure of *philiatic* love just discussed. This is one of the results achieved in different ways by two recent commentaries on this dialogue.

Rowe and Penner claim in their commentary: 'What it is for Lysis to be friend with Menexenus is for him to believe truly that the good of Menexenus is a high-level means to his own ultimate good' (Penner and Rowe 2005, p. 272). Lysis' friendship with Menexenus is thus grounded in a desire for the good. Lysis loves Menexenus, not for the latters' sake, but for the sake of his own ultimate good. Thus, friendship, according to this interpretation, would be construed on the basis of an instrumental account: I do not value my friend for her own sake but only as a means to my own ultimate good. Hence, according to Rowe and Penner, the *Lysis* does not offer a *per se ipsum* account of friendship.

Michael Bordt, although offering a different interpretation, agrees that there is no *per se ipsum* account of friendship in the *Lysis* (Bordt 1998). Like Rowe and Penner, he argues that the striving towards the good is a crucial element in the notion of friendship in the *Lysis*. In a way that Plato does not clarify, the friends' relation to the good constitutes their friendship. Yet unlike Rowe and Penner, Bordt does not claim that friendship is instrumental to the (selfish) achievement of the good. Rather, in his interpretation, the common striving for the good somehow constitutes friendship. Thus, both friends are primarily directed, not to one another, but to a third thing, namely the good. Hence, also according to Bordt, friendship in the *Lysis* is not of the *per se ipsum* type.

Unfortunately, as Bordt concedes, in the *Lysis* we do not learn how precisely a common striving for the good constitutes friendship. Yet I think we can find in the *Republic* an account that picks up precisely this idea: friendship is not grounded in two people's loving one another for the respective other's sake but in a third thing (be this third thing the good or something else).

3 Friendship between guardians

3.1 Collective intentions

Let me first introduce the idea of the unity of friendship that I suggest we find in the *Republic*. According to this notion friends are engaged in a common project, have a common goal, act together and share their emotions. Their common activity is brought about by collective intentions, i.e. by intentions that they literally share and that we might call *we-intentions*. They all pursue the same goal together and structure their own activities, and perhaps even their whole lives, accordingly as parts of this common project. Before I move to an interpretation of the crucial passages in the *Republic*, let me briefly say something more about what I mean by 'being engaged in a common project' and by 'collective intentions'.[11]

Imagine two friends playing chess together every Wednesday night. It might well be that they rightly consider each other friends on the basis of their regularly playing chess together. They both care about chess and that is all they talk about. I want to argue that the unity of this friendship is based on their being engaged in playing chess together regularly. It does not matter, for the unity of their friendship, what each person's character is because friendship, on this account, is not based on sharing character traits, such as Aristotelian virtues. In other words, there need not be something *about* my friend on the basis of which I am her friend. Friends are thus not primarily directed to one another in such a way that their being directed to one another is what constitutes their friendship. Rather, their being engaged in regularly playing chess together, in our example, is a *third* thing to which both friends are appropriately related. This does not preclude that they share certain traits (for example, their passion for playing chess) but, on this account, the sharing of these traits only plays a role in their friendship if it is grounded in a common project (in their actually playing chess together). Thus, one important difference to a *per se ipsum* account of friendship consists in the fact that friends are not friends primarily because they are attracted to one another but rather, in our example, because they are both attracted to playing chess and because they do it together.[12]

The intentions that they have in common are collective in the sense that they both have literally the same intention, namely to play chess together on Wednesday nights. According to the Platonic version that I am going to discuss, such *we-intentions* are not reducible to a number of *I-intentions*, for example, to the conjunction of A's intention to play chess with B and B's intention to play chess with A. Another example suggested to me by Martin Stone is that of dancing tango. The we-intention of dancing tango together is not just the sum of the two I-intentions, to wit that I have the intention of dancing tango with Sue and Sue has the intention of dancing tango with me. Now I shall not provide arguments for non-reductionism of we-intentions.[13] All I am going to argue is that we find this sort of intention in Plato and that the non-reduction is crucial for the notion of friendship that Plato proposes in *Republic* V to which I now shall turn.[14]

Book V discusses Socrates' claim that the guardians, as a collective of friends, have everything in common, in particular, and provocatively, wives and children. In what follows I am less interested in the community of wives and children in particular but rather in the more general idea that the guardians form a collective of friends – an idea that is already indicated early on in the text by the Pythagorean saying that friends have everything in common (*Rep.* IV, 424a2 and V, 449c5). What this means is at least partly that the guardians are engaged together in a common project, namely in the ruling of the just city of Kallipolis. Moreover, they have a common goal, namely the good, or happiness, of the city and thus crucially also of the collective that they form together.[15] This goal structures the collective activity of the friends.

Before discussing the friendship between guardians further, let me make three preliminary exegetical remarks. First, I will not make any distinction between guardians and citizens. I am not sure whether, in book V, we can identify the two classes. Socrates seems to switch between the use of the term 'guardian' and the term 'citizen' in such a way that an identification of citizens with guardians seems to be in order. But even if the class of citizens is not identical with the class of guardians, clearly all guardians are also citizens, and hence what is true of the citizens is also true of the guardians.

Second and in the same vein, I will not discuss the producers. The question of whether the guardians and the producers are friends with one another as well is a difficult one. On the one hand it seems that the unity of the city is guaranteed by the unity of the guardians and that thus the guardians do not need to be friends with the producers. For at 465BC we learn that 'if these [i.e. the guardians] are free from dissensions among themselves, there is no fear that the rest of the city will ever start faction against them or with one another' (Shorey's translation). The unity of the city and the absence of dissension is, of course, Plato's political aim in which friendship plays a key role: he wants to use the unity of friendship to assure the unity of the city. However, as Vlastos already saw, there is a passage in book VIII where Socrates talks about strife between guardians and producers: 'They compromised on the plan of distributing and taking for themselves the land and the houses, enslaving and subjecting *perioeci* and serfs their former *friends* and supporters, of whose freedom they had been guardians' (*Rep.* 547B).[16] If we assume that the term 'friend' in this passage is used in the strict sense, then this would be a good reason to assume that guardians and producers in the ideal city are friends with one another too. Again, I do not think that this poses problems for what I say, which is strictly focused on the friendship between members of the guardian class.

Third, in book V we have not yet learned about the distinction between philosopher rulers and mere guardians. Thus, the guardians we meet in book V have not yet ascended to the Forms and still lack a proper understanding of the Good and the Just in the light of which, as we are going to learn in later books, the city of Kallipolis is to be governed.[17] I believe that the picture drawn in book V would have to be somewhat modified in the light of the later distinction. For example, the motivational structure of the philosopher rulers will clearly differ from that of the guardians of book V. Yet even so, the philosopher rulers will rule the city together and thus also have a common project, possibly shared with the rest of the guardians.

3.2 Collective actions and emotions

At 457C Socrates explains that the guardians, male and female alike, must be 'engaged in everything together' or, in Shorey's translation, 'have all pursuits in common' (*panta epitêdeuein*).[18] Here is an example of their common pursuits: at *Rep.* 566C we are told that 'within the city and when they [i.e. the guardians] go forth to war they ought to keep guard together and hunt together as it were like hounds, and have all things in every way, so far as possible, in common.' It is true that Socrates in this passage emphasizes that men and women do everything together but we can conclude that this *a fortiori* holds true of all guardians.

Their community of action is accompanied by a community of feeling. So we learn that the guardians share one experience of pleasure and pain (*Rep.* 464D). Thus the guardians not only do everything together, they also share the pleasures and pains with their fellow guardians. This fits nicely with our modern intuitions concerning friendship. For friends are deeply concerned with what is good and bad for their friends and for their friendship and they feel accordingly. What is good or bad for my friend literally affects me too.

Now the idea of a community of feeling already points beyond the idea of being *merely* engaged in a common project. For Socrates' discussion shows that the community of guardians should not be identified with the sort of community that is formed, for example, by a business company. This is important because it is of course possible that people work together in a common project without being friends. The CEO, the accountant, and the factory workers work together within the structure of their company; even if we assume that they have a common goal and that everyone works hard to achieve it, the engagement within the company that unites the CEO, the accountant and the factory workers is still not sufficient to constitute friendship. Accordingly, being engaged in a common project (taken in a weak sense) is necessary for the unity of Platonic guardian friendship but not sufficient. We also need collective intentions and emotions (and thus engagement in a strong sense).[19] To discuss this further we need to look at how guardian friendship is conceived against the background of family relations.

3.3 Family as a model for friendship

Socrates emphasizes that the guardians are kinsfolk, calling one another brother and sister etc. Some of them are indeed blood related, but others are not strictly speaking relatives, and thus sharing more genes with some than with others does not seem to be the reason why Socrates proposes the idea of their being kin. The crucial point rather is that they live together and are thus, just like a family, engaged collectively in a common project, namely that of leading a good life together.[20]

Friends, just like family members, belong together and thus distinguish themselves as a collective in important ways from non-friends. This sense of belonging together plays an important role in the *Republic*'s discussion of the friendship between guardians. When talking about how his ideal city differs from other states, Socrates asks whether in other states any of the people belonging to the ruling class could be considered outsiders (*allotrioi*) and receives the answer that in many states this will be the case. Not so in Kallipolis. Here no guardian will ever be considered an outsider; all guardians belong together (are *oikeioi*: *Rep.* 463B). The reason given shows how important it is for Socrates that guardian friendship is modeled on the basis of family relations: 'for no matter whom he meets, he will feel that he is meeting a brother, a sister, a father, a mother, a son, a daughter, or the offspring or forebears of these' (*Rep.* 462C). Family members, just like friends, belong together in a much stronger sense than co-workers in a business company.

This stronger sense is well expressed in the case where a citizen in Kallipolis fares well or ill: then 'people will pronounce in unison the word of which we spoke: It is mine that does well; it is mine that does ill' (*Rep.* 463E). Thus, each guardian is immediately affected by what happens to her co-guardians and friends. It is not only the case that one guardian suffers and the other guardians merely feel empathy for her; rather the very same affection is felt by all of them together. This point is vividly illustrated by a comparison with an organism:

> If the finger of one of us is wounded, the entire organism that binds body and soul together into a single system under the ruling part within it is aware of this ... All of it feels the pain as a whole, though it is a part that suffers, and that is how we come to say that the man has a pain in his finger. (*Rep.* 462CD)

When there is pain in the finger then the whole organism feels pain, not only the finger itself. By analogy, when a friend feels pain then the community of friends as a whole is affected by the suffering of this one friend. Thus, such emotions are in this sense not completely individualized – they are literally shared by the community of friends even though they have a particular *locus* in the one suffering friend: 'when anyone of the citizens suffers aught of good and evil..., [the state] will be most likely to speak of the part that suffers as its own and will share the pleasure or the pain as a whole' (*Rep.* 462DE). 'All the citizens rejoice and grieve alike' because 'the community of pleasure and pain [is] the tie that binds them together' (*Rep.* 462B).

It is remarkable that Plato, in the above analogy, talks of parts and wholes to bring out what is special about a community of friends. I think there are two related ways in which a collective of friends can be considered a whole of which the parts are friends.[21] First, as discussed, the collective of friends shares feelings (and, I would add, intentions) in the way just described. In so far as they feel, intend, and act together, they can be seen as one collective subject: a (non-reducibly) collective entity and thus a whole whose parts they are.[22] But we can secondly see that friends form a whole if we focus on what I said earlier about their being engaged in a common project. For the comparison with an organism allows for the notion that, in a friendship, each friend has a particular role to play and only when all friends do what they ought to will the collective goal be achieved.[23] Thus, the common project gives a structure to the friendship, which allows for differentiation between friends.[24] This may be attractive because it can explain how people of quite different status can be friends (and how their different status might be constitutive of their friendship). But even if we are not so much interested in the idea of differentiation between friends, friends are collectively active in such a way that their collective activity is grounded in collective intentions – intentions that, just like the emotions discussed above, are literally and non-reductively shared.

3.4 Degrees of friendship

One might find this a rather radical and perhaps odd notion of friendship, one that has nothing to do with the sort of friendship that ordinary people have. Accordingly, one might wonder whether Plato's model has any bearing on ordinary non-guardian friendship. Even though Plato does not elaborate such thoughts, I think that it is possible to account for ordinary friendships on the basis of guardian friendship. Guardian friendship is radical because guardians share their whole lives together and their whole lives are devoted to one grand project. This is clearly not the case with our ordinary friendships. Nor need it be. For we can account for ordinary friendship along Platonic lines if we allow for degrees of friendship. This in itself seems to be a reasonable move to make because it is a familiar fact that some friendships are very close, others less so and some hardly distinguishable from mere acquaintances. On the basis of the Platonic account, we might make two kinds of adaptation to arrive at a notion of friendship that captures that of more ordinary friendships. First, the closeness of a friendship might be due to how deeply and for how long we are engaged together in a common project and to what extent we are involved together in the project in terms of our collective emotions and intentions. There will rarely be a friendship that takes up our whole life (as it is in the case of guardian friendship). Second, our lives are usually not as unified as those of Platonic guardians. Most people will be engaged in a number of projects simultaneously and over time and this with different people and to various degrees. Accordingly, they will form all sorts of different friendships. Again, this is, I think, compatible with the Platonic model because all we need for each of these friendships is that it arises, in the way specified, out of the collective engagement in a common project.[25] Guardian friendship, i.e. a shared life devoted to one grand project, is much closer and deeper than any other friendship and can thus serve as the paradigm case of friendship.

4 Conclusion

In the *Lysis* we found Plato develop a notion of *philia* on the basis of the meaning of its verb, *philein*, i.e. to love. Since he understands loving, much like *eros* in the *Symposium*, as a sort of desire that cannot ultimately be satisfied by people, he does not primarily aim at giving an account of *philia* as friendship in that dialogue. Rather, Socrates tries primarily to clarify what notion of *philia* we need to explain the fact that we love such things as wine, horses, wisdom, and perhaps Forms. It is an account, I think, that is developed further in the *Symposium* even though in that dialogue Plato focuses on the related notion of *eros*.

In the *Republic*, by contrast, we do find an account of *philia* as friendship. Desire does not play any essential role in it, for according to this notion, a friend's love is not primarily directed towards his or her friend. Instead of trying to find a notion of *philia* which is based on the meaning of the verb *philein*, Plato uses in the *Republic* that connotation of the word *philia* that may be grounded in the adjective *philon* if it is true that the latter conveys a sense of belonging.[26] Quite independently of linguistic considerations, however, the crucial fact about friends in the *Republic* is that they belong together and the question is what makes them do so. I have argued that friends are together engaged in a common project (in the strong sense) and thus form a whole whose parts they are, involving collective intentions, emotions, and actions.[27]

At the very beginning of this chapter I discussed the *per se ipsum* account of friendship and how it is based on friends' loving one another for the sake of the respective other. His discussion in the *Lysis* and in the *Symposium* explain why Plato does not want to base his notion of friendship on this sort of love. The *Republic* does not indicate a change of mind: Guardian friendship is not of the *per se ipsum* type. What I have not shown yet is that neither is it instrumental. It is not instrumental because the intentions, actions, emotions, and perhaps even lives of friends are literally and crucially collective. To make this important difference clear, just look at how different the following two statements are: (i) I want my friend to do something which serves my own ends and my friend wants me to do something which serves her own ends. (ii) We (that is: my friend and I) want to do something together which serves our common end. On the Platonic account discussed here, (ii) is not reducible to (i), and accordingly the guardian-account of friendship is not instrumental.[28] Guardian friendship is thus a third account, distinct from the *per se ipsum* and from the instrumental type.

One appealing feature of this view on the unity of friendship is that it can account for the fact that we sometimes indeed become friends with people who are quite different from us. In such a friendship neither our similarity nor the difference between us is the reason for our friendship. Moreover, it might be hard or even impossible to see why we have become friends if we only compare the sort of person we are with the sort of person our friend is. But surely, in every friendship, perfect or not, friends will be engaged (in the strong sense) together in something or other and thus this must be a crucial element in any friendship. I have argued that this common engagement (properly understood) is also an excellent candidate for accounting for the unity of friendship.[29]

Notes

1. For Plato on friendship, see Price (1989), El Murr (forthcoming) and Konstan (forthcoming).
2. The classic paper for this discussion is Cooper (1999) who rejects the view that imperfect friendships in Aristotle are purely instrumental.
3. For Montaigne, see Chapter 4 of the present volume.
4. All translations of passages from the *Symposium* by Nehamas and Woodruff (1989); all translations from the *Lysis* by Lombardo (1997) and those from the *Republic* by Shorey (1930).
5. In both love and friendship, the *per se ipsum* account is related to the quality theory according to which we love friends (or lovers) because of certain non-relational loveable properties they possess. It is more restricted in that it postulates that these properties must be such as to make the friend what

she is in herself. For a discussion and critique of quality theories see Kolodny (2003), pp. 138–42 , Hurka (1997) and Chapter 11 of the present volume.

6. For a detailed explanation of the whole ascent in the *Symposium,* see Sheffield (2006).
7. For the following see also Konstan (2000). Two important commentaries on the *Lysis* are Bordt (1998) and Penner and Rowe (2005).
8. For this see Konstan (forthcoming).
9. The *Lysis* is still important for discussions of friendship, of course, but I claim that friendship is not Plato's primary interest in the dialogue.
10. See Annas (1977, p. 536). See also *Smp.* 200A.
11. For a contemporary account of friendship which is similar to the one that I suggest Plato proposes, see Helm (2010).
12. For an illustration of a friendship based exclusively on playing chess together, see the magnificent movie *Shatranj Ke Khilari* (The Chess Players), directed by Satyajit Ray, (1977).
13. For contemporary discussions of collective intentions see, for example, Searle (1990), Gilbert (2009) and Pettit (2009); for plural agency and friendship, see Helm (2010).
14. My focus is exclusively on the *unity* of friendship. Thus, there might well be further essential elements in friendship. For example, perhaps the project must be good for the friends; perhaps it must have some high degree of significance in their lives etc.
15. This does not imply that the city is identical with the collective of guardians.
16. Vlastos (1981, p. 13); El Murr (forthcoming).
17. On the philosopher rulers and their ruling Kallipolis, see Caluori (2011).
18. See also *Rep.* 451C. In a non-technical way, this view was widespread in antiquity. See for example Cicero *De amic.* 6.20; Sallust *Catiline* 20.4; Konstan (1997), p. 130f.
19. In what follows I mean 'being engaged in a common project (in the strong sense)' to involve collective intentions and emotions and 'being engaged in a common project (in the weak sense)' as not necessarily involving collective intentions and emotions.
20. Of course, their project also involves the continuous existence of the city over generations and thus procreation. Moreover, in both city and family the right upbringing of children is of the utmost importance. But these are matters I cannot go into here.
21. See Morrison (2001) for the relation of part and whole in the city.
22. This view also allows for the interesting possibility that the happiness of the collective of friends is not necessarily identical with the happiness of its individual members.
23. The goal need not be some future aim to be achieved; in some projects the collective activity itself is the aim (e.g. playing music together).
24. Note how Plato in talking about family relations also refers to the different functions within a family (father, mother, daughter, son etc.). I am not claiming that this sort of differentiation is necessary for friendship. It may only be necessary for some projects in which friends are engaged together.
25. It would be a natural extension of what is said in this chapter that, as Hurka suggests in his chapter in this volume, people are friends because of a

common history: see also Hurka (1997) and Kolodny (2003). Accordingly, we would have to add to the Platonic account that, even after having finished a common project, friends may well remain friends on grounds that they once were engaged together in a common project (in the strong sense).

26. See Frisk (1959–61) s.v. and Dirlmeier (1931). The meaning of the adjective *philon*, which usually means 'dear', is a much disputed issue. Remarkably, Homer uses it to qualify such things as hearts and garments and, on the traditional view, such expressions as '*philon* heart' are understood as 'one's heart'. The traditional view has been challenged by Hooker (1987) and Robinson (1990), followed by Konstan (1997), p. 29f. It has at least the scholion on *Il.* 1, 569 on its side: *<philon kêr: philon> to idion, hôs phila heimata* ('philon heart': 'philon' = 'one's own', as in 'one's garment').
27. An important topic I have not discussed is the relation between virtue, the good and the unity of friendship. Plato's guardians are of course highly virtuous people, and their aim is the good of the city. However, close friendships between Nazis seem at least possible, and if family is the model for friendship, we can easily remind ourselves of the existence of Mafia families. We would thus need to sort out whether (and to what extent) the virtuous character of the guardians is necessitated by the unity of their friendship or (and to what extent) by the ethical character of their project.
28. Thus, Platonic guardian friendship is crucially distinct from Aristotelian civic or political friendship, a type of friendship that is grounded in usefulness (*EE* 1242a; *EN* 1160a).
29. I would like to thank David Konstan, Don Morrison, Peter Turner and audiences at the New School in New York and at the National University in Seoul, Korea, for comments on and very helpful discussions of earlier versions of this chapter.

References

J. Annas (1977) 'Plato and Aristotle on Friendship and Altruism', *Mind* 86, 532–54.

M. Bordt (1998) *Platon:* Lysis. *Übersetzung und Kommentar* (Göttingen: Vandenhoeck & Ruprecht).

D. Caluori (2011) 'Reason and Necessity: The Descent of the Philosopher Kings', *Oxford Studies in Ancient Philosophy* 40, 7–27.

J. M. Cooper (1999) 'Aristotle on the Forms of Friendship', in id., *Reason and Emotion: Essays on Ancient Moral Psychology and Ethical Theory* (Princeton: Princeton University Press), 312–35.

F. Dirlmeier (1931) PHILOS *und* PHILIA *im vorhellenistischen Griechentum* (Munich: Druck der Salesianischen Offizin).

D. El Murr (forthcoming), '*Philia* in Plato' in G. Gurtler and S. Stern-Gillet (eds), *Ancient and Medieval Concepts of Friendship* (Albany NY: SUNY Press).

H. Frisk (1959–61) *Griechisches Etymologisches Wörterbuch* (Heidelberg: Winter).

M. Gilbert (2009) 'Shared Intention and Personal Intention', *Philosophical Studies* 144, 167–87.

B. Helm (2010) *Love, Friendship and the Self* (Oxford: Oxford University Press).

J. Hooker (1987) 'Homeric *PHILOS*', *Glotta* 65, 44–65.

T. Hurka (1997) 'The Justification of National Partiality', in R. McKim and J. McMahan (eds), *The Morality of Nationalism* (New York: Oxford University Press), 139–57.

N. Kolodny (2003) 'Love as Valuing a Relationship', *Philosophical Review* 112, 135–89.

D. Konstan (1997) *Friendship in the Classical World* (Cambridge: Cambridge University Press).

—— (2000) 'Plato on Love and Friendship', *Hypnos* 6, 154–169.

—— (forthcoming) 'Friendship' in G. Press (ed.), *A Companion to Plato* (London: Continuum Books).

S. Lombardo (trans.) (1997) *'Lysis'*, in J. Cooper (ed.), *Plato, Complete Works* (Indianapolis: Hackett).

D. Morrison (2001) 'The Happiness of the City and the Happiness of the Individual in Plato's *Republic*', *Ancient Philosophy* 21, 1–24.

A. Nehamas and P. Woodruff (trans.) (1989) *Plato: Symposium* (Indianapolis: Hackett).

T. Penner and C. Rowe (2005) *Plato's* Lysis (Cambridge: Cambridge University Press).

P. Pettit (2009) 'The Reality of Group Agents', in C. Mantzavinos (ed.), *Philosophy of the Social Sciences: Philosophical Theory and Scientific Practice* (Cambridge: Cambridge University Press), 67–91.

A. W. Price (1989) *Love and Friendship in Plato and Aristotle* (Oxford: Oxford University Press).

D. Robinson (1990) 'Homeric *PHILOS*: Love of Life and Limbs, and Friendship with One's *THYMOS*', in E.M. Craik (ed.), *'Owls to Athens': Essays on Classical Subjects Presented to Sir Kenneth Dover* (Oxford: Oxford University Press), 97–108.

J. Searle (1990) 'Collective Intentions and Actions', in P. Cohen, J. Morgan, and M. Pollack (eds), *Intentions in Communication* (Cambridge: MIT Press), 401–15.

F. C. C. Sheffield (2006) *Plato's* Symposium*: The Ethics of Desire* (Oxford: Oxford University Press).

P. Shorey (trans.) (1930) *Plato: The Republic: Books 1–5* (Cambridge: Harvard University Press).

G. Vlastos (1981) 'The Individual as an Object of Love in Plato', in id., *Platonic Studies* (Princeton: Princeton University Press), 3–34.

4
Montaigne's 'Perfect' Friendship

Ullrich Langer

In the history of the philosophy of friendship, few contributions have caught the attention of the popular and critical imagination as much as Michel de Montaigne's *Essais* (1580, 1588, 1595), and in particular a chapter entitled 'De l'amitié' (Book 1, chapter 27).[1] This attention brought to Montaigne's book is a curious phenomenon: in terms of the philosophy done in his own time, the *Essais* do not really qualify as philosophy, that is, as a treatise or dialogue containing consistent argumentation and commentary. Neither do they qualify as a compendium of moral philosophy, with its systematic presentation of topics and opinions. Nor do they qualify as a sourcebook for legal or political or ecclesiastic rhetoric, with sayings and examples arranged in alphabetical order, although some editions after Montaigne's death in 1592 include an elaborate index of topics designed to facilitate just such a use. The *Essais* are altogether something else, and often frustrate philosophers seeking unequivocal positions and elaborate arguments, since Montaigne proposes neither, really. Even his Pyrrhonian skepticism, the most obviously 'philosophical' argumentation we encounter, is not without glaring inconsistencies, or at the very least is an intermittent feature of his book.[2]

'De l'amitié' does not represent the only treatment of the topic of friendship in the *Essais*: several other chapters contain analyses of friendship or of examples of friendships (see 'De l'inégalité qui est entre nous' [I, 42], 'De la vanité' [III, 9], 'De l'expérience' [III, 13]). Remarks containing the words 'ami' and 'amitié' are strewn throughout the *Essais*, and the words had very wide meanings and uses in the sixteenth century. What characterizes 'De l'amitié,' however, is its wide critical and cultural reception[3] which, I think, is based on two factors. The first factor is existential: moral philosophy is being performed around a 'real' friendship, Montaigne's own relationship with his deceased friend Etienne de la Boétie.[4] Second, Montaigne formulates his 'feeling' of friendship in ways that essentially anticipate a private 'sublime' of human affection for another, and comfort our sense that there are, and perhaps should be, some areas of human emotional interaction that resist rational explanation. This private 'sublime' of affection runs counter to the classical philosophical account of friendship.

I will focus on this second factor, that is, on the way in which Montaigne's writing poses philosophical questions, or rather, the way in which philosophical positions are influenced by the language Montaigne uses to express them. In this specific instance, the question is that of personal identity and the fusion of the friends' identities in 'perfect' friendship. Let me outline the reasons for which personal identity – how one can define the friend as a singular person – is an important issue in the philosophy of friendship during Montaigne's time. This means that I will put off the discussion of Montaigne's chapter until I have outlined the positions that are in the background of his own analysis.

Classical accounts of friendship are fundamental in the moral philosophy of the sixteenth century, and the most rigorous account of friendship is to be found in Aristotle's *Nicomachean Ethics*, whereas more discursive treatments characterize Cicero's *Laelius de amicitia* and Seneca's *De beneficiis*.[5] In classical accounts, *philia* or *amicitia* is distinguished from desire, *eros/amor*, or simple good will, *eunoia* or *benevolentia*, and is said to be based on three motivating factors: friendship can be motivated by pleasure (*delectabile*), by usefulness (*utile*), and by virtue (*honestum*).[6] The first two are friendships in which the friend's identity as a person is less important than the pleasure or usefulness that the relationship procures. That is, once pleasure or usefulness cease to be produced by the friendship, there are no more grounds for the friends to be friends. Cases that are cited include lovers whose sexual pleasure with each other is the only motivation for their friendship, and thieves who are friends only as long as it is profitable for them to work together. In the third case the friend is loved for his/her own sake, *kath' hauton, propter seipsum*, and the friendship is said to be more durable because even if pleasure or usefulness gained through the relationship vary or diminish, the friendship itself is not in danger of ceasing. Being able to please or procure pleasure to the friend and being able to ensure profit or advantages to the friend are not thought of as constituting the person as such; these attributes are more easily separated from the person as such, although a friendship *propter seipsum* may very well entail pleasure and advantages. 'Honest' or 'perfect' friendship involves a sense, which I will come back to, that the friend is a singular person, and is loved as such – hence the wide-spread notion that friendships of this sort are quite rare and that one cannot have more than one 'perfect' friend at a time.

One of the reasons why one cannot have more than one 'perfect' friend at a time is the fact that this friend becomes a sort of double, an *alter idem* or *alter ipse,* of oneself.[7] Perfect friends are 'one soul in two bodies' and any multiplication of oneself beyond the friend is held to be unlikely or impossible. Hence the dictum attributed to Aristotle, 'for those who have many friends, there is no [true] friend.'[8] Another reason, or rather, a corollary of this notion is the principle that human beings have affection towards those who resemble them; implicitly, then, the greatest resemblance should produce the greatest affection, which would be 'perfect' friendship.

In light of these commonplace distinctions and notions defining friendship, inherited from the Aristotelian tradition, several questions arise for us. First of all, what does it mean to love someone for his/her 'own sake'? What is a person in his/her singularity, and how can that singularity constitute an object of the affection of friendship? Second, how can it be possible to love someone for his/her own sake if the basis for affection is resemblance? That is, if I love you *propter teipsum,* for yourself, then I do not love you because you resemble me, since each person is his/her own self. If I love you on the basis of your resemblance to me, then I do not love you for yourself. In what sense can there be 'one soul in two bodies'? Would that not vitiate the very basis of friendship for another for his/her own sake?

Classical moral philosophy did not really need to consider these questions for reasons that have to do with the definition of the person and with the type of relationship that friendship is held to be. I will begin by considering the second reason and then come back to the first. Friendship is an ethical relationship; that is, it considers the friend in an ethical way. Let me illustrate this point. One can have affection for another person 'for his/her own sake' in the sense that this person is one's relative; that he was born in a village one likes; that he has a funny way of walking; that his accent is charming, especially the way he pronounces his 'r'; that he drives an old station wagon; that he happens to like dogs who have long black hair; that he was once struck by lightning and lived to talk about it; etc. These features of the person are certainly part of his 'singularity', in that very few or no other persons can claim to have them, but they do not constitute a ground for an ethical relationship in the classical sense.

An ethical relationship is based on rationally chosen or rationally influenced behavior that manifests itself over a long duration of time. So what would count as the ground for friendship is that he became a good carpenter, that he writes poetry, that he is forthright in his dealings with his customers, that he is patient, that he despises tyranny, that he volunteers for the local charities, that he is well-liked by his neighbors and his dog, etc. These features also count towards defining the person in his/her singularity, and, indeed, these sorts of features are the only ones that count in a friendship. Some of these attributes are determined by what others say about him (being a good carpenter, being well-liked in the community); persons do not live in isolation and the quality of their choices is often measured by the impact they have on the community around them.

The definition of the person that arises from the ethical relationship of friendship is determined by activity that affects the community; a person who is a solitary contemplative and never speaks is never really an object of friendship. Hence the difficulty experienced by Aristotle in the final sections of the *Nicomachean Ethics* when, having ended up privileging the contemplative over the active life, he needs to retrieve friendship as a good for the wise man. The activity most worthy of praise by the community is that produced by rational choice over time, that is, by the person's virtue. Although great inherited wealth, a noble family, a fine physique, or the fact that a person was at the right place at the right time, might be very beneficial to a community, and thus praiseworthy, these are not the things that elicit the greatest praise. It is what the person consistently *did* with advantages given by nature or chance that counts, and constitutes the person's virtue. For the purpose of friendship, it is this sense of 'virtue' that defines the person.

This is seen most clearly in discussions of how friendship ends. When a friend becomes bald, when his stock investments take a plunge, when he takes up a different sport, for the purpose of the friendship, he does not become a different person; thus, friendship *propter seipsum* would not be in danger of ending. However, when he starts gambling, when he becomes abusive, etc., the friendship is in danger of ending, and if the friend's repeated efforts to persuade him not to gamble or not to be abusive fail, the friend is justified in ending the friendship. The person he loved as a friend is no longer there. The former friend has become a different person, or he/she is 'no longer of the same sort'.[9]

We need to keep in mind, then, that in the way that I have just described, the person 'as such,' for his/her own sake, is singular and cannot be duplicated or replaced. 'Perfect' friendship remains unique, and one cannot expect to have many such relationships. However, only a limited number of traits count as defining the person's singularity *qua* friend. Only more or less commonly recognizable and praiseworthy features of the person constitute that person as a friend in friendship *propter seipsum*, and these features are rational and consistent activities or behavior, not behavioral quirks or physical features. Virtuous personal features are not simply qualities that stand separately from the person; for the virtues to have any reality at all they must be enacted over time through choices made in contingent situations by a whole person.[10] In this sense, resemblance can be the basis of affection while the singularity of the other is respected, for similar choices are what determine resemblance and not attributes of the person that make her unique but are irrelevant to her virtue. I would be tempted to say that this conception is premodern and that a modern view, and especially a postmodern view, would refuse this hierarchy of personal traits: why privilege virtue over other traits in defining a person's distinctness? Moreover, a modern view would defend the notion that personal singularity is, *in fine*, an essentially non-rational and inaccessible otherness – I will come back to this notion since I think that Montaigne's language at least anticipates this position.

In the sixteenth-century intellectual culture that Montaigne knew, there was a general consensus that virtue constituted identity in relationships such as 'perfect' friendship, but there are signs that alternatives were certainly conceivable. The standard classical accounts of friendship were widely available, and the most sophisticated one, the *Nicomachean Ethics*, was a fundamental pedagogical text. One of the signs of alternatives to the classical accounts is the representation of friendship in fiction: in some narratives, characters are friends with all the trappings of a relationship *propter seipsum*, but at certain moments or through certain circumstances, it becomes clear that they are different from each other in precisely those activities that would count as virtuous, and yet the friendship persists.[11] Another source of questions about the identity of the friend as constituted by virtuous choices is the *paradox*, that is, the early modern genre of the mock encomium (or mock blame). Whereas friendship is something one generally praises, in the genre of the paradox friendship is blamed. One of these paradoxes explicitly states that despite claims to love the person *propter seipsum* in 'honest' friendship, one in fact loves virtue, not the person, for otherwise one would continue to love a person despite his bad choices.[12] This mock 'rhetorical' critique of friendship naturally connects to a religious critique, deriving from medieval theology. An alternative to friendship as a 'perfect' relationship to the other might be charity. The love of the other as creature of God is much more encompassing and less centered on rational choices of the friend, and at least in principle more respectful, then, of the person in her individuality.[13] One could argue that Christian charity is more accepting of 'otherness' than classical 'perfect' friendship. However, charity is essentially the love of God through the love of one's *proximus*, one's 'neighbor' or fellow human being: is charity, in the end, the love of a human being or rather simply an indirect love of God?[14] It does not seem to be an alternative to friendship with one person, based on virtue, and the persistence of writings on classical friendship attests to charity's conceptual insufficiency.

* * *

In 'De l'amitié' Montaigne is not concerned with charity, nor is he interested in pursuing the sort of paradoxes that his lawyer contemporaries enjoyed, but he is concerned at the outset, in a traditional way, with various types of friendships, which he characterizes as [*amitié*] *naturelle* (familial ties), *sociale* (civil ties), *hospitalière* (presumably, host-guest bonds), and *vénérienne* (erotic relationships) (p. 284–285). In fact, he concentrates on family ties, child–parent and fraternal friendship, and on erotic relationships between men and women and between men, as a background to the 'perfect' friendship that he enjoyed with Étienne de La Boétie. None of these ties can measure up to his friendship. In classifying types of human affective ties, Montaigne in fact follows the model of classical sources which were careful to proceed from general civil ties to more intimate ones, establishing a sort of scale of increasingly restricted relationships. He also is careful to segregate his friendship from those motivated by pleasure (*la volupté*) or usefulness (*le profit, le besoin public ou privé*) (p. 284), again following the classical distinctions I described earlier.

But from the beginning of the chapter, he also inserts autobiographical information, giving us hints of an etiology of his friendship with La Boétie. It began not with a personal encounter or a correspondence, but with Montaigne's reading of *De la servitude volontaire*, a radical tract composed by the young La Boétie deploring both the wide-spread practice of tyranny (while refusing to distinguish clearly between tyranny and monarchy, as classical and humanist political analysis would have done) and the servile and self-interested acceptance of rule by one person on the part of his subjects. This text impressed Montaigne so much that it became the source of their friendship, even before they met in person:

> Et si suis obligé particulièrement à cette pièce, d'autant qu'elle a servi de moyen à notre première accointance. Car elle me fut montrée longue espace avant que je l'eusse vu, et me donna la première connaissance de son nom, acheminant ainsi cette amitié, que nous avons nourrie, tant que Dieu a voulu, entre nous, si entière et si parfaite, que certainement il ne s'en lit guère de pareilles: et entre nos hommes il ne s'en voit aucune trace en usage. (p. 284)
>
> And yet I am particularly obliged to this work, since it served as the medium of our first acquaintance. For it was shown to me long before I had seen him, and gave me my first knowledge of his name, thus starting on its way this friendship which together we fostered, as long as God willed, so entire and so perfect that certainly you will hardly read of the like, and among men of today you see no trace of it in practice. (p. 136)[15]

Montaigne's account conforms perfectly to the expectations of classical 'perfect' friendship in the following ways. The text that was shown to him is a defense of liberty against tyranny; several celebrated friendships are asserted or confirmed in the face of a king or a tyrant (such as Damon and Phintias, willing to sacrifice themselves for the other, in face of execution by Dionysius the tyrant).[16] Tyrants are said to discourage friendship and are said to be incapable of friendship, which is a point made by La Boétie himself in *De la servitude volontaire*. In addition, the first knowledge Montaigne has of his future friend comes through a political treatise, that is, the product of rational choice and thought, and the demonstration of the connection between rational thought and the life of the community. Nothing can be more *virtuous*! *De la servitude volontaire* demonstrates a good knowledge of Xenophon and various classic moral philosophers, which means that La Boétie shares with Montaigne a humanist juridical education and a fondness for certain Stoic sources of moral thought. In other words, they *resemble* each other.

The fact that Montaigne was shown the treatise in manuscript form before meeting the person himself means that La Boétie enjoyed a solid reputation in the milieu of Montaigne's acquaintances and friends (i.e., in his network of bourgeois and nobles). In other words, he was already praised by those capable of judging, which in turn is a confirmation of his virtue. So everything worked: Montaigne is given certain proof of

La Boétie's intellectual virtue and of his valuation of friendship. And nothing quirky and 'personal' interferes: the fact that La Boétie might have looked creepy, might have had insistent body odor, was accompanied by odious servants, or happened to have been in a bad mood that day, did not derail their nascent friendship.

The essayist returns to this wondrous beginning of their friendship a few pages later:

> Nous nous cherchions avant que de nous être vus, et par des rapports que nous oyions l'un de l'autre: qui faisaient en notre affection plus d'effort, que ne porte la raison des rapports: je crois par quelque ordonnance du ciel. Nous nous embrassions par nos noms. Et à notre première rencontre, qui fut par hasard en une grande fête et compagnie de ville, nous nous trouvâmes si pris, si connus, si obligés entre nous, que rien dès lors ne nous fut si proche, que l'un à l'autre. (p. 291)
>
> We sought each other before [seeing each other] because of the reports we heard of each other, which had more effect on our affection than such reports would reasonably have; I think it was by some ordinance from heaven. We embraced each other by our names. And at our first meeting, which by chance came at a great feast and gathering in the city, we found ourselves so [taken, so known,] so bound together, that from that time on nothing was so close to us as each other. (p. 139)

In addition to the text of *De la servitude volontaire*, various 'reports' are given to the future friends about each other. These descriptions or news of the other person have a certain informational content, and that content alone does not explain the 'affection' provoked by the accounts. The friends already 'embraced' each other through their 'names'. Whereas in modern times, a proper name is generally assumed to simply designate an individual, in sixteenth-century France, and all the more obviously in noble culture, a proper name is a fulcrum of 'dignity'. 'Dignity' in the sense of accrued family history, and speech and action by the individual occupying that station, all of which are established and confirmed by reputation, 'gloire', 'renommée', 'honneur', etc.[17] Embracing each other by 'name' is a gesture of recognition of the other's dignity, which is the social equivalent of the person's virtue. Once again, without saying as much, Montaigne's account is modeled on 'perfect' friendship in classical accounts. When the first meeting finally takes place, it is in the setting of a 'fête et compagnie de ville' during which, next to a battlefield, precisely noble dignity can best be displayed.

However, the consciously hyperbolic language of this passage removes us ever so slightly from the parameters of classical virtuous friendship. The terms 'se chercher', recalling the efforts of the two halves of the Platonic Androgyne to find each other; the distinction between attraction based on rational reasons and attraction that exceeds them; the possible intervention of the heavens, or of chance; being 'taken', 'known' by the other, 'obliged' or bound to the other: this language resembles erotic attraction without ever saying so, but it also tries to communicate something beyond reasons and motivation, something inexpressible – and the language of passion is the closest one can come to the ineffable without resorting to invocation of the divine. This sense of inexpressibility of the 'perfect' friendship of Montaigne and La Boétie is most manifest in the passage just preceding the one I quoted:

> En l'amitié de quoi je parle, elles [nos âmes] se mêlent et confondent l'une en l'autre, d'un mélange si universel, qu'elles effacent et ne retrouvent plus la couture qui les a jointes. Si on me presse de dire pourquoi je l'aimais, je sens que cela ne se peut exprimer, qu'en répondant: Parce que c'était lui, parce que c'était moi. Il y a au-delà de tout mon discours, et de ce que j'en puis dire particulièrement, je ne sais quelle force inexplicable et fatale, médiatrice de cette union. (p. 291)
>
> In the friendship I speak of, our souls mingle and blend with each other so completely that they efface the seam that joined them, and cannot find it again. If you press me to tell why I loved him, I feel that this cannot be expressed, except by answering: Because it was he, because it was I. Beyond all my understanding, beyond what I can say about this in particular, there was I know not what inexplicable and fateful force that was the mediator of this union. (p. 139)

The commonplace account, which the essayist mentions himself (p. 294), of friendship as 'one soul in two bodies' is rendered by Montaigne as a 'mixing' and 'fusion' of souls: the ties that join the souls have been effaced. This 'mixing' of souls is explained in terms of motivation or justification, in the sense that the 'stitching' that joined them is an image of the reasons that impelled Montaigne and La Boétie to become friends. These reasons can no longer be found, or more pertinently, expressed. Whereas in other cases, at least as seen from the outside, one could say 'these persons are friends because they resemble each other in their consistent rational choices, in their virtue,'[18] in the case of Montaigne and La Boétie, seen from the inside as it were, no reasons can be expressed. But Montaigne could have stopped with that (indeed, before the 1595 edition, that is what the reader would have seen). Instead, he adds in the final version of the text: 'qu'en répondant: Parce que c'était lui, parce que c'était moi' ('except by answering, because it was he, because it was I'). This answer in fact conveys no semantic information; it does not convey any information about the virtue of the two friends (as had, implicitly, the reading of *De la servitude volontaire*). The two-part sentence designates two individuals through two personal pronouns, that is, it *points* to the two friends rather than *saying* anything about them. It is also perfectly symmetrical: the same amount of linguistic material is devoted to designating La Boétie as is devoted to designating Montaigne. There is, in addition, the matter of precedence: first La Boétie is referred to, then the author, as if, in the manner of sacrificing oneself to the friend, Montaigne let his friend come first. The sentence represents an alexandrine (a 12-syllable line of poetry), with a perfect 6–6 syllable distribution, and the words at the caesura ('lui') and at the rhyme ('moi'), that is, at the two most accentuated moments in the line, refer to La Boétie and Montaigne. The answer carries a force that is out of proportion with the semantic poverty of the sentence, just as the reports Montaigne received of his future friend had an effect greater than their 'raison.' The sentence is an example of what one would come to call the 'sublime' or the 'grand' style, a compression of affective force through a simple, apodictic expression.

In this way Montaigne does not express 'why' the two are friends, refusing to say, for example, 'because I was impressed by his virtue'. But he does express the 'perfection' of the friendship since the answer does convey the precise meaning of *propter seipsum*: what can be more *ipse* than 'c'était lui'? To modern readers, however, that means a disjoining of the 'self' from rational choices that the person makes. Montaigne seems to be saying that he loved La Boétie for 'himself' in a way not understandable through La Boétie's virtue, although in fact in the rest of the chapter all of the information surrounding his friend confirms, in traditional ways, his virtuous disposition. Montaigne's writing anticipates an ineffable definition of the individual, to whom one can refer, but of whom one can never give a full semantic account.

The other innovative feature of this passage is the language of 'fatal attraction': 'Il y a au-delà de tout mon discours, et de ce que j'en puis dire particulièrement, je ne sais quelle force inexplicable et fatale, médiatrice de cette union' (Beyond all my understanding, beyond what I can say about this in particular, there was I know not what inexplicable and fateful force that was the mediator of this union). A few lines later, Montaigne returns to this language, repeating as well the symmetrical representation of each partner of the friendship:

> ... c'est je ne sais quelle quinte-essence de tout ce mélange, qui ayant saisi toute ma volonté, l'amena se plonger et se perdre dans la sienne, qui ayant saisi toute sa volonté, l'amena se plonger et se perdre en la mienne: d'une faim, d'une concurrence pareille. (pp. 291–2)
>
> ... it is I know not what quintessence of all this mixture, which, having seized my whole will, led it to plunge and lose itself in his; which, having seized his whole will, led it to plunge and lose itself in mine, with equal hunger, equal rivalry. (p. 139)

The essayist's insistence on fatality, on the passiveness of the friends, whose wills were 'seized' by a 'je ne sais quoi', recalls Petrarchan love commonplaces. Aside from introducing hints of erotic love, this formulation also poses an ethical problem. Petrarchan love precisely reduces the lover to a passive object of love: he loses the control over his life that reason guaranteed him. Of course, this loss of control is mutual, and once it is mutual, it becomes a sort of parallel plunging into each other's wills, a 'concurrence'.[19] But it still poses a challenge to the sense of the friend's 'own sake': in the classical account of friendship *propter seipsum* the friend actively and consistently chooses behavior that is considered to be virtuous – indeed, that is what makes him into 'himself'. Montaigne points to the *passive* nature of the friends' attraction (despite many other instances in the same chapter where he insists on the voluntary nature of friendship): without this uncontrollable, fatal, inexplicable fusion of wills, the friendship would not be 'perfect'; it would be ordinary and common. It is as if a condition *sine qua non* of a free and deliberate choice of love of a person for his own sake contained its opposite: a blind loss of rational control, an abandoning of oneself to a superior force.

The following lines in the chapter are devoted to exploring the paradoxes of this fusion of wills, a voluntaristic version of Cicero's celebrated definition of friendship, 'omnium divinarum humanarumque rerum cum benevolentia et caritate *consensio*' (*De amicitia*, 6.20, my emphasis). Montaigne cites the example of Caius Blossius and Tiberius Gracchus (from Cicero, *De amicitia*, 11.37) and then delivers his own lengthy analysis. The example goes as follows: after the condemnation of Gracchus, his friend Caius Blossius is interrogated by the Roman consuls, and is asked by Laelius how much he would have been willing to do for Gracchus. Blossius answers that he would have done everything. Laelius follows up by asking what he would have done if Gracchus had commanded him to set fire to the temples. Blossius replies by saying that Gracchus would never have commanded him to do so. But if he had? insists Laelius. Blossius responds by saying that he would have obeyed his friend's command.

Montaigne's commentary is lengthy. First, he criticizes Blossius for having offended the consuls through his 'audacious confession', and insists that Blossius should have stuck by his earlier response, namely that he was confident that his friend would never have commanded him to set fire to the temples. According to the essayist, those, however, who find that his response is seditious do not really understand the extent to which in such a friendship one friend knows the other's 'will'. Montaigne explains:

> Ils étaient plus amis que citoyens, plus amis qu'amis ou qu'ennemis de leur pays, qu'amis d'ambition et de trouble. S'étant parfaitement commis, l'un à l'autre, ils tenaient parfaitement les rênes de l'inclination l'un de l'autre: et faites guider ce harnois, par la vertu et conduite de la raison (comme aussi est-il du tout impossible de l'atteler sans cela) la réponse de Blosius est telle, qu'elle devait être. Si leurs actions se démanchèrent, ils n'étaient ni amis, selon ma mesure, l'un de l'autre, ni amis à eux-mêmes. Au demeurant cette réponse ne sonne non plus que ferait la mienne, à qui s'enquerrait à moi de cette façon: Si votre volonté vous commandait de tuer votre fille, la tueriez-vous? et que je l'accordasse: car cela ne porte aucun témoignage de consentement à ce faire: parce que je ne suis point en doute de ma volonté, et tout aussi peu de celle d'un tel ami. (pp. 292–3)
>
> They were friends more than citizens, friends more than friends or enemies of their country or friends of ambition and disturbance. Having committed themselves absolutely to each other, they held absolutely the reins of each other's inclination; and if you assume that this team was guided by the strength and leadership of reason, as indeed it is quite impossible to harness it without that, Blossius' answer is as it should have been. If their actions went astray [or: went their separate ways], they were by my measure neither friends to each other, nor friends to themselves. For that matter, this answer has no better ring than would mine if someone questioned me in this fashion: 'If your will commanded you to kill your daughter,

> would you kill her?' and I said yes. For that does not bear witness to any consent to do so, because I have no doubt at all about my will, and just as little about that of such a friend. (p. 140)

Montaigne – for a moment, at least – disjoins friendship from ties to civil society, which allows him to explain the logic of Blossius's response. Although Blossius is sure that Gracchus would never have asked him to set fire to the temples, he would have done so on the friend's request, simply because Gracchus's request would have corresponded perfectly to his own will: implicitly, Blossius, too, would have chosen to set fire to the temples. But Montaigne also excludes the possibility that either Gracchus or Blossius could have chosen (and asked the other) to do so. The power to 'hold the reins of the friend's will' derives from 'la vertu et conduite de la raison' (the strength and conduct of reason), which reaffirms the classical sense of friendship *propter seipsum* as deriving from rational choices over time, that is, from virtue. So although in one sense the ties of friend to friend are stronger than the ties to the polity, in another sense what binds the friends is what binds the polity, that is, the activity that is virtue.[20] The friend would never have asked the other to violate divine law since the reason for which they are friends is, in part, the fact that both respect now and will respect divine law.

Montaigne then compares their situation to someone asking him if he would kill his daughter if his will asked him to do so. The comparison is in effect a *reductio ad absurdum*.[21] Since the friends' wills are fused, any difference between them entailing a difference manifest in the will would be equivalent to the friend not being a friend to himself. Since you are a friend of La Boétie, your wills are like one, and interchangeable, which means that being a friend to La Boétie is equivalent to being a friend to yourself. Anything that La Boétie might request would be equivalent to your requesting it yourself. One can imagine, then, La Boétie, or rather, Montaigne's will asking him to violate natural law and kill his daughter. Since the will is that which moves to action, Montaigne cannot say that he would not respond in the affirmative. But this does not imply that it would be possible for his will, as friend, to do so, since the will *qua* the will of the (perfect) friend is virtuous, that is, does not and would not advocate violating natural law. The 'certainty' of Montaigne, the absence of doubt concerning his and his friend's will, reflects, in classical friendship, a logical or definitional impossibility: given the definition of perfect friendship, whose members' identities are constituted by choices that are virtue, if a choice required the violation of natural or divine law, the friends' identities would be altered, and they would no longer be susceptible to perfect friendship. They would have become, in Aristotle's terms, someone of a different sort.

In Montaigne's formulation, however, this solution is replaced with one that appeals to an inner sense of certainty, impervious to arguments: 'Il n'est pas en la puissance de tous les discours du monde, de me déloger de la certitude, que j'ai des intentions et jugements du mien [de mon ami]' (p. 293) ('It is not in the power of all the arguments in the world to dislodge me from the certainty I have of the intentions and judgments of my friend,' p. 140).[22] This inner sense of confidence[23] corresponds to the sublime 'justification' for the friendship, and it avoids any real explanation. It is as if perfect friendship were sullied by its elucidation. Past models or precepts, and present and future comparisons, are threats to the singularity of the relationship: 'Rien n'est extrême, qui a son pareil' (p. 296) ('Nothing is extreme that can be matched,' p. 142). Indeed, Montaigne's double insistence on the 'extremeness' of the friendship and its complete internalization (being a friend to La Boétie means being a friend to myself), transforms the relationship to another into a radical sense of self, which in this precise case seems heightened by the painful absence of the deceased friend.

In sum, Montaigne's account in 'De l'amitié' of perfect friendship reproduces the paradigm of friendship *propter seipsum* that we find in classical sources and in their commentaries, medieval and humanist. One loves the friend 'for his own sake' precisely, that is, if and only if, the friend's enduring rational choices are praiseworthy, and one loves in the friend those choices. Nothing that Montaigne says about La Boétie – his reputation, his political writing, his poetry –, and nothing that Montaigne says about his own actions in response to this friendship – mainly, the editing of his friend's writings, his faithfulness to his memory – is contrary to the model of classical perfect friendship.[24] Indeed, all of the information we have confirms this sense that the ground of their relationship is 'virtue' (in this case, love of liberty, respect for divine and natural law), and that they resemble each other in their choices.[25]

The apodictic manner in which Montaigne formulates his 'feeling' of friendship inaugurates, however, an increasing hesitancy to articulate the most striking human bonds in terms of classical virtue. These a-rational formulations also implicitly – and counter to Montaigne's own stated intentions – leave political or civil association in hands not of 'friendship' but of associations of (self-)interest, those common associations that do not rise to the standard of Montaigne's own feeling.

The pseudo-erotic language used by Montaigne inaugurates perhaps as well the assignment of the strongest bond between human beings to erotic love, and makes, in the end, friendship a much more difficult relationship to justify.

Notes

1. For the purpose of this essay I will be using the 1595 edition (*Les Essais de Michel Seigneur de Montaigne...* eds. Denis Bjaï, Bénédicte Boudou, Jean Céard, Isabelle Pantin, Paris, Librairie générale française, 2001). The numbering of the chapters in book 1 of the 1595 edition differs slightly from earlier editions.
2. For a discussion of propositions and procedures in the *Essais* that are not subject to skepticism, see Hartle (2003, pp. 13–25).
3. A good, if not exhaustive, summary of recent critical reception can be found in Scholar (2007). The most recent entry into the long line of critical interpretation of 'De l'amitié' is Gontier (2011), who emphasizes, more so than I do, the difference between Montaigne's account of 'perfect' friendship and classical ones.
4. See Defaux (1995) for an attempt to account for the importance of the death of the friend in the writing of the *Essais*.
5. See Fraisse (1974). Additional sources for accounts of friendship are sections of Aristotle's *Eudemian Ethics*, several pieces in Plutarch's *Moralia*, Plato's *Lysis*, and Lucian's *Toxaris*; they are less interesting for the philosophy of friendship as such. On the reception of classical friendship in the early modern period, see Langer (1994).
6. On this tripartite distinction, see Aristotle, *Nicomachean Ethics*, 1155b16–19. It becomes a commonplace in medieval and humanist commentary (e.g., Thomas Aquinas, *In X. libros Ethicorum ad Nicomachum*, VIII, lectio 3, etc.), and in moral literature of the early modern period.
7. See Aristotle, *Nicomachean Ethics*, 1166a31–32, Cicero, *De amicitia*, 21.80, and Erasmus, *Adagia*, 1.1.2, 'Amicitia æqualitas. Amicus alter ipse.'
8. In Diogenes Laertius, *Lives of the Philosophers*, V.21. Another version, understood as the standard one before Isaac Casaubon's emendation in 1593, is 'Oh my friends, no one is a [true] friend.'
9. See *Nicomachean Ethics*, 1165b21–22.
10. This point is made in somewhat different terms by Gontier (2011, pp. 55–6), who refers to the analysis of Aristotelian friendship in Cooper (1998); see especially pp. 328–329, for my purposes. Gregory Vlastos (1973) argues that Platonic love of persons makes it impossible to love 'whole persons,' but only 'that abstract version of persons which consists of the complex of their best qualities,' a flaw that 'Aristotle's conception of "perfect *philia*" does not repudiate' (pp. 31 and 33). For a lucid account of caring for another 'for her/his own sake' in Aristotle, and the principal objections to this aspect of his view of friendship, see also Gottlieb (2009, pp. 146–50), who argues against Vlastos' position.
11. I am thinking of the friendship between Pantagruel and Panurge, in Rabelais's books *Pantagruel* and the *Tiers livre*. See Langer (2005).

12. See Antoine Hotman, *Deux paradoxes de l'amitié et de l'avarice* (1598), discussed in my *Perfect Friendship*, pp. 84–5. Hotman's (mock) objection seems to anticipate Vlastos's argument that in classical care for a virtuous friend, one loves (universal) good character, and not the person herself (ibid., see n. 10).
13. Thomas Aquinas, Ethelred of Rievaulx, and Peter of Blois all compare charity and friendship, and sixteenth-century humanists follow suit, such as Jacques Lefèvre d'Étaples and Josse Clichtove (see my *Perfect Friendship*, pp. 100–101).
14. On medieval commentaries that also engage the relationship between charity and friendship, see Séré (2007) and Hyatte (1997).
15. Translations are from *The Complete Essays of Montaigne*, trans. Donald M. Frame (Stanford: Stanford Univ. Press, 1958). I have occasionally modified the translation.
16. See Cicero, *De officiis*, 3.10.45, among innumerable other mentions. Montaigne himself cites Harmodios and Aristogiton (from Plato's *Symposium*, 182c) and states that the violence of tyrants and the cowardliness of their subjects are the enemies of friendship (p. 290).
17. See Sterchi (2005).
18. E.g., 'Virtutis enim causa sunt amici,' as a paraphrase of Aristotle's *Nicomachean Ethics* states (*Aristotelis Ethicorum Nicomachiorum Paraphrasis, incerto auctore, antiquo & eximio peripatetico*... ed. and trans. Daniel Heinsius, Lyons, 1607, 9.4, p. 428). Also: 'virtus, inquam... et conciliat amicitias et conservat' (Cicero, *De amicitia*, 27.100).
19. Which recalls the friendship 'competitions' ('who is the better friend? Which is the most perfect friendship?') exemplified in Lucian's *Toxaris*.
20. See on this point also Scholar (2007), pp. 42–3. And the commentary by Jacques Derrida (1994): 'La raison et la vertu ne sauraient être *privés*. Elles ne peuvent entrer en conflit avec la chose publique. Ces concepts de la vertu et de la raison sont d'avance accordés à l'espace de la *res publica*' (p. 211).
21. See the commentary by Derrida: 'L'impossibilité de ce calcul, la ruine du sens courant des mots, l'avalanche des absurdités logiques et grammaticales, c'est à de tels signes qu'on reconnaît la différence entre l'amitié "souveraine et maistresse" et les "autres amitiez." La *philia* la plus dévouée à l'autre, la plus hétérotropique ou hétérophilique, n'est autre au fond qu'une amitié de soi, *philautie* sinon narcissisme – et ce n'est pas mal' (ibid., p. 203).
22. See also: 'Car les discours même que l'antiquité nous a laissé sur ce sujet, me semblent lâches au prix du sentiment que j'en ai. Et en ce point les effets surpassent les préceptes mêmes de la philosophie' (Montaigne, p. 298).
23. On the 'dissymmetrical' confidence in the friend, see Derrida (1994, p. 220).
24. One exception might be the rapidity with which the friendship developed ('la précipitation de notre intelligence, si promptement parvenue à sa perfection,' [p. 291]), a point made by Gontier (2011, p. 55). But before the friends met in person, they knew each other through others' reports and their writings. According to Montaigne, La Boétie wrote his Latin poem 'Ad Michaelem Montanum' to 'excuse' and 'explain' this rapidity, since it does

not conform to classical precepts about friendships developing slowly. This 'excuse' shows how present the classical model is.

25. In this respect I agree with MacPhail (1989).

References

Anonymous (1607) *Aristotelis Ethicorum Nicomachiorum Paraphrasis, incerto auctore, antiquo & eximio peripatetico*... ed., trans. Daniel Heinsius (Lyons).

Aristotle (1990) [1926] *Nicomachean Ethics*, ed., trans. H. Rackham (Cambridge, MA: Harvard University Press).

T. Aquinas, St. (1949) *In X. libros Ethicorum ad Nicomachum*, in *Opera omnia* (repr. New York: Musurgia).

M. T. Cicero (1979) [1923] *Laelius de amicitia*, ed., trans. W. A. Falconer (Cambridge, MA: Harvard University Press).

—— (1990) [1913] *De officiis*, ed., trans. Walter Miller (Cambridge, MA: Harvard University Press).

J. M. Cooper (1998) *Reason and Emotion: Essays on Ancient Moral Psychology and Ethical Theory* (Princeton: Princeton University Press).

M. de Montaigne (2001) *Les Essais*..., eds Denis Bjaï, Bénédicte Boudou, Jean Céard, Isabelle Pantin (Paris: Librairie générale française).

—— (1958) *The Complete Essays of Montaigne*, trans. Donald M. Frame (Stanford: Stanford Univ. Press).

G. Defaux (1995) *Montaigne et le travail de l'amitié* (Orléans: Paradigme).

J. Derrida (1994) *Politiques de l'amitié* (Paris: Galilée).

Diogenes Laertius (1972) [1925] *Lives of Eminent Philosophers*, vol. 1, ed., trans. R. D. Hicks (Cambridge, MA: Harvard University Press).

D. Erasmus (1993) *Adagia*, in *Opera omnia*, vol. 1.1, eds M. L. van Poll-van de Lisdonk, M. Mann Phillips and C. Robinson (Amsterdam: North Holland Publishing Co.).

J.-C. Fraisse (1974) *Philia: La notion d'amitié dans la philosophie antique* (Paris: Vrin).

Th. Gontier (2011) 'L'amitié, entre sentiment et discours philosophiques,' *Bulletin de la Société internationale des amis de Montaigne*, 54, 43–59.

P. Gottlieb (2009) *The Virtue of Aristotle's Ethics* (Cambridge: Cambridge University Press).

A. Hartle (2003) *Michel de Montaigne: Accidental Philosopher* (Cambridge: Cambridge University Press).

R. Hyatte (1997) *The Arts of Friendship: The Idealization of Friendship in Medieval and Early Renaissance Literature* (Leiden: E.J. Brill).

U. Langer (1994) *Perfect Friendship: Studies in Literature and Moral Philosophy from Boccaccio to Corneille* (Geneva: Droz).

—— (2005) 'Théorie et représentation de l'amitié à la Renaissance', in Bernard Schumacher, Jean-Christophe Merle (eds), *L'amitié* (Paris: Presses universitaires de France), 47–62.

E. MacPhail (1989) 'Friendship as a Political Ideal in Montaigne's *Essais*', *Montaigne Studies* 1, 177–87.

R. Scholar (2007) 'Friendship and Free-Thinking in Montaigne', in Corinne Noirot-Maguire, Valerie M. Dionne (eds), *'Revelations of Character': Ethos, Rhetoric and Moral Philosophy in Montaigne* (Newcastle: Cambridge Scholars Publishing), 31–46.

B. Séré (2007) *Penser l'amitié au Moyen Âge. Étude historique des commentaires sur les livres VIII et IX de l'Éthique à Nicomaque* (Turnhout: Brepols).

B. Sterchi (2005) *Über den Umgang mit Lob und Tadel: Normative Adelsliteratur und politische Kommunikation im burgundischen Hofadel, 1430–1506* (Turnhout: Brepols).

G. Vlastos (1973) *Platonic Studies* (Princeton: Princeton University Press).

Part III

Friendship and Reason

Part III
Friendship and Reason

5
Relationships and Emotions

Michael Slote

I am not going to confine my discussion here to friendship, but wish to talk about the nature and implications of the emotion(s) that both love and good/strong friendship involve. My hope is to be able to illuminate the topic of friendship, but to do so by placing friendship within the context or topic of close relationships generally. Most philosophers recognize that emotion is important to these relationships, but they haven't, I think, seen how all of this bears on issues of human rationality and early human development. And that is what I shall be speaking about here.

1

Let me begin by speaking about the role of moral development in friendship. The idea that friendship implicitly involves a concern for morality or moral principles can be found in writers as diverse as Aristotle and Rawls.[1] But I want to push this issue back further in individual psychology than other philosophers have attempted to do. Rawls, for example, assumes that children need to be loved by their parents if they are to develop a genuine commitment to (correct) principles of justice, but he leaves this fact hanging in the midst of an otherwise fairly rationalistic account of moral/political development, and I would like to say a lot more about how parental love fits in here. And how it also fits into a proper understanding of the psychological preconditions of human friendship. Then, after saying some things about this topic, I shall stop talking about the psychological preconditions of love and friendship and start talking about what such relationships by their very nature (or metaphysical necessity) entail. The picture that will emerge is much less rationalistic than has been generally presupposed or accepted in discussions of friendship and love, but I hope by the same token that it will be more balanced and realistic than those other discussions.

Discussions of moral education like Rawls's rely heavily on the work of Piaget and, to some extent, also of his follower Lawrence Kohlberg.[2] They see moral learning and education as largely a matter of progressing through various stages of moral development to (hopefully, but far from always) a final stage in which the learning individual can articulate complex, rational, universal moral principles like Kant's Categorical Imperative. But the problem here, and this is something Kohlberg himself eventually came to recognize, is that increasing cognitive sophistication about moral principles doesn't necessarily bring with it the motivation to adhere to such principles. To that extent and for that reason, Kohlberg eventually brought in considerations of empathy in order to explain how moral motivation grows and remains in place, but this didn't fit all that well with the original Piagetian emphasis on cognitive development, and that fact has led me, at least, to think that we ought to emphasize empathic processes more fundamentally than Kohlberg did if we are to understand moral development.

At this point, the psychological literature on empathy becomes relevant. Many (but not all) psychologists of moral development subscribe to an 'empathy–altruism hypothesis' according to which sympathy for and altruism toward others depends on the development and encouragement of natural human tendencies toward empathic identification with others.[3] The idea, in other words and very briefly, is that we feel sorry, say, for those who are suffering and are motivated to help them only if our capacity for 'feeling their pain and suffering' develops too. And the literature of psychology and also the previous literature of philosophy tell us something useful and interesting about how this can occur.

According to psychologist Martin Hoffman, if a parent notices their child hurt another child, then, if they have a good relationship with their child, they can intervene and focus their child's attention on the harm/pain she/he has caused, and given the natural human capacity for empathy, this will mean that the child will feel bad (a form of primitive guilt) for what he/she has done.[4] And according to Hoffman, if this happens a few times, the child will build up a motivational resistance to harming others that counts as a kind of moral disposition. Hoffman calls the process of parental intervention and moral education 'inductive discipline'; but what he doesn't mention is that parents like this will also teach their child a subliminal lesson in caring about others. Hume in the *Treatise* noted that the attitudes and beliefs of others tend to infect or infuse themselves into those around them – and this happens basically in the same way that the pain of another can emotionally infuse itself into us as 'feeling their pain'.[5] So a parent who cares about and who deliberately teaches a child to care about the well-being of others is also setting an example for that child, is offering an example for more or less conscious modeling. All of this helps the child care about others and represents a kind of moral advance or development. But let us now ask what happens if this doesn't occur – and how this issue bears on the preconditions and possibility of human love and friendship.

As I pointed out, Hoffman assumes that inductive discipline or 'induction' occurs in the context of a good parent-child relationship. And presumably the parent will be a good model of caring about others only if the parent also cares about – *loves* – their child. But if the relationship between parent and child isn't good because the parent in fact doesn't love their child, other forces and other possibilities come into play, and a description of them can help us better understand both moral development and the preconditions of genuine human friendship and love. The basic fact here – one that Hoffman and Hume, for example, don't call attention to, but that Rawls pretty clearly presupposes – is that children need love. And as many have pointed out and much empirical literature indicates, this need won't be satisfied simply by satisfying a child's material wants. The child really needs to be loved by their parents (or, possibly, parental figures) – and will react very negatively if this doesn't occur. And I want to explore the implications of this for friendship, love, and morality.

If the child doesn't receive parental love, that is a kind of psychological abuse, and such abuse in many cases will be compounded by physical and/or sexual abuse as well. So what happens if and when all or most of these elements are present? Well, I think the child naturally reacts with rage and anger, but what this does, surely, is get in the way of the child's developing a capacity for love. Let's consider what can happen to make someone into a sociopath or serial killer (I am not going to talk about genetic abnormalities that can or might push someone in the same direction). If they aren't loved and are mistreated, anger/rage can build up, and such feelings are inconsistent with (the development of) empathy. As we know from even 'normal' adult individuals, it is difficult to empathize with those one is angry with (say, those who have harmed one's family or oneself or who hold religious beliefs one finds abhorrent). And so I am saying – or sketching the idea – that someone who isn't loved and who is abused is going to be too angry to become capable of normal empathy. They won't get to the stage where inductive discipline can make them more empathic and altruistic, because their capacity for empathy has been frozen (or has atrophied) in the wake of all the mistreatment they have suffered and all the rage and anger they enduringly feel as a result. (I don't say this always happens. Some psychologists hold that some mistreated individuals react less with anger than with a sense of pity and empathy for others who suffer the same fate. But this is unusual and perhaps praiseworthy, and it isn't what occurs with most abused and unloved children.)

By contrast, consider what can happen to make a child capable of learning from inductive discipline, what can allow a child to have a good enough relationship with their parent(s) so that induction and parental modeling can then help make the child *more* empathic and *more* altruistic or moral. What presumably happens is that the parents act lovingly toward their child and the child, who in some deep way needs and wants loving treatment, responds with a kind of primal gratitude. The child can empathically feel how their parents feel about them, in other words, feel the lovingness the parents have directed toward them, and as an empathic result that registers as love in the child. Such reciprocating love is a form of gratitude (there is no space to go into the details), but the important point is that the love the loved child feels in empathic response to and by way of imbibing their parents' love will not develop in a child who isn't loved and who is also abused or mistreated. So if the need for love is answered, the capacity for love and for empathy develops or can develop in the child, but if that need goes unanswered and is crushed by cruel or uncaring parental treatment, the child will typically be too angry to develop a capacity for loving and empathy toward others. And all of this obviously bears on issues about love and friendship and what is necessary for them to develop or flourish.

What I am in effect saying is that the failure to receive love, to have that need met, can lead to an incapacity for empathy and altruism, and this basically means a person incapable of morality as we know it and incapable of any kind of genuinely close friendship or love. But one has to be careful. It is often said that the sociopath or psychopath is incapable of empathy, and such people are often also thought to be incapable of genuine moral or altruistic feeling, but aren't sociopaths known to be able to get inside of people's heads and to be capable of manipulating or hurting them on that basis? And isn't getting into someone's head a form of empathy?

Yes, to be sure. But psychologists (like Hoffman) tend to distinguish two kinds of empathy, the projective kind that involves putting oneself in someone's shoes or into their head and the 'associative' kind that involves feeling the other's pain or joy or what have you. The latter involves a certain emotional receptivity to or toward the other that getting into someone's head doesn't seem to require. So we can say that the sociopath or serial killer has a form of empathy as long as we recognize that it is a rather cold and intellectual form of empathy – and doesn't involve them being invaded by or infused with the feelings or emotions of other people. Genuine sympathy and altruism depend on the capacity or actuality of feeling what others feel, and the empathy–altruism hypothesis is best understood, therefore, in terms of emotionally receptive associative empathy. Sociopaths and serial killers seem to lack this kind of empathy and to be therefore incapable of the emotional connections with others that moral altruism, love, and friendship all require or presuppose. And all of this hinges, I am saying, on whether a child's need for love is met or left unsatisfied (or trampled on).

It is fairly well known that love and friendship require or involve a certain capacity for altruism, and it is not too far a step from that assumption or conclusion to the idea that love and friendship also require a capacity for or disposition toward associative/receptive empathy. But I have been arguing here that a certain form of psychological development is necessary (at least in most cases) for these phenomena to take place. Students of moral development stress the need for parents to use inductive discipline and perhaps also to model empathic altruism for their children – in order for those children to develop into altruistic and moral individuals. But they generally fail to focus on a major psychological precondition of such development, namely, the satisfaction of the child's need/desire for parental love. And we have argued here that such a precondition is essential not only to the development of morality but to the development of a capacity for genuine friendship and love relationships, as well. Where a child isn't loved, they can fall into a deep and enduring rage at how they have been treated, and this can interfere with or undercut their empathic capacities/dispositions and leave them unable to feel love or deep affection for anyone else. Human love and friendship have to be understood against such a developmental psychological background, and this means that emotions play a crucial historical/causal role in determining whether an individual will be capable or incapable of love and friendship. That tells us something very important, I think, about the nature of love and friendship in at least the human instance.

But I now want to shift gears. I will still be talking about emotion or the emotions, but the emphasis won't be on the causal preconditions of love and friendship, but on what actually or already existent love and friendship cause us to be like. Love relationships and close friendships involve warm feeling and empathic practical concern for (the welfare and wishes of) loved ones or friends – we all know, or should know, that. But the empathy we feel for or towards those we are close to or intimate with has implications for how we see the world, and some of this may have implications for our views about the nature or extent of human epistemic rationality. We will focus on these issues in our next section.

2

Hume thinks that we take in the feelings of others, that they can spread by contagion from one person to another. But he doesn't limit the process – which he called sympathy, but we nowadays would refer to as empathy – to feelings like joy or pleasure. He argues that attitudes and beliefs have the same tendency to spread from one person to another, and he thinks that the sheer proximity of another individual automatically affects us in this way. But he never explicitly considers or discusses the effect of love and friendship on such processes. Like many contemporary psychologists, he holds (roughly) that we are more inclined to feel sympathy/empathy for those we know or resemble than for strangers or distant others. And he sees this as making us more likely to help, to act benevolently toward, people we know or are intimate with. But he doesn't translate this into his discussion of the effects of beliefs and attitudes: he never says that we are more likely to take in the attitudes and opinions of those we love or care deeply about than to do so with strangers, mere acquaintances, etc. And yet we know (don't we?) that children are more likely to take in their parents' views and attitudes than those of strangers, and one might well think, therefore, that greater feeling makes for greater empathy not only in regard to whom we are likely to altruistically help but also in regard to whom we are more likely to end up agreeing with. That seems to be a sensible enough conclusion. So other people have a certain tendency to influence us via the empathy we naturally (or as a result of a favorable empathic development) have toward other people, but this effect is intensified in regard to people we love. And the tendency is usually not self-conscious. The child takes in parental opinions or attitudes without particularly or consciously desiring or striving to do so and without, typically, even knowing that this is happening. It's a kind of osmosis.

But if this is just osmosis, what kind of epistemic justification can beliefs arrived at in this way really have? And if there is, in fact, such a general human tendency, intensified in relation to those we love, to take in opinions without critically reflecting on their validity, on how good the evidence in their favor actually is, doesn't this mean that most of us – maybe even all of us – are irrational or less than fully rational or justified in holding many of the opinions we do? Philosophers are always pointing to sources and causes of epistemic/evidential irrationality, but the potential source I am speaking of here has not, I think, been previously mentioned (not even by Hume), and since, given the above assumptions, this is a very widespread phenomenon, the present discussion may indicate a broader or deeper source or aspect of human irrationality than other philosophers (or psychologists) have ever mentioned. But do we in fact have to assume that these processes are epistemically less than or other than rational? Let's consider.

Think of the evidence of testimony. Many philosophers (Hume notable among them) hold that we should trust someone's testimony as to matters of fact only if we have evidence that *they* are trustworthy. But other philosophers have disagreed. Thomas Reid held that testimony has evidential value on its own or in its own right, and this means that we have some epistemic justification for believing what someone tells us independently of whether we have evidence that they usually speak the truth or have evidence for what they say that is separate from the fact of their saying it and that their testimony merely corroborates.[6] Thus when a loving parent tells a child that God loves him or that the mail never comes on Sundays, it can be argued that the child has two sources or kinds of reason to believe what they are told: whatever evidence they have that their parents have been reliable about other matters plus the sheer fact that their parents are telling them a given thing. And couldn't what a child unself-consciously imbibes from their parents play a similar epistemic and justificatory role? Seeing that their parent thinks highly of Ronald Reagan (and feeling how strong that parental conviction is), couldn't the child osmotically take in a similar conviction, and couldn't the child then be epistemically justified in thinking highly of Reagan (thinking he was a very good president) on the basis of this empathic process? Empathic osmosis would then play a justificatory role that is similar to what Reid attributed to testimonial evidence, and we would have discovered a new source of epistemic justification that hasn't previously been attended to or recognized.

But notice this. Testimony may have evidential force of its own, but that force is pretty clearly limited. What people testify to or claim may give the hearer or reader *some* reason to agree, but that reason can surely be overridden by counterevidence indicating that the person who has told one something was mistaken or deliberately lied. If someone tells us when we are young that the Declaration of Independence was signed on July 4, 1776, then we have reason, epistemic justification, for believing that; but when we later learn that the Declaration was signed at a later date (this is in fact the case), the earlier 'testimony' is overridden, overturned, and someone who persisted in believing that the Declaration was signed on July 4 after hearing a fuller account of what happened that placed the signing on August 2, 1776, would clearly not be epistemically justified in doing so. Yet what children imbibe from parents or other loved ones seems precisely to *be* in this way impervious to counterevidence. What we empathically take in from our parents about Ronald Reagan or the Virgin Mary or any other significant topic will tend to strongly resist any counterevidence. So even if what one takes in from one's parents has some epistemic force or justification, there may be something less than fully rational, in epistemic terms, about such belief if it is resistant and even impervious to counterevidence in the way that testimonial evidence (considered in separation from empathic factors) clearly isn't.

But what we have said so far may not settle this matter. Someone might still maintain that beliefs taken in from parents or other loved ones (including friends) have a strong epistemic justification, that those holding such beliefs are in no degree epistemically irrational or unjustified in holding *strongly* to them in the face of what a more objective observer would or might call counterevidence. And this is an interesting possibility because it challenges received historic views about evidence and rationality in a way that Reid's ideas (I believe) do not. Most of us philosophers are children of the Enlightenment. We think we are supposed to be objective or impartial about evidence and to come to empirical or other beliefs only on the basis of evidence that is objectively valid. And we think emotion has a mainly negative and only very occasionally a positive effect on what we know or have reason to believe. Emotion can make us less than objective about various matters, we know that, and our tradition has a tendency to think that we should try to stay away from strong feeling(s) when we judge empirical matters. Of course, we are willing to grant that an emotion can *sometimes* be epistemically helpful: as when anger with someone can lead one to notice things about them one hadn't realized before. But in that case the emotion or feeling isn't itself a form of or basis for epistemic justification, and the idea that what our love for our parents makes us empathically take in from them is ipso facto justified and justified in a way that allows (or requires) one to resist all or almost all counterevidence, that idea *does* treat a kind of emotion as the very basis of epistemic justification – which is a far cry from anything any epistemological rationalist would be willing to accept. If love can ground empathically derived beliefs that one is epistemically entitled to treat as practically sacrosanct, then our whole epistemological tradition has been mistaken about the sources and nature of epistemic or theoretical justification, and that is certainly reason in itself to resist such a strong revision of what all or almost all of us philosophers have believed.

So the idea that our empathy with those we love can justify us epistemically in holding strongly to what we take in via such empathy does seem somewhat questionable. It challenges a whole tradition, and on the face of it, it is indeed far from obvious that justification can occur on such a basis. But there is also a further consideration. We may often take in beliefs from loved ones in a way that is practically impervious to counterevidence and counterargument, but it is also true that we tend to exaggerate or overestimate the merits and prospects of those we love. In other words, our beliefs *about* our friends or loved ones (as opposed to beliefs that come *from* them) tend to favor them in a way that more objective observers would not. Every parent thinks their child is the smartest or prettiest in their class; and the mother of a convicted killer will resist believing in the evidence against her son or daughter in a way or to an extent that others who know the case never would. Similarly, we remain hopeful about (or on behalf of) our loved ones' prospects in life beyond anything that available evidence would support. And don't say that all of this is because those who love have evidence that isn't available to observers who are less emotionally involved. Often, the parent who believes in their son's innocence of the murder they have been convicted of will in fact know of other morally unsavory incidents in their son's previous life that would further support the belief that he has killed the person he is convicted of having killed. But they will tend to downplay those other incidents as well as the evidence for his having murdered the person he has been accused of murdering – and all of this will be due to their feelings about their son.

Now in parallel with what Thomas Reid said about testimony, some philosophers have been willing to consider the possibility that the evidential partiality that comes with loving someone should be included within our understanding of the sources of epistemic/rational justification.[7] In other words, it could be argued, first, that love and/or close friendship by its very nature (and apart from issues about rivalry) makes us overestimate the merits and prospects of those we feel strong positive feelings toward: if someone is too quick or willing to go along with evidence against a given person, that may criterially undermine any claim that they love that person. And one could then go on to say that what counts or would count as irrational overestimation or (epistemic) charity from a more impartial or objective perspective can nonetheless be justified, epistemically justified, from or within the perspective or point of view of someone who actually loves a given person.

As I indicated, some philosophers seem open to this sort of thing. But I think the idea in fact flies in the face of common sense and intuition, and surely most of us know that. Love may not be actually *blind*, but almost everyone other than philosophers recognizes that love can *prejudice* us in favor of those we love, that a parent isn't a good or reasonable judge of their child's looks or intelligence or even their general life prospects, that love gets in the way of dealing or thinking in a fully rational way about the prospects or merits of those we love. So much is just common opinion, and I think we should take such opinion seriously. Philosophers have a certain aversion to irrationality – that is part of why most of them are in the business they are in. And I believe that can make one reluctant to think that so many people, that almost everyone, is evidentially irrational in matters regarding their loved ones. But I think we need to bite the bullet on this one. The parent who believes their child is the brightest in their class and who does so in great measure out of their great love for their child (also perhaps for egoistic or egotistical reasons of pride) is typically not epistemically justified in what they believe. And as with beliefs taken in osmotically from parents or (as can happen in adulthood) from other people we love, the fact that such beliefs so strongly or even irrecusably resist counterevidence is some reason to come to this conclusion.

I am proposing, then, that we view beliefs about the merits or prospects of loved ones and beliefs that are empathically taken in from loved ones as in the same epistemic boat. If, as I have suggested, the former sort of beliefs are typically less than epistemically justified, then I think we should say the same thing about the latter. The cases are parallel enough to recommend such similar treatment, and in that case we don't have to say that love is a special and newly discovered source of epistemic justification. Saying this would go against our philosophical traditions, our fundamentally Enlightenment-like approach to epistemological questions, our very strong tendency to believe that epistemic rationality cannot essentially involve or include the emotional factors that enter into love and friendship. And I am arguing that there is no good reason why we should say this sort of thing.

However, and I think this is the most important point to be made here, that doesn't mean that the Enlightenment/rationalist tradition of Western epistemology remains entirely intact. Far from it. Love and close friendship are extremely important to and in our lives, and if they by their very nature cause us to be subject to epistemically irrational or unjustified influences and ways of thinking, then our lives will be less fully rational than many philosophers, both historically and today, have hoped. W. K. Clifford famously argued that one should always believe in accordance with one's evidence or epistemic reasons, but we have pointed out above that someone who loves another person is going to take in their beliefs in a way that resists and won't accord well with empirical evidence or epistemic reasons and that such a person will also tend to think better of the merits and prospects of the loved one than can be justified by evidential or epistemic reasons.[8] So if Clifford is really right to say that we shouldn't think contrary to available good evidence, then we shouldn't really love other people. And that is absurd.

What makes more sense, rather, is that we should continue to love even if that ipso facto makes us evidentially (to some extent) irrational. And of course we typically have no real choice about whether to continue to love or whether, even, to love in the first place. If parents love us, we are most typically going to love them in return, and all this will happen without the explicit consent or choice of the person who loves. And similar things also happen to adults. So rather than deplore love and friendship because they essentially involve us in certain forms of epistemic irrationality, I think – uncomfortable as this thought may be for us philosophers – that we need to accept the idea, the fact, that a substantial degree of epistemic irrationality (I am not talking here about practical irrationality) is inevitable in our lives. And because such irrationality is necessary, is essential, to the very existence or flourishing of relationships of love and friendship, we might even come to see it in a (somewhat) favorable light, as a kind of *beata culpa*. (Some Christians view Adam's disobedience as a *beata culpa* because it made necessary the beautiful redemption of Jesus's self-sacrifice for our sins.)

In any event, these considerations ought to make us reconsider and, I think, reject Clifford's view about what people should believe or not believe. And that view was emblematic of what rationalistic Enlightenment philosophy had to tell us about the justification of belief. According to the Enlightenment way of thinking, we should always be objectively/impartially rational about evidence and shouldn't, for example, believe in God merely on someone's say-so and without first considering whether we have any good epistemic reason or evidence for such belief. (Even the moral sentimentalist Hume is *this kind* of rationalist about what one should or should not believe.) But in that case, what we have been arguing here tells against Enlightenment rationalism in a rather strong way. Earlier on, I considered the idea that love and empathy can be a source of epistemic justification and noted how it went against Enlightenment/rationalist beliefs about the sources and bases of epistemic justification. But if we reject that idea and argue, instead, that love isn't a good source for epistemic reasons, then Enlightenment thought also comes under attack, but from a different angle. Its problem won't be that it unnecessarily and unjustifiably restricts the forms and bases of epistemic warrant, but rather that it accords epistemic rationality or warrant a more important and exclusive place in good human lives than it is reasonable to assume it has or to want it to have. If rationalism and Enlightenment thought aren't mistaken about the sources of epistemic warrant, then it turns out that such warrant is less important or crucial to our lives than they have thought or assumed. And such warrant plays less of a role because so much of what we value and what is valuable in human lives essentially involves beliefs and attitudes that lack theoretical/epistemic warrant or justification because of the way they are influenced or determined by emotions like love and caring (and the relationships in which such emotions/motives are embedded).

The present chapter, then, offers an overall picture of relationships of love and friendship that points to some previously underappreciated ways in which, either empirically or by their very constitutive nature, they are subject to emotional influences and tendencies. Everyone knows that these relationships involve emotions, strong emotions, and there has been a lot of discussion, for example, of how those emotions make us want to help the people we are in such relationships with more than we want to help other people. I believe there is no denying this. But that simply shows that love and friendship make an *efferent difference* in or to our relations with those we love or care about, and I have argued here that love and friendship make an *afferent difference* too. For we are more disposed to unconsciously (or consciously) model ourselves on those we are intimate with than on those we know or like less well, and, as I also pointed out, we are also more likely or disposed to take in their opinions and attitudes than the opinions and attitudes of people we are less strongly connected with.

But we also argued that genuine love and friendship make us less than fully rational with regard to the people we stand in such relationships with. And it is the feelings, the strong emotions, that such relationships involve that seem to make us (to some degree) irrational in various ways. We overestimate the merits and prospects of those we love – not because we tend to have misleading evidence about them, but because we tend to disregard or downplay evidence that (really) indicates a lack of merit or good prospects. Our willingness to believe or disbelieve on insufficient evidence is a sign, a necessary sign, of the strongly positive feelings we have about those we love or deeply care about, and I have suggested that, rather than deplore this fact, we accept it (and even welcome it!) as an essential condition of having good relationships. Given our original need for love, a need that (as I would argue) never goes away (the enduring anger of the serial killer is in fact evidence for that), a life led without good relationships of love and friendship is going to be marred as a life by that absence. Love and friendship may not be all that we need in life (the Beatles were probably wrong about that), but they are important goods within human lives. And by the lights of the present chapter, that means that some of the good, the best, things in life require us to be emotional in ways that compromise or undercut our fullest epistemic rationality. However, if I am not mistaken, that fact is not something we need to regret.

Notes

1. See Aristotle, *Nicomachean Ethics*, Books VIII and IX; Rawls (1971), sections 70 and 74.
2. See, for example, Kohlberg (1981 and 1984).
3. See, for example, Batson (1991) (but also various of Batson's subsequent publications).
4. See Hoffman (2000).
5. Hume (1978), pp. 320–4, 346, 499, 592, 605, inter alia.
6. Reid (1975).
7. See, for example, Stroud (2006).
8. Clifford (1999).

References

C. D. Batson (1991) *The Altruism Question: Toward a Social-Psychological Answer* (Hillsdale, NJ: Lawrence Erlbaum Associates).

W. K. Clifford (1999) *The Ethics of Belief and Other Essays* (Amherst: Prometheus Press).

M. Hoffman (2000) *Empathy and Moral Development: Implications for Caring and Justice* (Cambridge: Cambridge University Press).

D. Hume (1978) *A Treatise of Human Nature*, ed. L. A. Selby-Bigge (Oxford: Clarendon Press).

L. Kohlberg, *Essays in Moral Development*, Vol. 1 (1981), *The Philosophy of Moral Development*, and Vol. 2 (1984), *The Psychology of Moral Development* (New York: Harper and Row).
J. Rawls (1971) *A Theory of Justice* (Cambridge: Harvard University Press).
T. Reid (1975) 'An Inquiry into the Human Mind on the Principles of Common Sense', in R. Beanblossom and K. Lehrer (eds), *Thomas Reid's Inquiry and Essays* (Indianapolis: Bobbs-Merrill), vol. VI.
S. Stroud (2006) 'Epistemic Partiality in Friendship', *Ethics* 116, 498–524.

6
Friendships: Epistemically Dangerous Liaisons?

Curtis Brown

At least since Aristotle, friendship has been held to have epistemic benefits. Friendship has been thought to facilitate acquiring both knowledge of oneself and knowledge of others. More recently, however, it has been suggested that friendship also has serious epistemic disadvantages. Both Simon Keller (2004) and Sarah Stroud (2006) have argued that friendship brings with it an obligation to exhibit what Stroud calls 'epistemic partiality' toward one's friends, and that this partiality is epistemically irrational, at least according to mainstream views of rationality. I argue that, although it is true that friendship may require epistemic partiality, in several senses, in none of these senses is such partiality necessarily irrational or epistemically objectionable.

1 Epistemic advantages of friendship

My main focus in this chapter will be on the possible epistemic dangers of friendship, but I want to begin by considering its purported epistemic benefits. To a significant extent, the usefulness of friendship in gaining self-knowledge, its usefulness in gaining knowledge of others, and the danger that it may lead us to misjudge others, all stem from the contrast between the subjective perspective we naturally take on ourselves and the more objective perspective we naturally take on others. Friendship can help us to, and may even obligate us to, take up perspectives on ourselves and others that we would be less likely to adopt in its absence, and this shifting of perspectives brings with it both epistemic opportunities and epistemic dangers.

1.1 Friendship's contribution to self-knowledge

Friendship is explicitly (and famously) claimed, not just to facilitate self-knowledge, but to be essential for it, in Aristotle's *Magna Moralia*:

> Since then it is both a most difficult thing, as some of the sages have said, to attain a knowledge of oneself, and also a most pleasant (for to know oneself is pleasant) – now we are not able to see what we are from ourselves (and that we cannot do so is plain from the way in which we blame others without being aware that we do the same things ourselves; and this is the effect of favour or passion, and there are many of us who are blinded by these things so that we judge not aright); as then when we wish to see our own face, we do so by looking into the mirror, in the same way when we wish to know ourselves we can obtain that knowledge by looking at our friend. For the friend is, as we assert, a second self. If, then, it is pleasant to know oneself, and it is not possible to know this without having someone else for a friend, the self-sufficing man will require friendship in order to know himself. (1213a13–26)[1]

Here is a mundane example of the sort of self-knowledge Aristotle seems to have in mind here. On a recent visit to see my father, I noticed that he often puffs out his cheeks when he exhales, in a way that frankly looks a little silly. After observing this several times, I was suddenly struck by an uncomfortable thought: when I am feeling a bit anxious or uneasy, I often expel my breath by blowing rather than merely exhaling. I tried this in front of a mirror and, sure enough, it gave me exactly the same rather silly appearance I had noticed on my father.

Although the example is trivial, it exhibits the general pattern of reasoning that Aristotle seems to be calling attention to. The pattern is something like this:

> My father sometimes looks silly when he exhales.
> I am like my father.
> Therefore, (perhaps) I sometimes look silly when I exhale.

This argument is obviously not deductively valid. In fact perhaps it is not best regarded as an argument at all. It might better be regarded as a way of generating hypotheses which may be worth further testing. Indeed, this is precisely what happened in my own case: once I had hypothesized that I might have the same expression as my father, I then tested the hypothesis by literally examining myself in a mirror.

There are two main difficulties with Aristotle's understanding of the contribution of friendship to self-knowledge, at least on this interpretation. The first is that I am likely to be similar not only to my friends, but to other people as well. So if the above pattern of reasoning is an example of what he has in mind, then it is not clear why he thinks that friends are necessary for self-knowledge. As Zena Hitz (2011) notes, 'it seems that any argument for the value of friendship based on similarity will have difficulties limiting the relevant similarities to friends' (p. 10). I might have reason to think that I am very similar to people with whom I am not friends, and if so, I could apply the same pattern of reasoning to them. Although this point raises difficulties for the interpretation of Aristotle, however, it does not diminish the value of the above pattern of reasoning, which offers a way that friends can help us to achieve self-knowledge, even if this way of facilitating self-knowledge is not unique to friendship.

Hitz (2011) responds to this first difficulty with the Aristotelian view by suggesting that Aristotle 'understands friendship to involve collaborative activity, and so the friend is another self in the sense of being a helper rather than a mirror' (p. 10). But Hitz's main concern is not with the *Magna Moralia* account but with an argument in *Nicomachean Ethics* 9.9, and the kind of self-knowledge she focuses on is knowledge of one's essential nature rather than of one's character (Hitz 2011, p. 18, n. 59). As long as we are not concerned to argue that *only* friends can facilitate self-knowledge, there seems to be no reason to deny that friends can be mirrors as well as helpers and that in both roles they can help us to achieve knowledge of ourselves.

A second and perhaps more serious difficulty with the Aristotelian view is that we might not be similar to our friends, so that the second premise of the above argument might be false. Of course, it is a central feature of the Aristotelian account of friendship that we must be similar in character to our primary friends, but this is often questioned in the literature on friendship. Dean Cocking and Jeannette Kennett (1998), for example, claim that 'one's close friends need not be markedly similar to oneself, as is claimed by the mirror account' (p. 503).[2] Cocking and Kennett (1998) suggest that the mirror view of friendship should be replaced by an alternative account that emphasizes interpretation rather than reflection: 'You do not passively reflect my own characteristics; what you give back to me is not a reflection, but an interpretation of me, and for this you do not need to be like me. The better analogy here is not of a mirror but a portrait' (p. 509).[3]

Aristotle and his critics, then, offer several related ways in which friends can facilitate self-knowledge: by serving as mirrors, as helpers, and as interpreters. The crucial point I would like to emphasize about all of them, though, is that they all provide ways in which I can attain a perspective on my own character which is more like the objective, third-person perspective I naturally have on others, thereby to some extent overcoming the blindness to my own failings and overestimation of my own virtues that I am normally prone to. John Cooper (1984) puts this very well when he describes the Aristotelian view as holding that friendship can be 'the needed bridge by which to convert objectivity about others into objectivity about oneself' (p. 322).

1.2 Friendship's contribution to knowledge of others

Although the literature contains extensive discussions of the role of friendship in facilitating self-knowledge by helping us to achieve a more objective perspective on ourselves, there seems to be surprisingly little discussion of the converse, so to speak. But it seems equally noteworthy that if friendships can help us to take an objective perspective on ourselves, they can also help us to achieve a subjective perspective on others. And this too seems to bring potential epistemic advantages: if we can take a more first-person, subjective perspective on others, we may achieve a better understanding of their perspective on their own lives. Elizabeth Telfer (1970–71) puts this well:

> Friendship can enlarge our knowledge throughout the whole gamut of human experience, by enabling us in some measure to adopt the viewpoint of another person through our sympathetic identification with him. Through friendship we can know what it is like to feel or think or do certain things which we do not feel, think or do ourselves. And our knowledge is not merely knowledge by description, but knowledge by acquaintance, derived from our sympathetic sharing of his experience. (p. 240)

1.3 Transition to epistemic dangers

I have suggested that the epistemic benefits of friendship have to do in part with the relationship between subjective and objective perspectives. We find it difficult to take an objective perspective on our own characteristics, and we find it difficult to achieve a subjective understanding of what the world is like for others. Friendship can help with both tasks. It can help us to see our own virtues and flaws from an objective standpoint, and it can help us to understand and empathize with others based on a richer understanding of how they experience the world.

The success of these means to greater knowledge depends on the fact that each perspective is conducive to certain sorts of knowledge, even as it hinders others. Our understanding of our own experiences, motivations, and rationalizations from our first-person perspective gives us a genuine knowledge of ourselves that it is difficult for others to achieve, and friendship can help us to gain something approaching this perspective on the experiences, motivations, and rationalizations of others. On the other hand, our objective assessment of the strengths and weaknesses of others is often more likely to be just and accurate than their assessment of themselves (or our assessment of ourselves), and our friends can help us to achieve this valuable objectivity with respect to our own lives and characters.

But if each perspective facilitates certain kinds of knowledge and endangers others, then there is also the possibility that the transfer will work in the wrong direction. Perhaps there is little danger that we will overextend a third-person perspective on our own lives, using it to analyze aspects of our experience that are better understood subjectively. But it is all too possible that in extending a first-person perspective to our friends, we will also apply to them the very sorts of mistaken assessments we are so prone to with regard to our own character. Our natural tendency to ignore our own flaws and overestimate our strengths can easily be extended to our friends.[4] Then instead of gaining valuable objectivity about our own strengths and weaknesses through our interactions with our friends, we may find that we lose our objectivity about theirs. (To put the point in the crudest possible way, the mirror view suggests that we should reason: I am like my friend; my friend is not OK; therefore, I am not OK. But by the same token, we may reason instead: I am like my friend; I am OK; therefore, my friend is OK.)

Although losing objectivity precisely where it is most valuable is a genuine danger of friendship, nothing I have said so far supports the idea that it is a necessary or constitutive feature. It would seem that we should strive to apply each perspective to the domain to which it is most appropriate, understanding both our friends and ourselves subjectively, but assessing both ourselves and our friends objectively. However, matters may be more complicated than this. Simon Keller (2004) and Sarah Stroud (2006) have both argued that friendship does not merely make it more likely that we will make false judgments about our friends, but that it brings with it an actual obligation to form beliefs about our friends in ways that are epistemically irrational. It is this idea that I want to explore, and criticize, in the remainder of this chapter.

2 Epistemic dangers of friendship

Keller and Stroud both argue that friendship brings with it an obligation (not necessarily moral) to exhibit what Stroud calls 'epistemic partiality' toward one's friends. Both also argue that this epistemic partiality is epistemically irrational, at least according to mainstream views of rationality. Keller (2004) puts this by saying that 'good friendship sometimes requires epistemic irresponsibility' (p. 329), and that 'sometimes the norms of friendship clash with epistemic norms' (p. 331); Stroud (2006) argues that 'friendship constitutively involves belief-forming practices which are epistemically irrational or otherwise objectionable by the lights of mainstream epistemologies' (p. 500); a bit more strongly: 'Friendship positively demands epistemic bias...to put the point as succinctly (and brutally) as possible, friendship requires epistemic irrationality' (p. 518). I think that it's true that friendship may require epistemic partiality, in several senses. But I will argue that in none of these senses is such partiality irrational or epistemically objectionable. Friendship may sometimes lead people to genuine epistemic irrationality, but this is a pathology of friendship, not a constitutive feature.

2.1 A Bayesian approach

A surprising feature of both Keller's and Stroud's essays is the absence of any discussion of subjective probabilities or degrees of belief. Both almost exclusively treat belief as an all-or-nothing matter.[5] Why is this surprising? In part, because they are discussing the relationship between hypotheses and the evidence for them, and evidence rarely establishes or refutes a hypothesis; rather, it adds or diminishes support, altering our confidence in the hypothesis without necessarily making the difference between belief and disbelief, or between either of these and suspension of belief. If we want a nuanced discussion of whether and how friends respond differently to evidence than non-friends, it seems that we will need to consider degrees of confidence.

Another reason the absence of any discussion of degrees of conviction is surprising is that both Keller and Stroud stress that the effects of epistemic partiality are subtle. Stroud (2006) writes that 'the good friend's epistemic stance seems to involve a relative (although not, as we noted, an absolute) imperviousness to new evidence, a slowness to update her beliefs in the light of new data' (p. 514). These remarks seem to cry out for some acknowledgment of degrees of belief! A relative, but not absolute, imperviousness to evidence – doesn't it seem plausible to interpret this to mean that although the friend will adjust his or her degrees of belief to some extent in light of new evidence, the result will be higher or lower than that of a non-friend? And although her reference to slower updating of beliefs could be interpreted digitally (no change in belief until the evidence is substantial, then a move from disbelief to belief), surely it is more helpful to look at this difference at a finer-grained level: the friend and non-friend alter their convictions in the same direction in light of new evidence, but the friend's convictions move in that direction more slowly (in the case of negative beliefs, more quickly in the case of positive ones).

I thus propose to look at Keller's and Stroud's examples and arguments from an epistemological perspective different from the one they themselves bring to bear. In point of fact neither Keller nor Stroud is very specific about their epistemological point of view. Stroud does consider one specific epistemological view, Conee and Feldman's evidentialism (Conee and Feldman 2004), but neither commits herself to it nor discusses alternative views. (Given that she wants her conclusions to generalize to other epistemological views, evidentialism may be a poor choice to focus on, since it would appear to particularly favor her conclusions.[6]) Keller (2004) writes that 'it is very plausible to think that there is an epistemic norm telling us that our beliefs should, in standard cases at least, be responsive only to the evidence, or to what we take to be the evidence, for or against their truth' (p. 334), and mentions other epistemic norms he takes to be plausible (pp. 330–1), but without relating them to specific work in epistemology.

I propose to consider the issue from the perspective of Bayesian epistemology, which focuses on subjective probabilities instead of all-or-nothing beliefs.[7] I think that from this perspective we will see a very natural and plausible way of reconciling epistemic rationality with the phenomena to which Keller and Stroud call attention.

It will be helpful to keep in mind an analogy between the epistemic behavior of friends and that of scientists. (A key source of Bayesian insights in epistemology is work in the philosophy of science on the nature of confirmation.) Keller and Stroud are questioning the epistemic rationality of certain practices of belief formation and the evaluation of evidence, practices that they take to be constitutive of friendship. It seems reasonable to assume that when scientists formulate and test hypotheses, in conformity with the norms and practices of the sciences, they are acting in an epistemically rational way. So if it turns out that the practices of friends are similar to those of scientists, that is at least a prima facie reason to count the friends as rational too.

From a Bayesian point of view, what should a scientist (or other believer) believe, and to what degree, upon considering new evidence? There will be several determining factors. First, we need hypotheses to evaluate. Supposing we have a specific hypothesis H that we want to evaluate in the light of a specific piece of new evidence E, the Bayesian says that the probability we should assign to H given E is $P(H|E)$, the conditional probability of H given E. Determining this value requires a *prior probability* $P(H)$, the degree to which we believe H prior to considering the new evidence E. (The prior probability may or may not itself be the posterior probability resulting from the evaluation of a previous piece of evidence.) We also need a probability for E, which we can determine if we know $P(E|H)$ and $P(E|\neg H)$, i.e. the conditional probability of E given that H is true, and the conditional probability of E given that H is false (making its negation $\neg H$ true).[8]

With these ideas in mind, let us turn to Keller's and Stroud's specific claims.

2.2 Two examples

Keller's and Stroud's arguments that friendship is epistemically dangerous depend heavily on our reaction to examples. Each offers examples about which the reader is expected to agree (a) that a good friend should exhibit certain epistemic behaviors or dispositions, and (b) that these behaviors or dispositions are epistemically objectionable, at least by the standards of prominent epistemological views. It will be useful to have their main examples before us.

2.2.1 Samantha's poetry reading

Keller's (2004) primary example concerns a poetry reading:

> Rebecca is scheduled to give a poetry reading at a café. She is nervous about reading her poetry in public, but has decided to do it on this occasion because she knows that a certain literary agent will be present and she hopes that her work might catch his attention. She lets her good friend Eric know that she will be giving the reading, and asks whether he would mind coming along to be in the office.
>
> Eric, as it happens, is a regular visitor to the café, and has over time accumulated strong evidence for his belief that poetry read there is almost always mediocre, and that it is very unlikely that anything read there would make any literary agent take notice. He had not known that Rebecca fancies herself as a poet, and has no familiarity

> with her work. But he is her friend, and he makes sure that he is there for the reading. (p. 332)

2.2.2 *Sam's apparent insensitivity*

Stroud's (2006) main example concerns receiving information about a friend which puts the friend in a bad light:

> Suppose...that someone tells a damning story about a friend of yours. Your friend appears in a bad light in this tale; he is portrayed as having acted badly, even disreputably. The speaker is clearly rather shocked and disapproving of your friend's behavior; she has obviously formed an unfavorable judgment of your friend's actions and perhaps even his overall character. And it must be confessed that your friend comes off looking rather bad from the information conveyed.... Suppose, for instance, that a third party reports that your friend Sam recently slept with someone and then cruelly never returned any of that person's calls, knowingly breaking that person's heart. (pp. 503–4)

2.3 Epistemic partiality: favorable initial beliefs

Keller contrasts the epistemic attitudes and responses of a friend before, during, and after the acquisition of new evidence. Stroud emphasizes the response to evidence and the resulting beliefs but has less to say about the friend's attitudes prior to acquiring a new piece of evidence. I would like to begin with the appropriate attitudes of a friend prior to acquiring new evidence, so I will begin with Keller's example.

Recall that Eric has evidence that most of the poetry read at the café at which Rebecca is about to read is mediocre. Keller (2004) writes:

> If some stranger were about to give the reading, then Eric would believe that the poetry he is about to hear will probably be pretty awful, not of the type that is likely to impress a literary agent – and he would have good evidence for his belief. Seeing as he is Rebecca's good friend, though, and seeing as he is there to offer her support, he ought not, before she takes the stage, have those beliefs about her. He ought not be expecting that the poetry about to come out of Rebecca's mouth will be awful. Yet, the fact that Rebecca is Eric's friend, rather than a stranger, does not make it any less likely that her poetry will be awful, and there is no need to imagine that Eric, as a friend, should think that it does. (p. 332)

I believe that Eric's knowledge that most of the poetry read at this café is bad is a somewhat distracting and misleading feature of this example. It is true that if most of the people who read poetry at this location are bad poets, and if Eric randomly selects a poetry-reader from this population, then he should assign a high probability to the proposition that the reader is a bad poet. That is a straightforward inductive inference. But in the present example, the poetry-reader Eric is interested in is his friend, not a randomly selected sample. As far as I can see, Eric has no reason to think that Rebecca is a typical reader of poetry at this establishment, and therefore his knowledge concerning most of the poets represented there has no bearing on his opinion of Rebecca's poetry.

In any case, I would like to begin by setting this issue aside and asking what attitude Eric should have if he has *no* evidence about the quality of Rebecca's poetry. This will enable us to separate the question of what one should believe prior to acquiring evidence from the different question of how one should respond to a piece of evidence. In the passage just quoted, Keller does not say that Eric should believe that Rebecca is a good poet, only that in the face of evidence to the contrary, he should *not* believe that she is *not* a good poet. However, in a later passage he speaks more generally of a 'requirement that you be disposed to think well of your friends', arguing that this requirement 'can extend beyond the cases in which you already have good evidentiary reason to do so' (Keller 2004, p. 337). So what Keller seems to have in mind is that there is a general requirement that we think well of our friends; in the absence of any evidence, this will lead us to actually believe positive things about a friend, while if there is evidence to the contrary, it may only lead us to suspend disbelief.

Restricting ourselves to the case in which we have no evidence, we might try this as a first attempt at a general principle Keller would accept:

> If *H* is a positive hypothesis about a friend of *S*, and *S* has no evidence relevant to the truth or falsity of *H*, then *S* should believe *H*.

This is certainly too strong, however. For one thing, there are a great many positive things one might believe about a friend, and many of them are incompatible with one another (at least given our other beliefs). For instance, should Eric believe that Rebecca is a brilliant nuclear physicist in the absence of any evidence? But if so, then by the same token he should believe that she is a brilliant geneticist, a brilliant organic chemist, a brilliant mathematician, and so on. Given plausible beliefs about the amount of study required to achieve excellence in these fields, these hypotheses are incompatible with one another.

It looks as though we need additional constraints in the antecedent of our conditional in order to have a plausible sufficient condition for belief in the positive hypothesis *H*. There are few other aspects of the story that we might appeal to, however; we certainly can't restrict *H* to hypotheses about poetic ability, since the moral of the story is supposed to apply much more broadly. Perhaps the most plausible additional constraint we can derive from the story is that Eric is in a situation in which his belief in Rebecca's poetic ability will be helpful to Rebecca. This suggests that the relevant principle might be something more like this:

> If *H* is a positive hypothesis about a friend of *S*, and *S* has no evidence relevant to the truth or falsity of *H*, and *S*'s believing *H* will be helpful to the friend, then *S* should believe *H*.

This is my best guess at a general principle Keller would endorse concerning what friends should believe in the absence of evidence, expressed in terms of all-or-nothing belief. I am inclined to think that any formulation in terms of all-or-nothing belief will be too strong. That is, saying that *S* should believe *H*, period, may be stronger than Keller intends. It seems more plausible to say something weaker: for example, that *S* should be *inclined to think that H is true*; that *S* should be *open to accepting H*; or that *S* should be *more convinced of H than a stranger would be*. I think that a better formulation would move from all-or-nothing belief to degrees of belief. Although the following is deplorably vague, I believe that it comes at least a bit closer to being correct:

> If *H* is a positive hypothesis about a friend of *S*, and *S* has no evidence relevant to the truth or falsity of *H*, and *S*'s believing *H* will be helpful to the friend, then *S* should assign *H* a probability higher than .5.

If this principle is correct, then clearly the reasons for belief it provides are not epistemic reasons, and the 'should' in the consequent is not the epistemic 'should'. So the principle requires that there be non-epistemic grounds for belief. However, this leaves open the crucial question of whether acting in accordance with this principle is positively irrational, whether it is something that epistemically speaking one should not do. Only if this is the case will there be a conflict between what friendship requires and what is epistemically responsible.

How one answers this question will depend on one's views on epistemology. The one epistemological view Stroud discusses is evidentialism, and it is undeniably true that on an evidentialist view, believing something in the absence of evidence is irrational, is something that we epistemically should not do. Conee and Feldman (2004), for example, defends the view that 'if a person is going to adopt any attitude toward a proposition, then that person ought to... suspend judgment about it if his evidence is neutral (or close to neutral)' (p. 178).

But is this evidentialist view really plausible? Is it really plausible that it is never epistemically acceptable to believe a hypothesis if one's evidence is neutral? Set aside the demands of friendship for a moment, and consider analogous cases. In particular, consider the case of a scientist who hypothesizes that *H*, but has not yet subjected *H* to empirical test. It seems that the scientist might have many reasons to look with favor on *H*. One reason might simply be that *H* is the scientist's creation, and she is inclined to look favorably on her own creations. A different reason might be that she has a hunch that *H* is true, a hunch that is not based on evidence. Finally, there might be more substantive, but still non-evidential, reasons to favor *H*: perhaps it is simpler than rival hypotheses, or more conservative in the sense that it involves smaller changes to current theories than its rivals. Arguably, none of these reasons for belief is evidential. But would we really regard a scientist as irrational if she believed *H* for these reasons?

Her belief in *H* would of course be tentative, subject to change once *H* is actually tested; but that is true in the example of Eric and Rebecca as well. Moreover, '*S* believes that *H*' might be too strong to really capture the attitude that seems rational; '*S* is inclined to believe that *H* is true' and the like might be better descriptions of the appropriate attitude. As I mentioned above, this also seems to be true in the case of Rebecca and Eric. With these provisos, though, it seems to me that it is entirely epistemically reasonable for a scientist to have a more positive attitude toward *H* than toward rival hypotheses, even if there is as yet no relevant evidence, for any of the reasons just mentioned. If that is correct, then evidentialism is false, and it can be epistemically rational to hold a belief, or at least have a subjective probability greater than one has for rival hypotheses, even in the absence of positive evidence.

In any case, this is certainly a widely held point of view among Bayesian epistemologists and philosophers of science.[9] From a Bayesian point of view, we can regard Eric's initial beliefs about Rebecca's poetry as prior probabilities. It is a staple of Bayesian epistemology that priors can legitimately be determined in a variety of ways. They may be the result of evaluating prior evidence: my prior for this round of evidence-evaluation may also be my posterior from a previous round. But this is not essential. My prior might also be based on a hunch, or even bias or prejudice. From the point of view of determining whether I am assessing the evidence rationally, what matters is not the prior probability I assign to a hypothesis, but rather whether I update that probability appropriately given the nature of the evidence. Colin Howson and Peter Urbach (2006) express this position clearly:

> The prior distribution from which a Bayesian analysis proceeds reflects a person's beliefs before the experimental results are known. Those beliefs are subjective, in the sense that they are shaped in part by elusive, idiosyncratic influences, so they are likely to vary from person to person....it has been argued that the difficulty may be stemmed at the source by repudiating subjective in favor of purely objective prior probabilities...although the idea that scientific theories possess unique, objectively correct, inductive probabilities is eminently appealing, it has so far resisted determined efforts at a satisfactory analysis, except in the special cases of tautologies and contradictions, and there is now a wide consensus that no such analysis is possible (pp. 237–8).

2.4 Epistemic partiality: differential effects of evidence

Stroud and Keller both stress that friends will not only begin with a more favorable assessment than a neutral observer might have but will also respond differently to new evidence. It is certainly appropriate to stress this because the way people react to the evidence seems to be the most important single factor in determining whether they are being epistemically rational. But a crucial point that Stroud and Keller seem to miss (or at least do not mention) is that it is entirely rational for two people to assign different posterior probabilities to a hypothesis after assessing the same evidence, provided they had different prior probabilities for the hypothesis before taking the new evidence into account. It seems to me that this simple fact is enough to account for the responses to evidence of the friends in their stories, and thus that they have not shown that there is any epistemic irrationality involved in their examples of epistemic partiality.

The appropriate effect of prior probabilities on the posterior probability is fairly dramatic. Although assigning specific numbers may seem a bit silly, it will help in gaining a vivid sense of the effect of the prior probability. In Stroud's example, let us suppose that the friend assigns a prior probability of .9 to the hypothesis that Sam always acts honorably. And let us suppose that an 'objective' or disinterested observer would assign a prior probability of .5 to the same hypothesis since the disinterested observer has no reason, epistemic or otherwise, to favor one belief or the other.

Now, suppose that both the friend and the disinterested observer agree that the probability of someone saying what Sam said, given that they always act honorably, is fairly low, say .3. And suppose they also agree that the probability of someone who doesn't always act honorably making this remark is much higher, say .7. If both the friend and the disinterested observer update the probability they assign to the hypothesis in accordance with Bayes's Theorem, they will end up with very different results. The friend will assign the hypothesis a posterior probability of .79, while the disinterested observer will assign it a posterior probability of .3.

Tinkering with the numbers a bit, we can make the example even starker. Suppose both observers agree that $P(E|H) = .2$ and that $P(E|\neg H) = .9$. The disinterested observer will assign an extremely low posterior probability to the hypothesis, .18. Meanwhile the friend will still, entirely rationally, think it more likely than not that their friend always acts honorably: the friend's posterior probability will be .667.

As additional evidence comes in, if it all points in the same direction, the friend and the disinterested observer will converge on the same assessment (this is what is known as the 'washing out of the priors'). But if their belief formation processes are rational, as Bayesianism interprets this, then they actually *should not* converge on the same probability after assessing only a single piece of evidence. And as we have just seen, their posterior probabilities can differ very dramatically even if they are both evaluating the evidence in the same, equally rational way. My suggestion is, then, that the differential responses to evidence of friends and non-friends is not in fact a second sort of epistemic partiality: rather, it is simply a consequence of our first sort, the different prior probabilities that friends and non-friends may assign to hypotheses.

Matters would be quite different if the two observers actually followed different rules in updating their subjective probabilities. Suppose that a friend and a disinterested observer, even if they began with the same prior probabilities, and agreed on $P(E|H)$ and $P(E|\neg H)$, would nevertheless end up with different posterior probabilities. In that case, the Bayesian will be committed to the view that the friend really is being epistemically irrational (assuming that the disinterested observer updates in accordance with Bayesian conditionalization). But nothing in the examples discussed by Stroud and Keller gives us any reason to think that friendship requires this kind of epistemic irrationality. It seems quite plausible that their epistemically rational differences in prior probabilities are enough to explain the differences in their posteriors. We can imagine a case in which friendship leads someone to go beyond assigning high prior probabilities to positive views about a friend, and to respond irrationally to the evidence: but there seems to be no reason to regard such irrationality as *required* by friendship.

2.5 Epistemic partiality: constructing hypotheses and seeking evidence

Having considered whether a friend and a disinterested observer can rationally have different prior probabilities in the absence of relevant evidence and whether they may rationally assign different posterior probabilities upon considering the same piece of evidence, let us briefly consider two further sorts of epistemic partiality. The first is the possibility that people will more assiduously seek out alternative hypotheses to explain evidence that might appear to support negative conclusions about their friends than they would for non-friends. Stroud (2006) writes: '[W]e will go to greater lengths in the case of a friend to construct and to entertain less damning interpretations of the reported conduct than we would for a nonfriend. This takes effort: these alternative explanations may not be obvious, and we may need to devote considerable mental resources to working them up and considering their merits' (p. 506).[10] The second and final sort of epistemic partiality is that in addition to working harder to construct hypotheses to test, a friend may also be motivated to look harder for evidence by means of which to test those hypotheses.

Both of these final forms of epistemic partiality feature conscious effort in a way that the first two forms do not. A good friend will probably not consciously set out to assign high prior probabilities to positive estimates of a friend's character and abilities; a good friend will simply be more likely to find him or herself with such a higher assessment. But the construction of hypotheses and the gathering of evidence are activities which must be engaged in consciously and with effort. It seems very likely that both activities are more characteristic of the epistemic behavior of friends than of the epistemic behavior of disinterested observers.

One point to make about this is that in some cases, actively seeking out hypotheses to test and evidence by means of which to test them may make it *more* rather than less likely that we will discover the truth. This is a main theme of Troy Jollimore's (2011) detailed discussion of Keller's and Stroud's essays. As Jollimore writes: 'Although it is, in one sense, evidence of a certain epistemic imperfection – a perfect epistemic agent would approach *every* situation with the kind of open-minded, full, and generous attention that we, on the whole, reserve for our friends – it does not follow from this that such instances of special attention are to be condemned in epistemic terms' (p. 59).

But even aside from whether the active search for hypotheses and evidence is more likely to lead to the truth, it is worth noting that this same eagerness to find and test favorable hypotheses is characteristic of work in the sciences. Ever since Hans Reichenbach (1938) introduced the distinction between the context of discovery and the context of justification, and wrote that 'epistemology is only concerned in constructing the context of justification' (p. 7), it has been common in the philosophy of science to stress that scientific methodology is concerned only with how hypotheses get confirmed or disconfirmed, not with where they come from in the first place.[11] It doesn't matter so much where the hypotheses come from (even if they come from a desire to save one's pet theory, or to believe the best about one's friend); what matters is how we assesses the hypotheses in the light of the evidence. Similarly, we would not be surprised or critical if a scientist works harder at testing her own theories than those of others, so long as she does not fudge the data and properly updates her assessment of the theory in light of it.

If this behavior is epistemically rational for a scientist, then it seems that the similar behavior of friends is also epistemically rational. Keller's and Stroud's inventories of the kinds of hypotheses friends will seek for are very plausible, but give us no reason to think that the friends are doing anything epistemically objectionable.

Conclusion

We have seen why friendship may in some cases require epistemic partiality. And we have distinguished several distinct sorts of epistemic partiality: friends may assign different prior probabilities than non-friends; as a consequence of this, they may arrive at different posterior probabilities after considering exactly the same evidence as a non-friend; they may work harder to construct alternative hypotheses to evaluate than a non-friend would; and they may work harder to test hypotheses than a non-friend would. I have argued that all of these sorts of epistemic partiality are in fact entirely epistemically rational.

There is much room here for further exploration. What are the differences between the subjective, first-person perspective we typically have on ourselves, and the objective, third-person perspective we typically have on others? Is there a single distinction here, or are there several different factors that need not always go together? What kinds of knowledge is the subjective perspective conducive to, and what kinds might it inhibit? Similarly, what kinds of knowledge does the objective perspective facilitate, and what kinds does it make more difficult? Just how much epistemic partiality does friendship require, and under what circumstances? Can we formulate more precise principles to elucidate the epistemic requirements of friendship?

But although all these issues invite further consideration, we have seen that there is at least one mainstream epistemological view, subjective Bayesianism, on which the epistemic partiality sometimes required by friendship can be seen to be entirely epistemically rational. At a minimum, this calls into question the idea that *all* mainstream views in epistemology must hold that epistemic partiality is irrational. And although I have not offered a detailed defense of subjective Bayesianism against such alternative views as evidentialism, I believe that the similarities between the epistemic dispositions of friends and those of scientists, and indeed the intuitive reasonableness of the epistemic partiality exhibited by good friends, give us some reason to favor a Bayesian approach over an evidentialist one.

Notes

1. The authenticity of the *Magna Moralia* has been questioned, but regardless of whether the author is Aristotle, the views are Aristotelian, and scholars have not hesitated to use the work to gain insight into Aristotle's discussions of friendship elsewhere.
2. Nancy Sherman (1989) finds Aristotle himself acknowledging that, as she puts it, 'friends bear varying degrees of similarity to each other' (p. 142). She suggests that 'if another self need not be exactly similar, then self-knowledge might involve contrasting oneself with another' as well as seeing oneself in another (p. 143).
3. cf. Lynch (2005), pp. 160–1. Lynch seems to attribute something very like this interpretive view to Aristotle himself, but I don't see how she can square this with the texts.
4. As Cooper (1984) notes: 'one might doubt whether, if, as seems true, people tend to be biased in favor of themselves and blind to their own faults, they are any less so where those with whom they are intimate are concerned' (p. 322).
5. Stroud (2006) does once mention giving certain hypotheses 'greater credence [for a friend] than we would for a non-friend' (p. 506), but this is the only exception I have noticed.
6. Stroud (2006) explicitly declines to consider other epistemological theories, writing: 'I shall presume that the ... evidentialist strategy ... was the most

promising avenue for vindicating the friend's beliefs and belief-forming practices in epistemic terms' (p. 518). I think that this is nearly the opposite of the truth: evidentialism provides a distinctly *unpromising* approach to epistemic vindication of non-evidential influences on belief!

7. A useful introductory overview of Bayesian epistemology is Hájek and Hartmann (2010).
8. Almost nothing that I say will depend on the precise details of Bayesian updating, but for the sake of concreteness I will consider an example or two which involve actually calculating $P(H|E)$ in accordance with Bayes's Theorem: $\frac{P(E \mid H)P(H)}{P(E \mid H)P(H) + P(E \mid \neg H)P(\neg H)}$.
9. To be more precise, the view that prior probabilities may legitimately vary from one person to another so long as they conform to the laws of probability is held by 'subjective Bayesians'. 'Objective Bayesianism' might be more favorable to Stroud's and Keller's view. See Hájek and Hartmann (2010) for an introductory discussion, and Howson and Urbach (2006, chapter 9), for some of the details.
10. Stroud (2006) mentions the same idea again, more briefly, later in her essay, writing that the good friend will tend 'to fasten on possible hypotheses that present her friend in a more favorable light' (p. 516). Keller (2004) does not discuss this idea so explicitly, but does make the related suggestion that Eric 'will be disposed to interpret [Rebecca's poetry] in ways that make it look like a stronger piece of work' (p. 333).
11. Nevertheless, interest in the context of discovery has made a bit of a comeback: see Nickles (2000) for a quick overview of work in this area.

References

Aristotle (1984) *The Complete Works of Aristotle: The Revised Oxford Translation*, ed. Jonathan Barnes (Princeton: Princeton University Press).

D. Cocking and J. Kennett (1998) 'Friendship and the Self', *Ethics* 108, 502–27.

E. Conee and R. Feldman (2004) *Evidentialism* (Oxford: Oxford University Press).

J. M. Cooper (1984) 'Aristotle on Friendship', in Amelie Rorty (ed.), *Essays on Aristotle's Ethics* (Berkeley: University of California Press).

R. Feldman (2004) 'The Ethics of Belief', in Conee and Feldman (eds), *Evidentialism* (Oxford: Oxford University Press), 166–95.

A. Hájek and S. Hartmann (2010) 'Bayesian Epistemology', in Jonathan Dancy, Ernest Sosa, and Matthias Steup (eds), *A Companion to Epistemology*, 2nd edn (Oxford: Wiley-Blackwell).

Z. Hitz (2011) 'Aristotle on Self-Knowledge and Friendship', *Philosopher's Imprint* 11, 1–28.

C. Howson and P.Urbach (2006) *Scientific Reasoning: The Bayesian Approach*, 3rd edn (Chicago: Open Court).

T. Jollimore (2011) *Love's Vision* (Princeton: Princeton University Press).

S. Keller (2004) 'Friendship and Belief', *Philosophical Papers* 33, 329–51.

S. Lynch (2005) *Philosophy and Friendship* (Edinburgh: Edinburgh University Press).
T. Nickles (2000) 'Discovery', in W. H. Newton-Smith (ed.), *A Companion to the Philosophy of Science* (Oxford: Blackwell), 85–96.
H. Reichenbach (1938) *Experience and Prediction: An Analysis of the Foundation and the Structure of Knowledge* (Chicago: University of Chicago Press).
N. Sherman (1989) *The Fabric of Virtue: Aristotle's Theory of Character* (Oxford: Oxford University Press).
S. Stroud (2006) 'Epistemic Partiality in Friendship', *Ethics* 116, 498–524.
E. Telfer (1970–71) 'Friendship', *Proceedings of the Aristotelian Society* 71, 223–41.

7

How to Be a Non-Reductionist about Reasons of Friendship

Jeffrey Seidman

We take ourselves to have reasons to do things for and with our friends: reason to console a friend when she loses her job, for instance, or to help her celebrate when she gets a new one. And we take ourselves to have reasons for emotions centered on our friends: reason to worry when her job prospects are discouraging, and reason for relief when she lands on her feet. These are, we are apt to think, *normative* reasons: they not only explain our behavior, they make it *appropriate*. Indeed, in some cases, we think that to fail to respond appropriately to these reasons would be to *wrong* our friends.[1] And we suppose that these reasons *depend* upon our friendships, so that others, who do not share our friendships, do not face the same normative reasons. I have a reason to critique my friend's job application so that she can make it stronger, but you do not.

That the parties to a friendship are disposed to see certain considerations as reasons for action and for emotion is a constitutive feature of friendship. If, in the right circumstances, I do not see your grief as giving me reason to console you – a reason different from whatever reasons a stranger has – then I do not stand to you in the relation of friendship. But it is one thing to claim that a friend is disposed to see herself as having reasons to do and feel certain things; it is another thing to claim that she is right – that she actually *has* the normative reasons she takes herself to have. A theory of practical reasons that denied that we *ever* have reasons of friendship would be so radically revisionary of our self-understanding that it is hard to see why we should accept it. To heed such a theory and cease to take considerations pertaining to our friends as giving us special reasons would be to give up friendship itself; and it is hard to envisage how a theory could make us believe that we should, or could, do that.[2] But the fact that wholesale skepticism about the reasons of friendship is implausible does not imply that, when we see considerations pertaining to our friends as reasons, we are always right. A person in an abusive relationship may think that she has reason to protect her partner when the police enquire about him, and she may be mistaken. And so the phenomenon of friendship poses two related questions for the theorist of practical reason: (1) In *which* cases do we have the reasons that our friendships dispose us to see ourselves as having? (2) What explains the fact that we have reasons of friendship at all (in the cases in which we do)?[3]

In what follows, I will offer a normative principle in answer to Question (1). I will address Question (2) by offering an explanation for the fact that we make judgments about reasons of friendship in a manner that is responsive to this principle. To the extent that it is correct, this explanation does not, by itself, comprise a complete answer to Question (2). A more complete answer would show not only why we *do* make judgments in a manner responsive to the principle I will propose, but also that, upon informed reflection, it is reasonable of us to *endorse* doing so. To argue this, one would need to consider each of the reasons that might be suggested that we ought *not* to make judgments in accordance with this principle. I will not offer such an argument. In keeping with the working assumption that wholesale skepticism about reasons of friendship is unwarranted, I will assume that it is, in fact, reasonable of us reflectively to endorse the principle to which we are responsive when we make our best, considered judgments about when we have reasons of friendship. To the extent that this is correct, the explanation that I will offer comprises a true, if incomplete, answer to Question (2).

Before offering my own answer to Question (1), it will help to consider, by way of contrast to the answer that I will offer, a normative principle suggested by the work of Samuel Scheffler. In Section 1, I will present this principle, and I will argue that it invites a *reductionist* answer to Question (2) – an answer according to which the normative force of reasons of friendship is reducible to the normative force of some *other*, more basic kind of normative reason. In Section 2, I will offer an alternative normative principle, *Friendship*, in answer to Question (1). I will argue in Section 3 that *Friendship* in fact better accords with our considered judgments about when we have reasons of friendship than does the principle suggested by Scheffler's work, and that it does not invite a reductionist answer to Question (2) in the way that Scheffler's principle does. In Section 4, I will argue the we can explain the fact that the extension of our concept of a normative reason is governed, in part, by *Friendship* by pointing to the distinctive advantages of employing a concept governed by this principle (and I will suggest that similar considerations in fact explain why our concept is governed by a more general principle, of which *Friendship* is an instantiation). In Section 5, I will argue that, contrary to first appearances, the account of reasons of friendship that I offer does not amount to, or encourage, naturalism about normative reasons.

1 *Scheffler's Suggestion* and the difficulty of non-reductionism

In an illuminating series of articles, Samuel Scheffler has sought to explain a class of reasons he calls 'relationship-dependent reasons'.[4] These include not just reasons of friendship, but reasons that derive from family relationships, professional relationships, and interpersonal relationships of other kinds. Although Scheffler does not single reasons of friendship out for special treatment, the following principle is implied by his more general claims about relationship-dependent reasons.

> *Scheffler's Suggestion*: if an agent has net reason to value a friendship non-instrumentally, then the friendship gives her genuine reasons.[5]

The suggestion nicely tracks many of our ordinary judgments about when friends have the reasons they take themselves to have. It is plausible to suppose, for instance, that an abused partner in an abusive relationship does not have 'net' reason to value her relationship. (Even if she does have *some* reason to value it, it is natural to think that whatever reason she has is outweighed by the facts that make her relationship abusive.) In that case, *Scheffler's Suggestion* yields the plausible answer that the abused partner does not have the reasons of friendship that she may take herself to have. By contrast, it is plausible to suppose that most of us do have net reason to value our healthy, non-abusive friendships non-instrumentally. (Our reasons to value our friendships might include the consideration, which Scheffler emphasizes, that friendships are often sources of meaning and fulfillment in our lives, and they might include moral reasons or perhaps reasons of other sorts.[6]) And it is plausible to suppose that we do have reasons of friendship in these cases. So, *Scheffler's Suggestion* seems to give the right answer to Question (1) for a wide range of cases.

Scheffler offers a positive answer to Question (2) somewhat tentatively and only in passing, but he does argue *against* one, reductionist, answer to this question. The reductionist theory against which he argues is a form of voluntarism, according to which reasons of friendship are simply the reasons generated by discreet interactions, such as accepting benefits and making commitments, that typically occur in the context of friendships, but which also occur, and which generate the same sorts of reasons, outside of that context. This view is 'reductionist', because the normative force of reasons of friendship, on this proposal, is simply the normative force of reasons to repay benefits in kind, to honor one's commitments, etc.

Scheffler's own, 'non-reductionist' answer to Question (2) (or rather, to an analogous but broader question, encompassing reasons generated by relationships other than friendships), runs as follows:

> [T]o value one's relationship with another is to see it as a source of reasons for action of a distinctive kind. It is, in effect, to see oneself as having special responsibilities to the person with whom one has the relationship. Thus, in so far as we have good reasons to value our interpersonal relationships, we have good reasons to see ourselves as having special responsibilities.... But, it may be said, even if we have reason to see ourselves as having such responsibilities, that is compatible with our not actually having them. This seems to me misleading, however. If the non-reductionist argument establishes that we have good reason to see ourselves as having special responsibilities, then that is how we should see ourselves. There is no substantive difference, in this context, between the conclusion that we do have special responsibilities, and the conclusion that, all things considered, we have good reasons for thinking that we do.[7]

An objector may worry that this argument simply ignores the distinction between practical and epistemic reasons. Whatever reasons we may have to value our friendships and other relationships are surely practical reasons. It is a matter of dispute whether there can be practical reasons for *belief* at all (as opposed to practical reasons for trying to *bring it about* that one believes something).[8] But even if there can be practical reasons for belief, an objector might argue, these can have no bearing on the *truth* of the belief they support. A belief in God might be comforting, and so I might have net practical reason to believe that God exists, but this reason certainly does not count in favor of the truth of the proposition that God exists. So, the objector might claim, it is simply a mistake to jump from the claim that we have good (practical) reason, all things considered, for believing that we have reasons of friendship to the claim that we do.

The objection would hit its mark if our beliefs about reasons of friendship tracked facts that were wholly *independent* of facts about our friendships and their value. But it is precisely Scheffler's claim that this is not the case: our valuable friendships *generate* reasons that we would not have if we did not have those friendships, or if we had them, but they were not valuable.[9] The *same* facts – about the value of a friendship – that constitute reasons to value that friendship non-instrumentally and hence constitute reasons to *see* considerations pertaining to it as 'friendship-dependent reasons' *also* make it the case, on Scheffler's view, that those considerations *are* the friendship-dependent reasons we see them as.

While this reply saves Scheffler's view from the objection that he conflates practical and epistemic reasons, it serves to underline a different worry: it suggests that *Scheffler's Suggestion* is compatible with, and in fact invites, a reductionist answer to Question (2) – one different from the voluntarist reductionism that Scheffler considers and rejects. For if the reasons we have to value a friendship are what make it the case that considerations pertaining to a friend are reasons of friendship, then should we not see the reasons we have to value our friendships as normatively *basic*, and see the normative force of reasons of friendship as simply inherited from, or identical to, the normative force of these more basic reasons, whatever they are? Suppose, for instance, that some friendship is, as Scheffler suggests it may be, a deep source of fulfillment for me. This fact constitutes a prudential reason for me to value that friendship, and hence a prudential reason to see considerations pertaining to my friend as reasons of friendship; and on Scheffler's view, this fact makes it the case that the considerations pertaining to my friend are, in fact, reasons of friendship. Shouldn't we say, in this case, that I am *justified* in seeing considerations about my friend as reasons just because doing so contributes to my welfare? And isn't this just to say that the normative force of my reasons of friendship is, in this case, the (presumably basic) normative force of prudential reasons?

I do not think that these considerations show that a theorist who accepts *Scheffler's Suggestion* in answer to Question (1) is thereby committed to a reductionist answer to Question (2). Perhaps there is a way to answer the questions raised at the end of the previous paragraph.[10] But they do throw into relief the difficulty of giving a non-reductionist answer to Question (2) – especially if one holds that one has reasons of friendship if and only if one has normative reasons of some other kind. A viable non-reductionism about reasons of friendship must make room (as *Scheffler's Suggestion* does) for the fact that the brute existence of a friendship is not sufficient to guarantee that the considerations that a party to it *sees* as reasons of friendship *are* reasons of friendship. (The considerations that an abused partner sees as reasons may not be.) But it must do this without implying that the normative force of reasons of friendship is simply *borrowed* from, or reducible to, the normative force of some other class of reasons – for instance, from the normative force of whatever reasons an agent has to value her friendship.

2 An alternative normative principle: *Friendship*

Consider the following normative principle in answer to Question (1),

> *Friendship*: if an agent (i) has net, non-instrumental reason to believe some consideration to be a reason of friendship for herself to do or feel something *or* (ii) sees some consideration as a reason of friendship for herself to do or feel something and does not have net, non-instrumental reason *not* to believe that consideration to be a reason to do or feel that thing, then that consideration is, in fact, a reason of friendship for her to do or feel that thing.

I will argue in Section 3 that *Friendship* in fact accords with our considered judgments as to when we have reasons of friendship. Before arguing for this principle, however, I must pause to clarify it.

1. The condition that an agent 'has' net reason should be understood *objectively*. That is, it should be read so as to allow that an agent may have normative reasons of which she is ignorant, or that she may not have the reasons that she thinks she has (because considerations she believes to be normative reasons are not, or because they have a strength different from the strength she believes them to have).
2. The principle allows that an agent may be wrong about what reasons of friendship she has in either of two ways. Clause (i) of the antecedent of the conditional makes room for the fact that, because she is depressed, or obtuse, or simply ignorant of some fact, an agent may fail to recognize some consideration as a reason of friendship for herself, even though it is a reason of friendship for her. Clause (ii) of

the antecedent allows that an agent may see some consideration as a reason of friendship for herself even though it is not.

3. The reasons in question are 'agent-relative' reasons in one sense of that term: they are reasons for the agent in question, but not necessarily for anyone else.[11] The principle does *not* imply that if an agent sees some consideration as a reason for *everyone* to do or feel something, then absent reason to believe differently, it is such a reason.
4. While part (i) of the antecedent of the conditional and the second conjunct of part (ii) of the antecedent of the conditional both concern what the agent *believes* to be a reason, the first conjunct of part (ii) of the antecedent concerns instead what the agent *sees* as a reason. On the usage of 'seeing as a reason' that I borrow from T.M. Scanlon, an agent sees some consideration as a reason if it impinges upon her consciousness in a way similar to the way in which it would do if she believed it to be a reason: commanding her attention, figuring in the premises of practical deliberation that she finds herself engaging in, etc.[12] Typically, 'seeing is believing', and so an agent who sees some consideration as a reason *also* believes it to be a reason. But, as with cases of visual perception, 'seeing-as' and believing may come apart: just as a subject may continue, recalcitrantly, to see Müller-Lyer lines as of unequal length, even though she knows that they are equal, an abused partner may continue to see considerations about threats to her partner's welfare as good reasons to help him, even though she knows that they are not.[13]
5. *Friendship* offers a finer-grained answer to Question (1) than *Scheffler's Suggestion* aims to do. Whereas *Scheffler's Suggestion* tells us which *friendships* generate reasons of friendship, *Friendship* tells us which *considerations* are reasons of friendship.

3 *Scheffler's Suggestion* and *Friendship*

In a wide range of cases, *Scheffler's Suggestion* and *Friendship* give identical answers to Question (1) because, as Scheffler argues, to value a friendship *just is*, in part, to see considerations pertaining to one's friend as reasons of friendship.[14] So, if an agent has net reason to value a friendship (as the antecedent of *Scheffler's Suggestion* requires), then, *ipso facto*, she has net reason to see considerations pertaining to it as reasons. And it is plausible to suppose that, at least in *many* cases, where an agent has positive net reason to *see* some consideration as a reason of friendship, she has net reason to *believe* that consideration to be a reason of friendship[15] – satisfying disjunct (i) of the antecedent of *Friendship*.[16] In these cases, the two principles will agree that an agent has reasons of friendship.[17] Likewise, it is plausible to suppose that, at least in *many* cases, if an agent has net reason *not* to value a friendship, then she also has net reason *not* to see considerations pertaining to her friend to be reasons of friendship, and not to believe them to be. In these cases, too, *Scheffler's Suggestion* and *Friendship* will give identical answers to Question (1).

There is, however, an important class of cases in which the two principles will give divergent answers. Disjunct (ii) of the antecedent in *Friendship* allows that some consideration may be a reason of friendship for an agent even if the agent has no *positive* net reason to believe that consideration to be a reason of friendship – so long as she does see that consideration as a reason of friendship and has no positive reason *not* to believe that it is a reason of friendship. For *Scheffler's Suggestion*, by contrast, this is not enough: in order for some consideration that an agent sees as a reason of friendship to be a reason of friendship, the agent must have positive reason to value the friendship in question.[18] The two principles, then, give different 'default' answers to the question whether some agent has the reasons of friendship that she sees herself as having. *Friendship* accords a (defeasible) *presumption* of normative significance to the bare fact that an agent *sees* some consideration as a reason of friendship for herself, whether or not she has any positive reason to see it that way. *Scheffler's Suggestion* does not.

It might be argued that, in practice, the two principles will never, in fact, yield inconsistent answers to Question (1), because it is never the case that an agent has *zero* net reason to value a friendship. Friendships are intrinsically valuable, and they tend to make an agent's life go better, so typically an agent will have some positive net reason, however small, to value her friendships. On the other hand, if an agent's friend is morally bad, or if her friendship with him is built around some destructive shared project, then she will have net reason *not* to value her friendship, and also not to believe considerations pertaining to it to be reasons. There is no room for middle ground, in which an agent has neither reason to value a friendship nor reason not to, someone might claim.

This attempt to rule out, *a priori*, the possibility that an agent might have zero net reason to value a friendship – no net reason to value it, but no net reason *not* to value it either – is, however, hard to motivate. Not all of our friendships play significant roles in our lives, or contribute to anyone's welfare, or are plausible candidates in other ways for the possession of intrinsic value. Two people may, for instance, begin a friendship at a time when they have significant shared interests, or when circumstances throw them together. Over time, they may lose their shared interests or shared circumstances, or it may simply become the case that they no longer 'click'. Nonetheless, out of habit or inertia, they may remain friends, and both may continue to value their friendship, if only slightly: they may continue to make occasional efforts to spend time together, may continue to take some interest in the happenings in one another's lives, and each may continue to see considerations pertaining to the other's welfare as providing reasons of friendship (though perhaps not strong ones). Each may have other, much more robust friendships, which are central to the meaning each finds in his or her life. This old friendship, by contrast, may make *no* significant contribution to the welfare of either party: neither would live a worse life without it. Or perhaps the friendship contributes in some marginal ways to the lives of the friends, but perhaps they have other, equally marginal but counterbalancing reasons not to value it: perhaps the two make time to get together each year, each out of a sense of obligation to the other, even though doing so is a chore that keeps them from doing better things with the rare, spare weekend; or perhaps, when they get together, they invariably revert to the mildly morally bad behavior in which they engaged together as teenagers. Why should we allow, then, that an agent may have positive reason to value a friendship, allow that she may have reason *not* to value a friendship, but not allow that she may have zero *net* reason to value it? It seems at least possible that some of our friendships are, on balance, neither valuable nor bad, but simply *valueless*.

A defender of *Scheffler's Suggestion* might acknowledge that there can be friendships that one or both friends has no net reason to value; but she might argue, contra *Friendship,* that an agent who has no net reason to value her friendship does not, in fact, have the reasons of friendship that she sees herself as having. This claim would be easy to motivate for a reductionist about reasons of friendship. If the normative force of reasons of friendship is simply derivative from the normative force of whatever reasons one has to value a friendship, then when one has no net reason to value a friendship, the well from which reasons of friendship draw their normative force is dry. But we are here considering the prospects for non-reductionism, so it would be question-begging to argue against *Friendship* by assuming the truth of reductionism.

Moreover, I think our considered intuitions support the claim that even valueless friendships – friendships that one has neither net reason to value nor net reason *not* to value – do give rise to genuine reasons of friendship. Suppose that Alfred and Betty have, out of sheer inertia, maintained an old friendship for many years, even though neither any longer has any positive reason to value it. And suppose that Alfred finds himself in desperate need of a relatively small sum of money to stave off some catastrophe in his life – money that Betty, who is very wealthy, could easily loan him or give him outright. If Betty does not regard Alfred's need as giving her special reason to help – reason different from and stronger than whatever reason she might have to help a stranger with a similar need – then Alfred may feel that Betty has *wronged* him. This feeling, moreover, seems *justified*: after all, whether or not there is any value in their friendship, the two of them have maintained it until now. Betty's refusal to help now, in Alfred's time of need, seems a *betrayal* – in a way that her refusal to help a similarly situated stranger would not be. One might suppose that, because each has no positive reason to value their friendship, they both ought, before now, to have broken it off. I doubt that this is true. But even if it is true, it does not alter the intuition that, since they have *not* broken their friendship off until now, for Betty to fail to help Alfred (or at least to suppose herself to have some reason to help) would be a betrayal of their friendship, which Alfred might justifiably resent. And if this intuition is correct, it seems that it can only be because Betty does, in fact, have a reason of friendship to help Alfred.[19]

4 Explaining *Friendship*

Because *Friendship* allows that an agent may have a reason of friendship even when she has no positive reason to value her friendship and no positive reason to believe the consideration in question to be a reason of friendship, it does not invite the reductionist answer to Question (2) that *Scheffler's Suggestion* invites. But if reasons of friendship cannot be explained in the manner in which the reductionist seeks to explain them, how can they be explained? To answer, it will help to consider a more general normative principle, of which *Friendship* is a specific instantiation.

> *Apparent Reasons*: if an agent (i) has net, non-instrumental reason to believe some consideration to be a reason for herself to do or feel something *or* (ii) sees some consideration as a reason for herself to do or feel something and does not have net, non-instrumental reason *not* to believe that consideration to be a reason to do or feel that thing, then that consideration is, in fact, a reason for her to do or feel that thing.

Just as the examples of Section 3 suggest that *Friendship* gives the right answer to Question (1) (the question about when we have reasons of friendship), I think that similar considerations show that *Apparent Reasons* gives the right answer to a question analogous to Question (1) about a wider class of ('agent-relative') reasons: I think that it accords with our considered judgments about when we have not only reasons of friendship, but also reasons that stem from family relationships, from membership in larger groups (whether chosen or un-chosen), and from our personal projects and commitments.[20] And so I think that this is a principle to which we are in fact tacitly responsive when we make our best, considered judgments about the reasons that we and others have. Moreover, I think that it is reasonable of us reflectively to endorse making judgments in a manner that is responsive to this principle. I will not, however, seek to defend these claims here. The kinds of reasons covered by this principle differ from one another, and from reasons of friendship, in important ways, and so an attempt to defend the general principle would involve questions specific to these various sort of reasons which are beyond our current scope. What I want to argue instead is that if we assume, for the purposes of argument, that we are, in fact, responsive to *Apparent Reasons* when we make considered judgments about the reasons we have, and we ask *why* we make judgments in accordance with this principle, the most plausible answer we can arrive at provides an answer to a question analogous to, but more general than, Question (2): it explains why we have the broad class of reasons governed by *Apparent Reasons* at all. *Ipso facto*, it provides an answer to Question (2), about why we have reasons of friendship at all. I proceed in this way, rather than simply offering an explanation for *Friendship* alone, because the explanation I will offer is, in fact, general in its application, and I think that this generality is illuminating. But anyone who believes that our judgments about reasons of friendship are responsive to *Friendship*, but that our judgments about other sorts of reasons are not responsive to *Apparent Reasons*, may simply apply the explanation I will offer directly to *Friendship*, ignoring the detour via the more general explanatory claim.

Apparent Reasons is a principle governing the extension of our concept of a normative reason. Because it concerns only agent-relative reasons, and because it *presupposes* that an agent may have normative reasons *other* than those considerations to which the principle grants the status of reasons (namely, the other reasons referred to by clause (i) and clause (ii) of the antecedent of the principle), *Apparent Reasons* maps only one small corner of the extension of this concept. Still, in asking why we tacitly accept this principle, we are asking why we have a concept of a normative reason the extension of which is (partly) governed by this principle. Why does our concept of a reason have (this aspect of) the shape that it does? In particular, we may wonder why the concept extends so *broadly* as to include considerations whose only 'qualification' for being reasons lies in the fact that we *see* them as reasons and have no reason not to – as clause (ii) of the antecedent of *Apparent Reasons* claims that it does.

I think that the beginning of wisdom, in approaching this question, is to notice that the fact that we possess the concept of a normative reason at all is something that requires an explanation – after all, the non-rational creatures from which we evolved did not. One might seek to explain how our ancestors came to acquire this concept by looking for some distinctive advantage that it confers upon its possessors. Etiology of this kind is, however, an inherently speculative endeavor: even if we discover some distinctive advantage that a trait confers upon those who now employ it, there is no guarantee that the advantage played a role in the acquisition of the trait; it may, rather, be a lucky by-product of a development explicable in a wholly different way. Still, if a trait confers some distinctive advantage upon those who possess it, this fact will contribute at least to an explanation of the fact that they *continue* to possess the trait. So, we can approach the question of why we employ a concept of a normative reason, the extension of which is governed by *Apparent Reasons,* by asking: is there a distinctive advantage that such a concept confers on creatures that employ it?

A realist about normative reasons may be tempted to complain that the best answer to the question I have just framed is: 'To the extent that *Apparent Reasons* is correct, the "advantage" of employing a concept governed by this principle is simply that it allows us to *get things right* – to make true judgments about the reasons we have, rather than false ones'. But to propose that there is *more* to be said, by way of explanation, than this realist suggests is not to take sides in the debate among various stripes of realists, anti-realists, and constructivists about reasons. We might ask, for instance, what advantages there are in possessing the concept of a hurricane, the extension of which is governed by the principle that a weather system counts as a hurricane only if it has sustained winds of over 74 mph – without presupposing anti-realism about hurricanes. Or we might ask what advantage there is in possessing the concept of a demand-driven economic contraction (governed by the principles that govern it), without presupposing anti-realism about these. The advantage of possessing these concepts does not lie *merely* in the fact that having them allows us to make true judgments that we could not otherwise make. It lies also, for instance, in the fact that demand-driven economic contractions tend to be far more prolonged and painful than other kinds of recession and that escaping them requires different economic remedies. This fact most likely figures in an etiology of the fact that economists have *developed* this concept, and it certainly helps to *justify* economists and lay-people in employing it now – and so helps to explain the fact that they continue to *bother* to distinguish demand-driven contractions from other kinds. Likewise, the advantage of possessing the concept of a hurricane lies, in part, in the fact that hurricanes can kill us, and we are more likely to survive them if we can recognize and predict them. If weather systems did not become more destructive with higher wind speeds, we might never have developed this concept, and we might have no reason to continue to bother, now, to distinguish between hurricanes and other tropical storms.[21]

So, without begging any questions concerning realism about reasons, we can ask: is there a distinctive advantage that the concept of a normative reason, the extension of which is (partly) governed by *Apparent Reasons*, confers upon its possessors? Before we attempt to answer, it will help to prescind from this particular principle governing the concept's extension, and ask the more general question: what advantage is there in possessing the concept of a normative reason at all?

Skeptics of the airs that we put on when we accord ourselves the title 'rational animals' have long pointed out that our motivations do not differ all that greatly from the motivations of our non-rational cousins among the social animals, such as chimpanzees and baboons.[22] Chimpanzees and baboons seek sex, and social status, and care for their offspring. Chimpanzees and baboons both form enduring, differentiated, and qualitatively rich social bonds with others to whom they are not closely related by maternal kinship – bonds which researchers have recently argued are best understood as genuine friendships.[23] Chimpanzees and baboons will come to the aid of a friend when it is threatened by an aggressor, and will exhibit anger toward the aggressor. And so we can ask: what do we *add* to the story when we say, of a creature that feels anger when a friend is threatened by another of its kind (as chimps do) and that is *motivated* to protect its friend from this threat (as chimps are), that the creature sees the consideration that another of its kind threatens its friend as a *reason* to feel anger and to protect its friend (as we do)?

At least this much. An agent with the concept of a normative reason is able to ask the question: is this consideration *sufficient* reason to be angry, or to fight alongside my friend? There are two ways in which the answer to that question might be 'no'. First, there might be *other*, countervailing reasons *not* to fight – and, perhaps, not to feel anger. The question whether some consideration is sufficient reason to feel or act in some way thus invites, at the very least, the exercise of attention, imagination, and causal reasoning;[24] and the exercise of these capacities may result in *new* beliefs about reasons to which nothing in the agent's antecedent motivational impulses corresponds. (One might arrive at the belief that one has a reason not to help one's friend fight this particular aggressor, for instance, because one will likely need the aggressor's good will in the future. Or one might learn that the aggressor has, himself, been mercilessly provoked by others and so come to understand his action in such a way that it merits less anger than one initially felt.) Second, a consideration that an agent sees as a reason to feel anger, or to fight alongside his friend, might not be a sufficient reason to do so because it might not be a genuine, normative reason to do so at all – either in the context in question, or more generally. In a context in which aiding my friend in a fight would harm him by serving to reinforce the impression that he is weak and hence a good target for future aggression, the fact that my friend is fighting against an aggressor might constitute no reason at all to come to his aid. And in a context in which the aggressor's threat is a justified response to an unjustified provocation by my friend, the threat might constitute no reason for anger.[25]

The concept of a reason thus opens a space, between potentially motivating feelings and action, for the questions: Do I have sufficient reason to feel as I do (antecedently) feel? And do I have sufficient reason to act as I am (antecedently) motivated to act? Where an agent has conflicting antecedent motivations, the concept makes possible the question: what do I have *most* reason to do? An agent who seeks to answer any of these questions is more likely (A) to exercise her cognitive powers in ways that will allow her to discover *more* of the practical reasons that she faces than she is initially aware of, and (B) to exercise her powers in ways that will allow her to recognize those cases in which she does not have any reason at all to feel the way she feels or to act as she is initially motivated to act. It is possible that, on *some* occasions, exercising cognitive powers in the manner of (A) and (B) will cause an agent to replace true beliefs with false ones about what she has most reason, all things considered, to feel or do; and it is also possible that, on some occasions, forming true beliefs about what she has most reason to feel or do will not benefit an agent, or will even harm her. But it is overwhelmingly plausible to suppose that, *generally*, exercising one's cognitive powers in the manner of (A) and (B) makes it more likely that an agent will have true beliefs about what she has most reason to feel and do; and it is overwhelmingly plausible that *generally*, a tendency to exercise one's powers in these ways, and to form true beliefs about what one has most reason to feel and do, will be advantageous for an agent with that tendency. To the extent that this is correct, making the exercise of cognitive powers in the manner of (A) and (B) more likely is a distinctive advantage that the concept of a normative reason confers upon its possessors. We may say that conferring this advantage is at least part of the *work* of the concept of a normative reason.

With this crude sketch in hand, we can return to ask why our concept of a normative reason is governed by *Apparent Reasons*. That is, we can ask: why does our concept of a normative reason have the extension that it does? The answer, I want to suggest, is simply that a concept shaped in this way is *sufficient* to do the work that we have identified, of making (A) and (B) more likely for agents who employ it. Suppose that an agent is antecedently motivated in some way (for instance, by partiality toward a friend) and so sees some consideration as a reason for action. Insofar as her beliefs are responsive to clause (ii) of the antecedent of *Apparent Reasons*, she will look out for reasons *not* to believe that consideration to be the reason she sees it as. That is simply to say that such an agent will exercise her cognitive powers in the manner of (A) and (B). And suppose that an agent who does not already see some consideration as a reason for herself is prompted (perhaps by someone else) to ask whether that consideration is a reason for her. Insofar as her beliefs about reasons are responsive to clause (i) of *Apparent Reasons*, she will seek to answer this question by exercising her cognitive powers, in the manner of (A), in search of further reasons she has of which she was previously unaware.

It may be objected that a concept of a normative reason governed by a principle analogous to but more general than *Scheffler's Suggestion*, rather than by *Apparent Reasons*, would *also* accomplish the work of making (A) and (B) more likely, and so the explanation I have offered would also account for a concept governed by that general principle. Yet I argued in Section 3 that our concept of a reason is not, in fact, governed by *Scheffler's Suggestion*, and so it follows that it is not governed by the generalized version of this principle, either. If the explanation I have offered would do equally well at explaining our possession of a concept governed by a principle *different* from the one governing the concept we in fact employ, how can it be an adequate explanation of our possession of the concept governed by *Apparent Reasons*?

Two points may be noted in response to this objection. First, an explanation need not be complete in order to be true. It may be the case that, if it were not for a random turn down a fork in the evolutionary road, we might have developed an organ with a structure quite different from that of our eye, but that would nonetheless have had all of the advantages for us that our own eye has. The fact that we evolved the eyes that we have, rather than eyes of this other kind, would be a matter of brute contingency. But this fact, if it is true, does not diminish the illumination of an explanation of the fact that we possess eyes of the sort we do in terms of the evolutionary advantages that our eyes confer upon us.

Second, we can in fact identify a reason, beyond brute contingency, that our concept of a reason is not governed by the generalized version of *Scheffler's Suggestion*: such a principle would impose a cognitive burden on an agent *beyond* what is sufficient to accomplish the work of making (A) and (B) more likely. *Apparent Reasons* accords a consideration that an agent sees as a reason a presumptive title to normative significance: in virtue of the fact that it is seen as a reason, it is presumed to be a reason, *unless* there is some reason for the agent *not* to believe it to be. This principle imposes on an agent who is responsive to it the responsibility to be on the lookout for such a defeating reason; but an agent may discharge this responsibility by exercising normal care and yet failing to discover a defeating reason. A generalized version of *Scheffler's Suggestion*, by contrast, would accord no normative significance to the mere fact that an agent sees some consideration as a reason. And so the principle would impose on an agent who is responsive to it the cognitively more demanding responsibility of determining whether or not she has net reason to value the relationship that disposes her to see that consideration as a reason. Insofar as the work of a concept of a reason is to make (A) and (B) more likely, *Scheffler's Suggestion* thus involves a sort of cognitive *overkill*.

Still, an objector might complain that the account I have offered does not really explain why our concept of a reason is governed by *Apparent Reasons* because it does not answer the fundamental question: why should a normative principle accord any normative significance at all to the fact that someone *sees* some consideration as a reason?[26] As long as this question remains unanswered, the objector may maintain, we have not explained why we have agent-relative reasons of the sort governed by the principle, including reasons of friendship, at all.

The objection ignores the background against which the explanation works. Our ability to form beliefs about the reasons we have and to act in a manner that is responsive to them is, in the course of our evolution, a late innovation. If our primate cousins are any guide, it came to creatures who *already* possessed a sophisticated system of motivations – including motivations toward partiality to kith and kin.[27] The system of rational principles, such as *Apparent Reasons*, which govern our beliefs about the reasons we have, *supplements* and *corrects* our evolutionarily more basic motivations – in part, by prompting us to employ our cognitive capacities in the manner of (A) and (B). But in order to confer this advantage, it need not – nor is it plausible to think that it could – *replace* these more basic motivations entirely.[28] The principles by which we govern ourselves must give a place to our motivations, and that is what *Apparent Reasons* does: it accords a presumption of normative significance to the fact that an agent *sees* some consideration as a reason, precisely because this fact will often be the expression, in the domain of rational thought, of a pre-rational motivation. When we reason in accordance with this principle, we may end up with beliefs about reasons that do not reflect our prior motivations, but it is from perceptions of reasons which reflect these motivations that our reasoning *begins*.

5 Naturalism about reasons?

On the account that I have offered, reasons of friendship do not inherit their normative standing from the normative standing of some sort of putatively more basic reasons, such as prudential reasons or moral reasons. But if the account that I have offered avoids *this* sort of reductionism, it might nonetheless seem to embrace reductionism of a different kind – namely of claims about (at least some of) the normative reasons we have to *non-normative* claims about our psychology. For, as I've emphasized, clause (ii) of *Friendship* accords a presumption of normative significance to the mere fact that an agent *sees* a consideration in a certain way. And this might seem to commit my account to a very simple and particularly implausible form of naturalism about reasons.

As it stands, the charge is simply mistaken. First, while *Friendship* accords a *presumption* of normative significance to the fact that an agent sees a consideration in a certain way, whether that presumption is 'validated' depends on the answer to the *normative* question whether the agent has net, non-instrumental reason not to believe that consideration to be a reason of friendship for herself. There is no suggestion that *this* question can be answered by appeal to facts stated in purely psychological terms. The principle thus involves a modest form of holism about normative reasons: whether the consideration in question is, in fact, a reason depends upon what other reasons the agent has. But, second, the psychological fact to which *Friendship* accords a presumption of normative significance is the fact that an agent sees some consideration *as a reason*. Even if we focus solely on this part of the principle, *Friendship* offers no prospect of reducing claims about reasons to claims expressible in non-normative, naturalistic terms, because the principle itself *employs* the concept of normative reason.

If my account does not offer encouragement to a simple, reductive naturalism, according to which individual claims about normative reasons can be reduced to claims expressible solely in naturalistic terms, it might still seem to be committed to a more modest naturalism, according to which a holistic web of normative claims, or a part of one, can be explained, *en bloc*, in naturalistic terms, even though individual normative claims cannot be either reduced to these terms nor explained in these terms.[29] The suggestion that my account involves this more modest naturalism begins by noting that, as I have emphasized, the fact that we see certain considerations as reasons of friendship is a reflection, in the domain of rationality, of our pre-rational motivations – motivations that are, themselves, shaped by evolutionary pressures. So, evolutionary pressures explain the fact that considerations *of this kind* are at least *candidates* for being reasons – that they have the presumptive normative significance that *Friendship* accords them. Whether one of these considerations is, in fact, a normative reason depends, holistically, on what *other* normative reasons an agent has – and in particular, on whether the presumption is defeated by net reasons not to believe the consideration in question to be a reason. But what explains the normative status of these other, potentially defeating reasons? Insofar as the general claim, *Apparent Reasons,* is true, the fact that at least some other classes of considerations are candidates for being agent-relative reasons will be explicable, in an analogous manner, by evolutionary pressures. So, even if it is true that whether one consideration is a normative reason for an agent depends on what other normative reasons the agent has, it might nonetheless be the case that evolutionary pressures explain the shape of the web of our true beliefs about reasons – or that *part* of it constituted by our beliefs about *agent-relative* reasons, in particular.

If these considerations suggested that *all* of the pressures that shape our beliefs about agent-relative reasons were describable in naturalistic terms, then the account that I have offered would indeed support this modest naturalism. But they do not suggest that, for several reasons. First, the holism built into *Apparent Reasons* ensures that there is no prospect of isolating the portion of the web of normative claims concerned with claims about agent-relative reasons, and saying that this portion alone is shaped by purely natural pressures. For even if we suppose that the fact that agents see considerations of various kinds as agent-relative reasons can *always* be explained as a response to natural, evolutionary pressures, not all of the reasons that an agent may have for or against believing those considerations to be agent-relative reasons are themselves agent-relative reasons of the sort governed by *Apparent Reasons.* I might find that I see the consideration that someone is my friend's main competitor for a job she desperately needs as a reason to injure that person, and this may be the rational reflection of motivations explicable in naturalistic, evolutionary terms; but I may have an agent-neutral, moral reason not to believe this consideration to be a reason to injure her. So, a naturalistic account of the fact that I do not have the agent-relative reason would have to encompass a naturalistic account of such agent-neutral, moral reasons. Of course, some philosophers have argued, on independent grounds, for such an encompassing naturalism, and nothing in my own account disproves it; but neither does my account do anything to encourage it.

Second, even in the case of agent-relative reasons, it is doubtful whether the fact that agents see considerations of some kind as reasons can always be described as the rational expression of pre-rational motivations shaped by evolutionary or other natural pressures. Such natural pressures may well explain the appearances of reasons from which the earliest rational agents among our ancestors *began* reasoning. But in the interim, human beings have invented intellectual, aesthetic, and political pursuits, and forms of reasoning, which have no parallel in the lives of our pre-rational ancestors, and which echo nothing in their motivations. The 'pressures' which shape these new interests may be distinctively *rational* pressures (e.g. of consistency or coherence with existing normative beliefs), or they may be pressures exerted by agents' imaginings of new ways of living or new ways of understanding themselves. It is doubtful whether purely natural pressures can explain, for instance, the fact that an artist sees some consideration as an aesthetic reason to use soft cloth as her medium in a particular sculpture; but *Apparent Reasons* will accord this consideration the status of a reason, so long as she doe not have net, non-instrumental reason not to believe it to be one.

* * *

A non-reductionist view of reasons of friendship must reconcile two facts, which only seem to be in tension. On the one hand, we are social animals with a motivational make-up conditioned by this fact. Rational principles that can hope to have any claim on us must give a place to the promptings of our motivations – or to the appearances of reasons that are their rational expressions. On the other hand, we are rational animals with the capacity to reflect upon, and to reject, mere appearances of reasons. By acknowledging both of these facts, *Friendship* allows us to understand that the considerations we see as reasons of friendship are not always normative reasons, but that *when* they are reasons, they are normatively basic.

Notes

1. That is to say, we sometimes take ourselves to have *obligations* to our friends. This fact raises a host of questions, which I will not seek to answer: When do considerations pertaining to our friends oblige us, rather than merely permit us, to act (or feel) in some way? Should we understand these as *moral* obligations? When, if at all, do our reasons to discharge these obligations trump other sorts of reasons, including impersonal moral reasons?
2. This is a point emphasized by Samuel Scheffler (2010).
3. These questions should not be confused with the question: what reasons (if any) can an agent have to begin a friendship or to maintain a friendship that she is already in?
4. See Scheffler (1997, 1999, 2004, and 2010). All page numbers hereafter refer to the reprints.
5. The principle articulates only a *sufficient* condition for an agent to have reasons of friendship. The claims from which I draw *Scheffler's Suggestion* concern the conditions under which an agent has relationship-dependent *responsibilities*. Scheffler takes responsibilities to involve normative reasons, so his claims entail *Scheffler's Suggestion*. But, as Scheffler emphasizes, not all reasons import responsibilities.
6. Insofar as friendships are *constitutive* elements in good lives, this would give us prudential and perhaps moral reason to value them *non-instrumentally*.
7. Scheffler (1997, pp. 103–104) in reprint. In the quotation (and elsewhere in his writing on the topic), Scheffler writes interchangeably of 'seeing' ourselves as having responsibilities (and, elsewhere, reasons) and 'thinking' that we do. In Section 2, I will suggest that we should distinguish seeing some consideration as a reason from believing it to be one.
8. For a partial defense of the view that there can be practical reasons for belief, cf. Reisner (2009). For the contrary view, cf. Parfit (2011, vol. 1, pp. 420–32).

9. As Scheffler (2010) puts it: '[a] valuable relationship transforms the needs and desires of the participants into reasons for each to act on behalf of the other in suitable contexts' (p. 110).
10. Kolodny (2010a and 2010b) tries to show how a view like Scheffler's can avoid reductionism.
11. They are not 'agent-relative' in the strong sense, sometimes attached to that term, of applying to an agent only in virtue of properties that the agent could not share with others. If A and B are both friends of C, then some consideration about C might be a reason of friendship for both A and B alike.
12. Cf. Scanlon (1998), p. 39. See also Seidman (2009).
13. Cf. Evans (1982, p. 123).
14. See, for example, Scheffler (1997, p. 100). While I think that Scheffler is right that valuing a friendship constitutively involves seeing considerations pertaining to one's friend as reasons, the implication does not run the other way: it does not follow that, if an agent sees considerations pertaining to a friend as reasons of friendship, then she must value her friendship. The abused friend of our earlier example may find that she continues to see considerations pertaining to her friend as reasons even though she does not value her friendship with him. (In a case where an agent does not value a friendship, Scheffler will claim that the relationship cannot count as a friendship at all. Cf. Scheffler (1999), p. 122 in the reprint. I think that this claim is mistaken, but will not argue that here.)
15. While Scheffler writes of seeing a consideration as a reason and believing it to be a reason as if they were interchangeable, the claim that valuing a friendship involves seeing considerations pertaining to one's friends as reasons is plausible only to the extent that seeing is *distinguished* from believing. An agent may value a friendship that she believes she *ought not* to value, and so she may see considerations pertaining to her friend as reasons of friendship for herself, even though she believes that she ought not to see them that way, because she believes that they are not, in fact, genuine normative reasons for her.
16. Where disjunct (i) is satisfied, the second part of disjunct (ii) will, *ipso facto*, be satisfied as well.
17. The two principles may appear to yield different verdicts in a case in which an agent has reason to value some friendship, and hence to see (many) considerations pertaining to her friend as genuine reasons, but nonetheless has net reason not to believe some *particular* consideration pertaining to her friend to be a reason. The disagreement in this case is merely apparent, however, because, as noted in (5) of Section 2, the two principles answer Question (1) with a different fineness of grain.
18. Note that *Scheffler's Suggestion* offers only a *sufficient* condition for reasons of friendship. So, the principle does not entail that an agent *cannot* have reasons of friendship in a case where she has no reason to value her friendship; it just does not offer grounds for claiming that she does.
19. Consider an analogy: Michael Bratman (1987) argues that a previously-adopted plan may give one reasons for action even when it is true that, were one to reconsider the plan, one would recognize that one does not, now, have net reason to hold it.

20. This is roughly the class of reasons that Scheffler aims to address with a principle analogous to but broader than *Scheffler's Suggestion*.
21. Compare Wiggins (2001, p. 152): 'what sortal concepts we bring to bear upon experience determines what we can find there – just as the size and mesh of a net determine, not what fish are in the sea, but which ones we shall catch'.
22. That is to say, our motivations have many of the same *objects* as the motivations of chimps and baboons. This is not to say that desire in humans is the same as the mental state we call 'desire' in primates (nor that other motivating mental states in humans are the same as mental states we call by the same names in primates).
23. Cf. Smuts (1985); Cords (1989); Mitani (2009); Massen, Sterck and de Vos (2010).
24. In sophisticated creatures, it might invite other sorts of reasoning as well – e.g., *specificatory* reasoning (cf. Kolnai (1961–62), Wiggins (1975–76), Richards (1994)); or, perhaps, some distinctively *moral* form of reasoning (for instance, reasoning to determine whether a maxim meets the test of the Categorical Imperative).
25. For some qualification of the idea that a consideration which constitutes a practical reason in one context may be cancelled or 'silenced' by features of another context, see Seidman (2004).
26. This objection is related to a further objection, which I will consider in Section 5: In according normative significance to the fact that an agent sees some consideration as a reason, does not *Friendship* amount to an implausible reduction of the normative to the non-normative?
27. Compare, in this regard, Gary Watson's (1975) distinction between the 'valuational system' and the 'motivational system'.
28. Even Kant, as great a proponent of the power of pure practical reason as anyone, does not suppose that pure practical reason can, by itself, supply all of the maxims on which it is rational to act. Our maxims are proposed by our empirically-conditioned inclinations, and the Categorical Imperative serves as a *filter*, by which our maxims may be judged permissible or not.
29. For discussion of a view of this sort, cf. Blackburn (1984, chapter 5).

References

S. Blackburn (1984) *Spreading the Word: Groundings in the Philosophy of Language* (Oxford: Oxford University Press).

M. Bratman (1987) *Intention, Plans, and Practical Reason* (Cambridge, MA: Harvard University Press).

M. Cords (1989) 'Friendships, Alliances, Reciprocity and Repair', in Andrew Whiten and Richard Byrne (eds), *Machiavellian Intelligence II: Extensions and Evaluations* (Cambridge: Cambridge University Press), 24–49.

G. Evans (1982) *The Varieties of Reference* (Oxford: Oxford University Press).

A. Kolnai (1961–62) 'Deliberation Is of Ends', *Proceedings of the Aristotelian Society* 62, 195–218.

N. Kolodny (2010a) 'Which Relationships Justify Partiality? The Case of Parents and Children', *Philosophy and Public Affairs* 38, 37–75.

N. Kolodny (2010b) 'Which Relationships Justify Partiality? General Considerations and Problem Cases', in Brian Feltham and John Cottingham (eds), *Partiality and Impartiality: Morality, Special Relationships, and the Wider World* (Oxford: Oxford University Press), 168–93.

J. Massen, E.Sterck and H. deVos (2010) 'Close Social Associations in Animals and Humans: Functions and Mechanisms of Friendship', *Behavior* 147, 1379–412.

J. Mitani (2009) 'Male Chimpanzees Form Enduring and Equitable Social Bonds', *Animal Behavior* 77, 633–40.

D. Parfit (2011) *On What Matters*, vol. 1 (Oxford: Oxford University Press).

A. Reisner (2009) 'The Possibility of Pragmatic Reasons for Belief and the Wrong Kind of Reasons Problem', *Philosophical Studies* 145, 257–72.

H. Richards (1994) *Practical Reasoning about Final Ends* (Cambridge: Cambridge University Press).

T. M. Scanlon (1998) *What We Owe to Each Other* (Cambridge, MA: Harvard University Press).

S. Scheffler (1997) 'Relationships and Responsibilities', *Philosophy and Public Affairs* 26, 189–209, reprinted in his (2001) *Boundaries and Allegiances* (Oxford: Oxford University Press), 97–110.

—— (1999) 'Conceptions of Cosmopolitanism', *Utilitas* 11, 255–76, reprinted in *Boundaries and Allegiances*, 111–30.

—— (2004) 'Projects, Relationships, and Reasons', in R. Jay Wallace, Philip Pettit, Samuel Scheffler, and Michael Smith (eds), *Reason and Value: Themes from the Moral Philosophy of Joseph Raz* (Oxford: Clarendon Press), 247–69.

—— (2010) 'Morality and Reasonable Partiality', in Brian Feltham and John Cottingham (eds), *Partiality and Impartiality: Morality, Special Relationships, and the Wider World* (Oxford: Oxford University Press), 245–69.

J. Seidman (2004) 'Two Sides of "Silencing"', *The Philosophical Quarterly* 55, 68–77.

—— (2009) 'Valuing and Caring', *Theoria* 75, 272–303.

B. Smuts (1985) *Sex and Friendship in Baboons* (Hawthorne, NY: Aldine Publishing).

G. Watson (1975) 'Free Agency', *Journal of Philosophy* 72, 205–20.

D. Wiggins (1975–76) 'Deliberation and Practical Reason', *Proceedings of the Aristotelian Society* 76, 29–51.

—— (2001) *Sameness and Substance Renewed* (Cambridge: Cambridge University Press).

Part IV

Friendship and Morality

8
Friendship in Kant's Moral Thought

Oliver Sensen

Introduction

Imagine that after an accident you are able to save either your friend or three total strangers. Is it morally permissible to save the friend? What would Kant say? One is likely to assume that Kant – with his emphasis on duty and universal law – gives little weight to special relationships like friendship. Kant famously defines marriage as the 'union of two persons of different sexes for lifelong possession of each other's sexual attributes' (*Metaphysics of Morals* [*MdS*] 6, p. 277[1]), and it would not be surprising if his views on friendship were equally unromantic.

On the other hand, it is not clear from the outset that an emphasis on universal law would recommend that one should save the three strangers instead of the friend. After all, it might be a good general rule that everyone should look after his or her friend first, as it seems to be a good rule that children should be cared for by parents who love them rather than by strangers. But even if one could universalize saving the friend instead of three strangers, there seems to be a further problem in the way one would arrive at this conclusion. If one arrives by a universalization procedure at the conclusion in favor of saving the friend, this seems to be at odds with the spirit of caring for a friend. The friend wants to be saved because we care about her immediately, and because she is special to us, not because a universalization procedure says that we should. Having recourse to such a procedure at such a moment seems, in Bernard Williams's (1981) famous phrase, to be 'one thought too many' (p. 18). Finally, even if Kant can mitigate the first two worries, it seems that there frequently could be conflicts between the demands of his ethics and friendship: Since Kant seems to insist on an absolute prohibition of lying and promise-breaking, for instance, would one ever be allowed to lie or break a promise to protect a friend? There are then at least three challenges friendship seems to pose to Kant's ethics: (1) Does he value friendship as a special bond between two people at all, or does he suggest that duty requires one to relate to all human beings impartially? (2) Is he subject to the 'one thought too many' objection? (3) Would he not significantly restrict what one could do to help a friend?

The aim of this chapter is to present Kant's account of friendship and to consider whether friendship poses a challenge for Kant's moral thought. In order to do so I shall first discuss the three challenges (Section 1), then explain Kant's conception of friendship (Section 2), and relate it to the challenges (Section 3). I shall argue – to anticipate – that Kant has a more nuanced account of friendship than one might expect and that Kant sees friendship properly understood not as being at odds with his moral philosophy but rather as its culmination. Kant's conception of friendship contains all the elements we hold dear in ordinary life: He understands friendship to be a union of two people that entails sweetness; the two friends have esteem and love for each other, and they are willing to help each other in need and share a certain taste. But Kant argues that this form of friendship is unattainable in practice unless the feelings involved are limited by principles. This is not an external critique – Kant does not criticize our ordinary conception of friendship from a standpoint of morality; rather it is an internal critique. Only in limiting feelings by principles is friendship possible at all.

1 Friendship as a challenge to Kant's moral thought

The three challenges mentioned above do not address Kant's particular view on friendship, but the structure of his moral philosophy as such. Before I look at Kant's conception of friendship (in Section 2), I shall first consider the challenges in relation to the main features of Kant's moral philosophy. The first challenge, in effect, alleges that Kant's emphasis on universalization as he expounds it in his *Groundwork of the Metaphysics of Morals* leaves no room for special relationships like friendship. The emphasis on universalization comes out in his famous Categorical Imperative, which he calls the '*supreme principle of morality*' (*Groundwork* 3, p. 392), and which runs: '*act only in accordance with that maxim through which you can at the same time will that it become a universal law*' (*Groundwork* 4, p. 421). The assumption behind the first challenge is that Kant's Categorical Imperative requires impartiality in the sense that 'everybody [is] to count for one, nobody for more than one' (Mill 1969, p. 257). If that is Kant's view also, then in acting one should not give more weight to a friend than one would give to a stranger. Impartiality in this sense is part of an agent-neutral moral theory such as a basic form of act-utilitarianism. Agent-neutral theories do not look at the special relationship the agent has to the outcome, but merely evaluate the outcome from a point of view of the universe or a view from nowhere (cf. Nagel 1986, p. 153f.).

One example of such a theory is a standard form of act-utilitarianism.[2] The theory holds that, for each act, one should directly evaluate whether it brings about more utility than any alternative. There would be no class of actions (such as lying or stealing) that would be forbidden in itself, but any act could be justified by the greater utility of the outcome. The suffering of the agent in not helping a friend is to be taken into account, but might be outweighed by the pleasure of the friends of three strangers in hearing that their friends were saved. The agent-neutral impartiality – that everyone counts for one and no one for more than one – might demand that one help the strangers rather than one's friend.

However, Kant's universalization requirement is not agent-neutral in this sense. His Categorical Imperative requires an agent to test his maxims, and it provides a criterion independent of an action's consequences by which maxims may be ruled out as impermissible. In the *Groundwork* Kant explains the point of the requirement as testing whether one wants to make 'an *exception*' for oneself to a rule that one wills to remain a universal law (*Groundwork* 4, p. 424). For instance, if one's maxim is 'to promise to repay a loan, although one has no intention of doing so', one could not conceive this maxim as a universal law without a contradiction. If everyone adopted this law, the borrower would know that one has no intention of paying back the loan, and would not lend the money. Thus, as Kant explains, 'we do not really will that our maxim [of false promising] should become a universal law,... but that the opposite of our maxim should instead remain a universal law, only we take the liberty of making an *exception* to it for ourselves' (*Groundwork* 4, p. 424). Similarly, a maxim of not helping others – if everyone adopted it – would prevent one from receiving any help although a finite being is sure to need help at some point. In the case of lying one could not even conceive the maxim as a universal law without contradiction (the maxim would be obsolete) while in the case of helping one could conceive such a maxim, but as a finite being one could not will it (independently of any particular desire one has).

What this means is that maxims can be rejected independently of the utility of the outcome. If not everyone could adopt the maxim, then it is impermissible, on Kant's view. Kant's ethics focuses more directly on what type of action the agent aims to perform. His universalization test is agent-relative as opposed to agent-neutral, and his version of impartiality (testing whether one's maxim could be adopted by all) is different from agent-neutral impartiality (cf. Hill 2012, p. 202).

The important implication of this for friendship is that the requirement to universalize one's maxim could be compatible with helping friends before others. This is for two reasons: (1) Since Kant's ethics does not focus on which action brings about the best outcome, one is not required to help as much as one possibly can. On Kant's view, helping others is a duty, since one cannot universalize the maxim not to help. As a finite creature, one will need help at some point. In universalizing the maxim not to help others, everyone would adopt a law by which others would cease to give one the help one needs: 'a will that decided this would conflict with itself, since many cases could occur in which one would need the love and sympathy of others and in which, by such a law... he would rob himself of all hope of the assistance he wishes for himself' (*Groundwork* 4, p. 423). However, the extent to which one should help cannot be settled *a priori*, and therefore helping others is a wide or imperfect duty, which 'leaves a playroom... for free choice in following... the law, that is, the law cannot specify precisely in what way one is to act and how much one is to do by the action' (*MdS* 6, p. 390). In contrast to act-utilitarianism, Kant does not endorse a '*negative responsibility*' (Smart and Williams 1973, p. 95), i.e., that one is responsible for any outcome on which one could possibly have a causal influence (such as preventing someone else from murdering a person), in contrast to merely being responsible for what one does in a narrower sense (such as not murdering someone).

(2) While one cannot universalize the maxim not to help others, it could be a law for all to help the people who are closest to them first. It is permissible, according to Kant, to act on a rule to help one's family or friend first: 'in acting I can, without violating the universality of the maxim, vary the degree greatly in accordance with the different objects of my love (one of whom concerns me more closely than the other)' (*MdS* 6, p. 452).

So, the first challenge – that Kant's moral theory does not leave any room for friendship at all – does not seem correct. Kant's theory is not an agent-neutral account in which one has to regard one's friend as one person among others. Kant's universalization requirement can make room for special ties like friendship. But even if one is often allowed to prefer helping one's friend, does one always have to apply the universalization test to see whether it is allowed? This is the second challenge, that Kant's ethics requires 'one thought too many'.

1.1 The second challenge: one thought too many

Even if Kant's theory leaves room for the importance of special personal relationships, the further question is whether he can account for them in the right way. It is one thing to value friendships, but another to value them *because* they are in conformity with a universalization test, rather than for their own sakes. If after an accident one helps the friend rather than the strangers because it is allowed by the Categorical Imperative, would the friend not object that one was acting on account of something other than friendship? Is it not an integral part of friendship that one helps a friend for the friend's sake (in contrast to helping her for morality's sake), and can Kant account for that key aspect of friendship?

This second challenge relates to a different aspect of Kant's moral philosophy. According to Kant, there are two requirements in order for an action to have full moral worth. The first is that the action be in accordance with the Categorical Imperative, and that it not violate the universalization requirement sketched above. The second is that one perform an action simply because it is morally right: 'in the case of what is to be morally good it is not enough that it *conform* with the moral law but it must also be done *for the sake of the law*' (*Groundwork* 4, p. 390). The first requirement tests whether what one does is morally permissible, while the second refers to the motive or cast of mind from which one should act. One should not only do the right thing, but do it simply because it is right, according to Kant. If one only does what is right, but not from the right motive, the action would only have *'legality'*, but not *'morality'* (cf. *Critique of Practical Reason* 5, p. 71).

The second challenge refers to the requirement concerning the motive or cast of mind from which one should act in order for an action to have full moral worth. It is the requirement to do the right thing *simply because it is right* that seems to conflict with friendship. If after an accident one helps the friend out of an abstract motive to do the right thing, and not out of an immediate concern for the friend, something essential seems to be missing. Friendship is thought to be a personal bond. One delights in the friend, cares for her for her own sake, and would immediately – without hesitation – offer any help she needs. To act instead out of an abstract motive to do the right thing – as Kant seems to demand – would be 'one thought too many'. This is why Kant's contemporary, the German poet Schiller, reacted polemically to Kant's moral philosophy in saying: 'I like to serve my friends, but unfortunately I do it by inclination. And so often I am bothered by the thought that I am not virtuous.'[3]

However, maybe Kant can escape this apparent conflict. He himself does not address the problem, even in his reply to the more general critique in Schiller's essay 'On Grace and Dignity'.[4] But there are two considerations one can point out in his defense. First, it is not clear that Kant means that one always has to reflect in each situation on whether one's action is morally right. Second, it is not clear that on Kant's views one always has to act from the motive of duty. Let me explain both points in turn. First, it is not clear that we have to apply the universalization test each time we are about to act, according to Kant. We are used to reading Kant as an alternative to utilitarianism. Whereas in act-utilitarianism one calculates for each act which alternative will bring about more utility, it seems that for Kant we must ask in each situation whether one's maxim can be universalized. But it is not clear why this should be so. If lying or promise-breaking is never allowed, according to Kant, then it seems that one does not have to figure this out each time one decides what to say or do. Accordingly, some Kantians interpret the maxims one must evaluate not as concrete plans for action, but rather as more general underlying principles (cf. O'Neill 1989, p. 84; Höffe 1992, chapter 3). Kant famously defines maxims as 'propositions that contain a general determination of the will, having under it several practical rules' (*Critique of Practical Reason* 5, p. 19). According to this reading, one's maxim would then not be 'to play tennis on Sundays at 10am', but 'to take care of oneself and exercise', which can have several practical rules of implementation under it. One can exercise by playing tennis or a different sport, and one can play tennis at various possible times. In the examples Kant himself gives of testing a maxim, it often seems as if the maxim were a very concrete rule such as 'playing tennis on Sundays at 10am'. But nothing he says seems to require that one be testing more than the more general underlying principle: Should one develop one's talents or not; should one help others or not? Kant's universalization test would then be applied in a 'cool hour' of reflection (Butler 2006, p. 117), not in each situation. On this interpretation one can mitigate the charge that Kant's universalization test is one thought too many. For in that case one does not have to stop in the heat of the action to determine whether it is permissible to rescue the friend rather than the strangers. This is something one has already decided in a cool hour of reflection, and after the accident one can act out of immediate concern for the friend. The friend might still hope that one would help him even if it were not allowed by the universalization test, but Kant would at least be able to soften the one thought too many charge.

There is a second way in which Kant could avoid the objection. It is not clear that his theory demands that one always act from duty. Again our image of Kant's moral philosophy is shaped by his *Groundwork*. There he famously starts out with the claim that nothing can be unconditionally good except a good will (*Groundwork* 4, p. 393), and he goes on to elucidate the good will as acting from duty. However, he does not draw the conclusion that one should *always* act out of duty, and never from inclination. The conclusion he draws is that one should be able to universalize one's maxim, the requirement of legality (see above). A morally right action (to tell the truth etc.) does not have the full moral worth if it is done out of inclination, but still the action deserves praise and encouragement (cf. *Groundwork* 4, p. 398). As long as one fulfills the requirement of legality, one has met the standard of reason. This point is important because it too can help to mitigate the challenge posed by the 'one thought too many' objection. If one does not always have to act from the motive of duty, and if the moral law allows rescuing one's friend instead of strangers, then one does not have to save the friend from the motive of duty, but one can save him out of inclination.

In sum: It is not clear that Kant falls victim to the 'one thought too many' objection. His moral theory can allow that after an accident one can save a friend out of inclination. But could one also save the friend in doing an otherwise immoral action, such as telling a lie or breaking a promise? This is the third challenge friendship poses for Kant's moral thought in general.

1.2 The third challenge: lying for a friend

Would Kant's theory allow lying in order to protect a friend, or breaking a promise in order to attend to a friend instead? So far I have considered a case in which friendship conflicts with a positive duty of helping strangers in need. For Kant, positive duties – which require that one do something – are wide duties that leave room for judgment, and friendship can trump helping strangers under certain circumstances. But what about cases in which friendship conflicts with negative duties, i.e., actions one ought not to do? According to Kant, a negative duty is strict and 'admits no exception in favor of inclination' (*Groundwork* 4, p. 421 note). If negative duties do not allow for exceptions, then this seems to hold in the case of friendship as well. Kant famously argues that one must never lie, not even when a murderer asks one whether his victim is in one's house (cf. Kant 'On a Supposed Right to Lie from Philanthropy' 8, pp. 425–30). This seems to imply that one should not lie to protect a friend, even under extreme circumstances, and this seems to be at odds with common opinion. Now it is true that common opinion does not hold that friendship trumps everything, for instance, that one should protect a friend who committed atrocities;[5] but we ordinarily hold that one is justified in lying to a would-be murderer who asks if our friend is in the house.

Even interpreters of Kant are mostly uncomfortable with Kant's apparent claim that one should never lie, and they try to find room within Kant's framework for exceptions.[6] For instance, one could argue that Kant's essay 'On a Supposed Right to Lie' merely addresses a *legal* right to tell a lie about the situation in which a murderer comes to the door, not a moral prohibition. The problem with this reading is that in his moral writings Kant seems to confirm the absolute prohibition against lying, calling it 'the greatest violation of a human being's duty to himself' (*MdS* 6, p. 429), or saying about a lie in an ethical sense: 'To utter one cannot be called in any wise permissible' (*Vigilantius* 27, p. 701). Another strategy could be to point out that in his *Metaphysics of Morals* Kant addresses casuistical questions after the prohibition of lying, thereby possibly granting that circumstances might yield a different conclusion. The problem with this strategy is that there Kant merely addresses cases of politeness and etiquette (cf. *MdS* 6, p. 431). Kant seems to take very seriously the conception of positive responsibility; telling a lie leaves an 'indelible stain' upon one's soul, in Adam Smith's phrase (Smith 1984, p. 138).

However, even if this was Kant's claim,[7] one can ask whether this position is sufficiently supported by Kant's arguments. If we go back, what the universalization test aimed at was to rule out making an exception for oneself. But why could the rule not be more specific, such as 'do not lie unless a life is at stake'? There is a parallel in the case of killing. Even if killing is wrong, Kant allows for exceptions in cases of self-defense, war, or even capital punishment (cf., e.g., *MdS* 6, p. 235f.; 6, p. 333f.). Could something similar not hold for lying as well? The problem is that the cases of lying and killing are not parallel. Kant had ruled out lying because, in universalizing the maxim, one would defeat the whole purpose of lying. This is not the case with a maxim of self-defense. Everyone could have the maxim 'not to kill unless it is the only way to stop the attacker'. But one cannot universalize a similar exception in the case of lying. If one universalizes the maxim 'do not lie unless a life is at stake', the murderer at the door would know the maxim too, and again the purpose of the maxim would be defeated. In order to allow for an exception in the case of lying, Kant would need to separate his key claim (that one should not make an exception for oneself to a general rule) from his more controversial universalization test (that one can find necessary rules by asking whether all could adopt them). However, Kant himself does not seem to allow for this separation.

Friendship does seem to pose a problem for Kant's moral thought, then, when it conflicts with certain prohibitions (like lying, promise-breaking, etc.). So far I have considered in the abstract how one could try to make room for friendship in Kant's moral theory. But how exactly does Kant understand friendship? Maybe this gives a clue how to resolve the conflict. Is there a reason why morality should set limits to friendship?

2 Kant's conception of friendship

Kant does indeed present friendship as being restricted by morality, but he does not argue the case on the basis of a superiority or higher importance of morality; rather, he argues that friendship is only *possible* under the confines of morality. Kant discusses friendship in his late *Metaphysics of Morals* (1797). He repeatedly lectured on friendship in his course on ethics, and we have lecture notes taken by students which record his lectures. One set of lecture notes, taken by Collins, dates around 1775, six years before the publication of the *Critique of Pure Reason* and the beginning of Kant's critical period. Another set of notes is from 1793/4, eight years after the *Groundwork* and three before the *Metaphysics of Morals*, taken by Vigilantius. Since the lecture notes were not published by Kant himself, I shall focus on the account given in the *Metaphysics of Morals*, and supplement it with passages from the lectures where they shed light on Kant's account in his published writings.

Kant defines friendship as follows: '*Friendship* (considered in its perfection) is the union of two persons through equal mutual love and respect' (*MdS* 6, p. 469). This view, as such, does not seem to be at odds with our ordinary conceptions of friendship. But Kant adds two elements that remove it slightly from our common notion. First, Kant goes on to elucidate friendship as 'the complete confidence of two persons in revealing their secret judgments and feelings to each other, as far as such disclosures are consistent with mutual respect' (*MdS* 6, p. 471). This might seem too narrow, because one might think that the mere enjoyment of being together or helping each other in need is just as essential as the showing of confidence. And, second, he does not present love and respect as *feelings* one has for the friend, but as the *maxims* of benevolence and treating others as equals. This aspect might seem too dry because friendship seems to involve a sweetness of sentiments that an account that intellectualizes love and respect would not capture.

Why does Kant present friendship in these ways? He is aware of ordinary conceptions of friendship, of classical conceptions and of the conceptions of romance writers, and he himself divides friendships into those based on need, on shared tastes and moral friendship of disposition.[8] The reason is that he takes seriously certain aspects of friendship: that it should involve equality and be lasting and stable, for instance, and he argues that only the moral friendship of disposition can achieve that. I shall discuss three key elements of friendship.

2.1 Friendship and feelings

From a contemporary perspective, the most striking feature of Kant's conception of friendship is probably that it curbs the role of emotions and feelings. In the ordinary conception of friendship, the longing for the friend as well as the sweetness in being with her seem to be among the most attractive features of friendship and to capture the imagination of romance writers. Kant retains a role for feelings and sweetness, of course, but he argues that one should limit them with principles. The reason is that Kant takes seriously a feature of friendship that is also part of the common conception: that friendships should be lasting and stable. We want a friend to be faithful and to remain a friend even in difficult times, and especially then; and we entrust her with secrets we would wish to remain secret (cf. *MdS* 27, p. 472). Accordingly, Kant claims that a lasting friendship cannot be based on feelings: 'the love in friendship cannot be an affect; for emotion is blind in its choice, and after a while it goes up in smoke' (*MdS* 6, p. 471). Feelings change, they are relative and contingent (*Critique of Practical Reason* 5, p. 26), and would not be a solid foundation for a friendship: 'friendship is something so delicate... that it is never for a moment safe from interruptions if it is allowed to rest on feelings' (*MdS* 6, p. 471). Similarly a friendship that is based on a shared taste would not be lasting and stable: 'In friendships of taste, the amity vanishes because in process of time the taste is lost, and alights upon new objects, and then the one displaces the other' (*Collins* 27, p. 429). In Section 3 I shall reflect on the plausibility of Kant's conclusions; for now my focus is on presenting his arguments.

Because of the instability and unreliability of feelings, then, Kant does not accept them as a sufficient basis for ideal friendship, and he does not present the love and respect that belong to such a friendship as feelings. In the *Metaphysics of Morals* Kant discusses friendship right after the duties of love and respect one owes to others. He explains the duty of love as a maxim to help others in need, and he argues that 'love is not to be understood as *feeling*... since others cannot put one under obligation to have feelings' (*MdS* 6, p. 449). Similarly, the respect owed to others is not a '*feeling* that comes from comparing our own *worth* with another's (such as a child feels... toward his parents, ... or any subordinate toward his superior)' (*MdS* 6, p. 449). Rather it is a '*maxim*... of not exalting oneself above others' (ibid.). This does not mean that feelings wholly drop out of the picture or are deemed irrelevant. One ordinarily chooses a friend 'in accordance with one's dispositions and taste' (*Collins* 27, p. 428). But ideally the civilized man would be disposed to have equal well-wishing for all: 'The civilized man seeks a general friendship and amenity, without having special ties' (Ibid.). Such a man would display 'a high degree of perfection. But people are still very much inclined to form particular ties' (*Collins* 27, p. 430). Kant struggles with the issue. It remains natural to enter particular friendships based on feelings, even if one would ideally be well-disposed towards all. Friendships based on feelings are in danger of 'closing the human heart towards others who are not of our company' (*Collins* 27, p. 428). This is an external critique of friendships based on feelings, a critique from the standpoint of universal morality. But Kant's ideal friendship is not in conflict with morality's demands.

2.2 Equality

A second element of Kant's account of friendship that might seem surprising is that he limits the love in a friendship by a demand for respect. In our ordinary conception we do not usually think that love and respect are at odds with one another, but that they go hand in hand and are both important: One esteems the ways in which the other is capable of enriching one, and loves her for it. Kant argues, on the contrary, that love and respect are opposing demands, and friendship is a middle position between the two: 'For love can be regarded as attraction and respect as repulsion, and if the principle of love bids friends to draw closer, the principle of respect requires them to stay at a proper distance from each other' (*MdS* 6, p. 470; cf. p. 449). The reason why friendship requires a balance of love and respect is the requirement of *equality* that is commonly regarded as important to friendship. Kant understands equality to demand that friends have an equal standing towards each other: 'friends must not demean each other' (*Vigilantius*

27, p. 682), and the love and the respect they have for each other is equal (*MdS* 6, p. 469). Because of these requirements, Kant sees a need to constrain love by respect.

But why does he hold this? Kant's claim that love and respect have to be equal grows out of his understanding of respect as a *moral* notion. To respect someone amounts to 'not exalting oneself about others' (*MdS* 6, p. 449), or not demeaning others. Kant's point is that love – here understood as helping the other – can create an imbalance in the relationship in that the benefactor is now raised above the beneficiary:

> The relation of friendship is that of equality; but if one friend now helps the other in his troubles, he has become my benefactor, and I am in his debt; ... and by then the true relationship is at an end, and friendship no longer exists. (*Collins* 27, p. 426)

In benefiting the other, the equality and equal standing is destroyed: 'if one of them accepts a favor from the other, then he may well be able to count on equality in love, but not in respect; for he sees himself obviously a step lower in being under obligation without being able to impose obligation in turn' (*MdS* 6, p. 471). One owes gratitude to the benefactor when one receives a favor, and this introduces inequality in a relationship that by definition should be between equals. So far from seeing the help one friend gives another as strengthening a friendship, Kant would argue that it upsets the fundamental balance on which friendship depends.

Kant's emphasis on equality also rules out the view that true friendships are based on needs or on an expected advantage, and he suggest that in order to secure the friendship, it is prudent rather to endure hardships than to ask a friend for help. This does not mean that there is no role in friendship for helping the other in need, but it is something that one should seek to avoid asking of the friend. Nonetheless, one has confidence that a friend would help if called upon:

> Yet in every friendship we must still presuppose this friendship of need, not in order to enjoy it, though, but to trust in it; I must, that is, have confidence in each of my true friends, that he would be able and willing to look after my affairs, and promote my interests; though in order to enjoy that confidence, I must never ask him to do it. (*Collins* 27, p. 425)

In short, Kant argues that for friendship to exist, the love for a friend – or the longing for the other and wish to do him good – must be tempered by respect, which entails a keeping of distance from the friend. The reason for this is that the equality that is necessary for friendship is otherwise in danger of being destroyed. In Kant's presentation, then, friendship is more reserved than in the accounts of romance writers, but this more reserved quality is due not to a prior commitment to morality, nor to a disdain for friendship, but rather to the requirements friendship itself imposes. This also affects how Kant understands a third key element of friendship: the union between two people and its sweetness.

2.3 The union of friends

A third central element of friendship is the union of two people. In our ordinary conception of friendship there is a sweetness in being together with a friend. One delights in the presence of one's friend, and thinks about her good rather than one's own. It is as if two people become one, and it is this togetherness that accounts for the joy of friendship. Kant recognizes the importance of this element (cf. *MdS* 6, p. 471), but modifies and again intellectualizes it. The reasons are the same as mentioned before. If friendships rest on feelings, they are not secure and stable. So one's feelings have to be restricted by the principle of respect:

> Although it is sweet to feel in possession of each other that approaches fusion into one person, friendship is something so delicate... that it is never for a moment safe from interruptions if it is allowed to rest on feelings, and if this mutual sympathy and self-surrender are not subjected to principles or rules preventing excessive familiarity and limiting mutual love by requirements of respect. (*MdS* 6, p. 471)

Again the reason is not a foreign element by which Kant seeks to restrain a friendship based on feelings, but one of friendship's *internal* requirements, respect which is demanded by equality. Friendship is then not the fusion of two people into one, but being 'fully in communion' with a friend (*Collins* 27, p. 427). This consists in 'the complete confidence of two persons in revealing their secret judgments and feelings to each other, as far as such disclosures are consistent with mutual respect' (*MdS* 6, p. 471). One remains a separate person in one's self-conception, but one can share one's thoughts without restraint. The feeling of sweetness is a consequence of sharing one's thoughts with the friend: 'The sweet delight in the enjoyment of friendship is afforded only by the harmony of judgment' (*Vigilantius* 27, p. 683).

Kant gives two reasons why we want to be able to share our thoughts with others. First, we are social beings, which makes us inclined to share our thoughts with others. But one cannot risk it in larger societies, since others might use what one said against one (cf. *MdS* 6, p. 471). One therefore longs to have someone with whom one can share one's thoughts with confidence: Someone who has a friend 'is not completely alone with his thoughts, as in a prison, but enjoys a freedom he cannot have with the masses, among whom he must shut himself up in himself' (*MdS* 6, p. 472). Having a friend allows one to share one's private thoughts and sentiments, and in this respect one's thoughts have a privileged status since every sentiment must be communicated via thoughts (cf. *Vigilantius* 27, p. 677). The second reason why one wants to share one's thoughts with a friend is that only in sharing one's thoughts can one rectify one's judgments and make progress in understanding: 'If I possess such a friend... he will already be helpful in rectifying my judgment, when I have gone astray' (*Collins* 27, p. 427).

The condition for achieving this union with a friend – even if one differs from him on a particular point – is that friends share the same basic principles and moral outlook. The sweetness of friendship is a result of this agreement on principles: 'The sweet delight in the enjoyment of friendship is afforded only by the harmony of judgment, i.e., that the feelings and thoughts of the parties are derived from the same *principia*' (*Vigilantius* 27, p. 683). If friends share the same basic outlook, they can share their thoughts about politics and religion, for instance, without restraint. However, respect sets limits here too. Kant notes that it is prudent not to reveal things that can be used against oneself if one were to fall out with the friend, and the intimacy relates only to a lack of reserve in expressing one's basic views, not to decorum or anything that could diminish the respect the other has for oneself (cf. *Collins* 27, p. 427). Because friendship entails being able to share these views and be intimate enough that one can keep secrets from other people, one can only have a small number of true friends, according to Kant.

But the biggest advantage of Kant's conception of friendship is that it 'actually exists here and there in its perfection' (*MdS* 6, p. 472). The advantage of Kant's conception of friendship is that it captures what makes friendship possible at all.

3 Friendship as a challenge to Kant's moral thought

We can now return to the initial question and reflect upon the extent to which friendship poses a challenge to Kant's moral thought. In the first section I argued that there is no intrinsic incongruence between Kant's moral thought and friendship, but that Kant would not allow doing something immoral (as he defines it) in order to help a friend.

In the second section I looked at his own positive account of friendship to see whether this would help to resolve this conflict. Rather than setting friendship against morality, in his own account of friendship Kant moralizes friendship. He is aware of our ordinary conceptions of friendship: that friends help each other in need (which he calls a friendship of need), that they enjoy doing things together (a friendship of taste), and the sweet feelings of the union of two people (the friendship of romance writers). But he argues that these forms cannot account for other elements that are a necessary part of the common conception of friendship: faithfulness and the equality of friends. The ordinary conceptions by themselves do not yield a secure and lasting friendship, and they are in constant danger of raising one person above the other and introducing an imbalance in the relationship. The perfect equality required for friendship is therefore not found in experience if one focuses on feelings. Kant does not try to argue against sweetness, helping and shared taste in friendship, but he construes them in a more reserved way such that they are not based on feelings. He focuses on the ideal, a friendship that contains all the components, and which has the further advantage of actually being possible in experience.

But does Kant's treatment of friendship resolve the conflict between his stance on lying and our ordinary view that it can be permissible to lie in order to save a friend? For Kant friendship is a moralized relationship that ideally all human beings would have towards each other. It is only that people form special ties because they share the same basic outlook and invest time in each other. One should not lie to a friend, for '*honesty*... is an absolute duty' (*Vigilantius* 27, p. 678), but Kant does not address the case in which one could lie to a third party in order to protect a friend. On the other hand, nothing suggests that he would consider it permissible. Friends need to have moral dispositions in order to be friends; a morally good person is more likely to follow the principles that establish trust, for instance (cf. Wood 1999, p. 277), and presumably friends do not give those principles up to help each other. So the challenge remains: There is a conflict between a common conception according to which it is permissible to lie in order to save a friend, and Kant's outlook of morality and friendship. This does not mean that we ordinarily think that lying is *always* allowed to help a friend, e.g., even to cover up crimes, but Kant seems to say that it is never allowed. This is not so much a critique of Kant's account of friendship as a critique of his moral theory more generally (see Section 1 above).

But Kant's account of friendship also raises a new issue. Our ordinary sense of friendship seems to pose a problem not only for Kant's moral theory but also for his particular account of friendship. While he tries to make room for all the elements that we hold dear, including the sweetness of friendship, the union of two people, and the importance of helping a friend and sharing tastes, he construes these elements in a way that makes them appear much more reserved, since they are not based on feelings (see Section 2 above). Kant's reason, to recall, is that feelings change: They cannot guarantee a stable and lasting friendship and are unlikely to be exactly the same over time. But does friendship need this absolute certainty and equality? Three questions arise: First, might it not be enough if there is a gray zone or range for true friendship to exist, rather than a strict mathematical equality? Second, does one need certainty about this equality in order to enjoy friendship? Could it be that friendship lives off of hope and trust as well as moments in which one experiences a unity with the other, rather than the certainty about a permanent state? Finally, does helping the other out of feelings really endanger the equality in a friendship rather than strengthen it? If both friends help each other, does it not bring them closer together? In sum: The question is whether there could be a workable friendship based on feelings after all.

Again, Kant can grant that we long for such a perfect friendship based on feelings. Such a friendship, Kant says, 'is an ideal of one's wishes, which knows no bounds in its rational concept but which must always be very limited in experience' (*MdS* 6, p. 472). He can grant that we will continue to long for this kind of friendship, even if it is not clear that it will ever be realized. But his concern is not to provide a phenomenological description of our wishes and longings. He treats of friendship in his moral philosophy, and places the emphasis on what we can and should aim for. He calls his form of friendship '*moral friendship*' (*MdS* 6, p. 471), and he says that it is a duty to strive for it (*MdS* 6, p. 469). His focus on what one can and should aim for gives rise to a further reservation against the ordinary conception of friendship with its emphasis on feelings. In his moral philosophy Kant's aim is to find out what one can say *a priori*, and to find the pure principles of morality: 'the *metaphysical* first principles of a doctrine of virtue, ... this has to do only with its pure rational principles' (*MdS* 6, p. 468). But one cannot determine *a priori* to what extent one should help a friend: 'that (pragmatic) friendship, which burdens itself with the ends of others, although out of love, can have neither the purity nor the completeness requisite for a precisely determinant maxim' (*MdS* 6, p. 468). Principles based on needs, for instance, cannot determine the right course *a priori*. If one friend helps the other out by babysitting, but does not have children herself, what is the proper way of returning the favor?

So Kant's conception of friendship – in advocating a certain degree of reserve – is one that is dictated by the head, but is it likely to convince the heart? Of course, Kant grants that there is the friendship of the heart, and his moral philosophy is not intrinsically opposed to it (cf. Section 1 above). But Kant does not seem to allow lying to help a friend, thereby setting up a possible conflict between the head and the heart. But – in Kant's defense – even in cases where our ordinary judgment would allow lying in order to help a friend, we also hope that some scruples are left in telling a lie. After all, as Kant reminds us, friendship should not close our heart to others (cf. *Collins* 27, p. 428). The conflict between the head and the heart to which Kant's account leads is not necessarily an objection against his account: It is all too familiar from our ordinary life.

Notes

1. All references to Kant cite the volume and page number of the Prussian Academy Edition of his collected works (Berlin: de Gruyter, 1902ff.). Unless otherwise stated, translations of Kant's published works are from Kant (1996), and translations of his lectures from Kant (1997).
2. For a clear description of such a view see Smart and Williams (1973, pp. 3–42).
3. Schiller *Xenien*, 'The Philosophers', trans. from Wood (1999, p. 28).
4. Kant replies to Schiller in his *Religion within the Boundaries of Mere Reason*; cf. note 6, p. 23. On this topic see Baxley (2010, pp. 98–115).
5. For dilemmas like this cf. Felten (2011).
6. Two important discussions are Wood (2008, pp. 240–58) and Hill (2012, pp. 195–202).
7. For the background on Kant's views on lying cf. Kuehn (2001, pp. 39 and 403).
8. Cf. *Collins* 27, pp. 424–7; *Vigilantius* 27, p. 680f. Scholars argue that Kant gets this distinction from Aristotle, cf. Wood (1999, p. 275); Denis (2001, p. 3). On Aristotle's account of three types of friendship see Kathryn Sensen (2009).

References

A.M. Baxley (2010) *Kant's Theory of Virtue* (Cambridge: Cambridge University Press).

J. Butler (2006) *The Works of Bishop Butler*, ed. D.E. White (Rochester: University of Rochester Press).

L. Denis (2001) 'From Friendship to Marriage: Revising Kant', *Philosophy and Phenomenological Research* 63, 1–28.

E. Felten (2011) *Loyalty* (New York: Simon & Schuster).
T. Hill (2012) *Virtue, Rules, and Justice* (Oxford: Oxford University Press).
O.Höffe (1992) *Ethik und Politik* (Frankfurt a.M.: Suhrkamp).
I. Kant (1996) *Practical Philosophy*, ed. Mary Gregor (Cambridge: Cambridge University Press).
—— (1997) *Lectures on Ethics*, trans. Peter Heath (Cambridge: Cambridge University Press).
M. Kuehn (2001) *Kant: A Biography* (Cambridge: Cambridge University Press).
S. Marcucci (1999) '"Moral Friendship", in *Kant-Studien* 90, 434–41.
J. S. Mill (1969) 'Utilitarianism', in J. M. Robson (ed.), *Essays on Ethics, Religion and Society* (Toronto: University of Toronto Press).
T. Nagel (1986) *The View from Nowhere* (Oxford: Oxford University Press).
O. O'Neill (1989) *Constructions of Reason* (Cambridge: Cambridge University Press).
K. Sensen (2009) 'On the Nature of Friendship in Aristotle's *Nicomachean Ethics*', in S. Krause and M.A. McGrail (eds), *The Art of Rule* (Lanham, MD: Lexington Books), 43–74.
J. J. C. Smart and B. Williams (1973) *Utilitarianism For & Against* (Cambridge: Cambridge University Press).
A. Smith (1984) *The Theory of Moral Sentiments*, ed. D. D. Raphael and A. L. Macfie (Indianapolis: Liberty Fund).
B. Williams (1981) *Moral Luck* (Cambridge: Cambridge University Press).
A. Wood (1999) *Kant's Ethical Thought* (Cambridge: Cambridge University Press).
—— (2008) *Kantian Ethics* (Cambridge: Cambridge University Press).

9 Consequentialism and Friendship

Alastair Norcross

Consequentialist theories, such as utilitarianism, typically emphasize impartiality. In Bentham's words 'each person is to count for one and no one for more than one.' This has led some to suggest that consequentialism cannot accommodate the value we typically place on friendship. After all, it seems to be of the essence of friendship that, to each other, friends 'count' for more than strangers. The consequentialist, it is claimed, will simply calculate impartially, and thus will have no room for friendship. This criticism is misguided and betrays an overly simplistic view of consequentialist moral psychology. Given the important contribution to human happiness of friendship, and the clear distinction between the consequentialist criterion of act evaluation on the one hand and decision procedure on the other, consequentialist theories have ample resources to account for the importance of friendship.

Friendships require partiality. This is a truism. At least part of what it is to be a friend to someone is to be disposed to do things for that person that one wouldn't do for a stranger. It is to weigh that person's interests more heavily in one's deliberations than the interests of a stranger. Another part of what it is to be a friend is to be disposed to behave in certain ways towards one's friends without subjecting such behavior to moral scrutiny, at least at the time of action. Consequentialist theories, such as utilitarianism,[1] might seem to have difficulty accommodating friendship. Consider a variation on an often discussed case. You hear that a friend is sick in hospital. You know that your friend would be cheered by a visit, so you go, bearing flowers (or grapes, or magazines, or whatever). Evidently cheered, your friend thanks you for coming. You reply, 'Of course I came. It was my moral duty. I calculated the utilities, and determined that I couldn't do any more good by any alternative available to me at the time.' This would hardly be what your friend was hoping to hear. It would also probably be false. Were there really *no* other alternatives that would have done more good? Weren't there *many* needy strangers who would have benefited more from your attention? What this illustrates is that both the impersonal and the supposedly calculating nature of utilitarianism are, on the face of it, opposed to the kinds of dispositions central to friendship. Thus, we can separate two distinct supposed problems for utilitarianism. First, there is what I will call the **criterial problem.** Given the standard utilitarian criterion of rightness, that an action maximize impersonal utility, the kinds of acts of partiality distinctive of friendships are unlikely to be right. Second, there is what I will call the **motivational problem.** Even if an act of friendship is right, at least part of what is distinctive about such acts is that they be motivated by partial concern for the friend and not by considerations of impersonal morality. These would only be problems, of course, if friendship has real moral value, such that the world would be worse for the lack of it. Given the current state of the world, this is not at all obvious. Given the extent and degree of suffering in the world, perhaps it would be better if we abandoned the kind of partiality involved in friendships, at least for now. This is a distinct (and depressing) possibility. However, it is also at least possible that the kinds of commitments involved in friendships make a net positive contribution to the world (or will make such a contribution in a distant, and better, future). In which case, it would be interesting to see whether utilitarianism can accommodate them.

1 Rule-utilitarianism and friendship

At this point, the utilitarian who is eager to make room for friendship in her theory may be tempted to experiment with rule-utilitarianism. Consider what is clearly the most thoughtful and well-presented version of the theory, Brad Hooker's (2000):

> RULE-CONSEQUENTIALISM.[2] An act is wrong if it is forbidden by the code of rules whose internalization by the overwhelming majority of everyone everywhere in each new generation has maximum expected value in terms of well-being (with some priority for the worst off). (p. 32)

Although the question of which code would, if internalized, maximize utility is complex, it is at least possible that such a code would include some kind of rule favoring acts of friendship. If, as I suggested above, the kinds of commitments involved in friendships do make a net positive contribution to the world, it is plausible that the internalization of a rule favoring acting on these commitments in some way will be part of the ideal code.

According to rule-consequentialism, the moral status of an action, such as standing by a friend in need, doesn't depend on the consequences of that action, but on the consequences of internalizing a code of rules. A rule-consequentialist friend could thus truly reason, on at least some occasions, that an act of friendship is right, because it is an act of friendship. She will not be disposed to evaluate the consequences of such an act, and certainly not to do something else merely to produce a smidgen more good.

It is important to note that the turn to rule-consequentialism, at best, addresses the criterial problem. Recall the hospital visit. Suppose you say to your friend, 'Of course I came. It was my moral duty. Visiting you was an act of friendship, and a rule enjoining acts of friendship is included in the ideal moral code'. This appears to be just as inimical to true friendship as the original, act-utilitarian version. It is not at all clear, though, that rule-consequentialism succeeds in its own right. Problems arise in cases in which, for example, the consequences of failing a friend are better than those of standing by the friend. Hooker's answer to such cases lies in his disaster avoidance rule. No doubt, the optimal code will include a rule to avoid disasters, which can override other rules in the code. So, it won't be wrong to fail a friend, if standing by the friend will lead to a disaster. What counts as a disaster will be relative to the seriousness of the situation in which the friend finds himself. If your friend simply fancies a beer with you, it might not take much to justify responding to the needs of strangers rather than the whim of your friend. If your friend is in serious peril, on the other hand, it would take a lot more to justify failing to come to his aid. The more serious the situation, the greater the disaster to be avoided. Although this gives the intuitively correct results (how could it not when it is phrased so loosely?), we still have to confront the familiar 'rule-worship' objection. Presumably, the disaster avoidance rule does not say that just *any* comparative loss of utility counts as a disaster. If it did, then we would have act-utilitarianism, or at least a theory extensionally equivalent to it. So, there must be cases in which more good would come of failing a friend than of standing by him, but in which it would nonetheless be wrong to fail him. Why would a utilitarian – someone who believes that well-being, or welfare, or flourishing (whether prioritarianly adjusted or not) is the only intrinsic good – believe that it is wrong to bring about more of the good rather than less *in any case*? The question is not whether a good utilitarian actually confronted with such a case would fail a friend, or even would believe that it is right to do so. Perhaps a good utilitarian would not perform the requisite calculations in such a case, or would even do something she knows to be wrong (more on that shortly). The question is whether a utilitarian would believe of an option under the description 'failing a friend but maximizing the good' that it is wrong. Of course Hooker could reply that a rule-utilitarian could believe such a thing, because that is what rule-utilitarianism implies (that at least some optimal instances of rule-breaking are wrong). But that would simply beg the question against the criticism, which is that a utilitarian wouldn't be a rule-utilitarian.

There is, of course, a lot more to say about rule-utilitarianism, and, even after it is all said, there may be some who still believe it gives a better account of the moral value of friendship than act-utilitarianism. However, I don't have world enough or time to say it all here. What I want to do now is to explain how act-utilitarianism can account for friendship and what it has to say about the commitment to friends even in circumstances in which a little more good would come of ignoring such commitments.

2 Act-utilitarianism and 'one thought too many'

Suppose it is true, as seems at least possible, that something like a disposition to form and be involved in friendships promotes overall well-being. A utilitarian would want such a disposition to exist, at least in most people. In order for this general disposition to flourish, individual agents must have personal commitments that include the disposition to favor friends over strangers even in cases in which somewhat more good will come of favoring the strangers. Thus, a utilitarian would approve of the existence of such commitments in individual agents. Even though such commitments will sometimes lead agents to sacrifice utility, there would be less overall utility if the agents lacked those commitments.

So far, so good, but there might appear to be a difference between the case of me approving of *your* commitment to your friends, and me approving of my own commitment. The point has been most notably pressed by Bernard Williams and Michael Stocker. Williams (1981) describes a situation in which a man chooses to rescue his wife rather than some other person: 'It might have been hoped by some (for instance, by his wife) that his motivating thought, fully spelled out, would be the thought that it was his wife, not that it was his wife and that in situations of this kind it is permissible to save one's wife' (p. 18). What is being criticized is not the agent's action, but his decision procedure: the conscious application of a principle of morality in a situation in which the agent should act simply on his natural affection. If the agent is a utilitarian, he doesn't simply act on his commitment to his wife, but he also justifies such a commitment on utilitarian grounds. This, according to Williams, leaves him with 'one thought too many'. The problem here is not just that the wife might have hoped that her husband's commitment to her would have provided the sole motivation for his action. Rather, it seems that the kind of conscious evaluation of his commitment that appears in Williams's example is actually inconsistent with having the commitment in the first place. What it is to have a strong commitment to someone is, in part, to be disposed to perform certain actions without subjecting either the actions or the disposition to independent moral scrutiny.

Although Williams's example involves a stronger personal commitment than mere friendship, similar considerations apply to the kinds of personal commitments involved in friendships. Does the utilitarian who acts to help a friend, as opposed to a stranger, think to herself that this option is right, because it involves helping a friend, and that friendship has utilitarian value? And if so, does she also have 'one thought too many'? Both the motivational and criterial problems seem to be at issue here. First, must a utilitarian subject her motivations to moral scrutiny while making decisions about what to do? Second, what form should such moral scrutiny, when and if performed, take for a utilitarian? Personal commitments, such as friendship, can seem to raise motivational concerns for many moral theories. The Kantian, who consciously applies the categorical imperative to her decision to help a friend in need, appears to have the same problem as the utilitarian (either of the act or rule variety), who subjects her decision to utilitarian evaluation in the same situation. 'My option is right because it involves helping a friend, and helping a friend is my duty, according to the categorical imperative', appears just as alien to true friendship as does 'my option is right because it involves helping a friend, and friendship has utilitarian value'. In fact, we might go further and question whether an act-utilitarian can coherently think such a thing at all. She can think that she should have a disposition to form and maintain friendships because of the general value of such commitments, but she can't think that any particular act of friendship is for that reason right. She believes of any action that it's right just in case it maximizes the good. But this objection confuses the evidential sense of 'because' with the constitutive sense. It is perfectly consistent for a utilitarian to think that the fact that an act is one of friendship is evidence that it is right, without thinking that its rightness is *constituted* by its being an act of friendship. Of course, it might be objected that the connection between friendship and rightness is more than just evidential, and thus that the utilitarian fails to account for this. But that would simply beg the question against utilitarianism. Perhaps, though, the objection can be resurrected in a less question-begging form. Whether or not the connection between friendship and rightness is more than just evidential, the utilitarian benefits of a general commitment to form and maintain friendships can only be (or at least are more likely to be) realized, if individual agents don't (usually) think of the connection as only evidential. The idea here is that an agent who thinks to herself 'she's my friend, which is evidence that my favoring her is right, because the general commitment to form and maintain friendships has utilitarian value', is always prepared to favor a stranger (or do something else entirely), if she sees that more good will come of it on this occasion. But the utilitarian value of the general commitment to form and maintain friendships depends in part on the commitment being robust enough to lead to favoring one's friends on at least some occasions on which more good could be done by favoring strangers (or oneself). This seems to require that the agent not rehearse the utilitarian justification for having the commitment to friendship on every occasion when the commitment might come into play. So the possibility of the act-utilitarian having one thought too many when it comes to decisions concerning friends threatens the theory with pragmatic self-defeat.

The answer to these objections (like the answers to many other objections) is to be found in Sidgwick (just think of the trees that could have been saved, if only Williams, Stocker, and their ilk had read and properly understood *The Methods of Ethics*!). Speaking of the value of a special concern for one's 'near and dear', Sidgwick (1981) cites many reasons why such concern has utilitarian value. 'On these grounds', says Sidgwick, 'the Utilitarian will evidently approve of the cultivation of affection and the performance of affectionate services' (p. 431). Is Sidgwick recommending that, on every occasion, or even most occasions, on which an agent does or might feel the promptings of self-love or natural affections, he should mentally run through the arguments for cultivating such feelings in calculating what to do? I don't think so. He does not say so, and seems to imply the contrary. He defends 'spontaneous beneficence', which could hardly exist if the agent were to subject his feeling to utilitarian assessment every time it prompted him to some action. He claims that 'we feel that the charm of Friendship is lost if the flow of emotion is not spontaneous and unforced' (ibid., p. 437). He stresses the connection between natural affection and the activities which it prompts in his claim that such activities are pleasurable because they are prompted by affection. Perhaps the clearest indication that Sidgwick didn't think that the utilitarian agent must always apply utilitarian reasoning is to be found in the following passage:

> [T]he doctrine that Universal Happiness is the ultimate standard must not be understood to imply that Universal Benevolence is the only right or always best motive of action ... it is not necessary that the end which gives the criterion of rightness should always be the end at which we consciously aim: and if experience shows that the general happiness will be more satisfactorily attained if men frequently act from other motives than pure universal philanthropy, it is obvious that these other motives are reasonably to be preferred on Utilitarian principles. (Ibid., p. 413)

If, on a particular occasion, we do not consciously aim at Universal Happiness, we can hardly justify our actions on that occasion with reference to Universal Happiness. That is, we cannot, on that occasion, employ a conscious reasoning process which involves recognizing that certain justifications for what we are doing are utilitarian justifications and therefore to be heeded. If we take this view of Sidgwick's, together with a recognition that certain forms of motivation are valuable as direct motivations, we can see that a good utilitarian agent need not have one thought too many. This applies equally with respect to personal commitments, such as commitments to friends and family, and to commitments to moral rules such as rules of fidelity or justice.

3 Esotericism

At this point, we have to confront the dreaded specter of 'esotericism'. Both Williams and Stocker claim that utilitarianism is an 'esoteric' theory, and that this is a problem for the theory. Williams is aware of the claim that utilitarianism might demand that moral agents not employ utilitarian reasoning on all occasions. Indeed, he regards this as a grave defect in the theory. He writes: '[I]t is reasonable to suppose that maximal total utility actually requires that few, if any, accept utilitarianism' (Williams 1973, p. 135). In which case, he claims, it is a matter for discussion whether 'utilitarianism is unacceptable, or ... no one ought to accept it' (ibid.). Thus we are confronted with two different claims:

> FALSE: If utilitarianism is true, it would be best if at least most people didn't believe it to be true.
> DEFECT: The truth of FALSE exposes a defect in utilitarianism.

Williams claims that there are 'some powerful reasons' for thinking that the prevalence of 'utilitarian thinking as a personal and social phenomenon ... could be a disaster' (ibid. p. 130). However, his arguments show only that utility will probably not be maximized if every action is motivated by the conscious desire to maximize utility; they certainly don't show that utility can only be maximized if no-one believes utilitarianism.[3]

Michael Stocker (1990), in a discussion of maximization, also seems to endorse both FALSE and DEFECT:

> Maximizers hold that the absence of any attainable good is, as such, bad, and that a life that lacks such a good is therefore lacking. The basic moral psychological reason for denying this is that regret over the absence or lack is a central characterizing feature of narcissistic, grandiose, and other defective selves. (p. 321)

Stocker admits that it may be argued that this shows, not that maximization is wrong, but that being a maximizer is itself not maximizing. He adds:

> I see it as a severe problem for a theory if, by its own lights, it cannot be embraced and followed .... What I have trouble in understanding is why we should be expected to think that a theory which is so esoteric as the one now in question is worth serious consideration as our ethical theory. (Ibid.)

What is Stocker claiming here? He moves from the possibility that being a maximizer may not be maximizing to the claim that maximization cannot be embraced and followed by its own lights. The tone of his remarks ('so esoteric as the one now in question') suggests a claim as extreme as Williams's claim that utilitarianism entails that no one believe it. But the evidence for this claim, that being a maximizer may not be maximizing, supports, at best, the claim that utility will probably not be maximized if every action is motivated by the conscious desire to maximize utility

Although Stocker clearly seems to embrace DEFECT, he offers no argument for it. Even if it is true that utilitarianism requires that most people don't believe it, why should that count against the theory? The most we get from Stocker is the rather cryptic claim that such a theory would be 'esoteric'. Williams (1973) offers a little more, but his arguments for DEFECT seem to center on the mistaken impression that act-utilitarianism is solely concerned with 'the situation of decision' (p. 125). This is illustrated by the following piece of reasoning:

> [The direct utilitarian] tells us that the answer to the question 'what is the right thing to do?' is to be found in that act which has the best consequences. But it seems difficult to put that to any use in this connection, except by taking it to imply the following: that the correct question to ask, if asking what is the right thing to do, is what act will have the best consequences. (Ibid.)

Thus Williams claims that the distinction between act-utilitarianism and other forms of utilitarianism is a matter of motivation. If this were the case, then FALSE, if true, would be a problem for act-utilitarianism. But it is obviously not true that act-utilitarianism is only concerned with motivation. Traditional utilitarian theory has, as its basic goal, the maximization of utility, and if this can only be achieved by no-one believing the theory, then that is what the theory demands.

Williams predicts that utilitarianism will

> retire to the totally transcendental standpoint from which all it demands is that the world should be ordered for the best, and that those dispositions and habits of thought should exist in the world which are for the best, leaving it entirely open whether those are themselves of a distinctively utilitarian kind or not. (Ibid., p. 135)

If we allow the utilitarian to specify what she means by 'for the best', I don't think she would object to this formulation as a basic characterization of utilitarianism. Utilitarianism must leave open the question of which dispositions and habits of thought are 'for the best'. That doesn't mean that it cannot take a stand on the issue, just that it must always be prepared to change its view in the light of new psychological evidence. Not only may our knowledge of and opinions about human nature change, but human nature itself may change. The fact that utilitarianism can accommodate itself to such change should be seen as an asset of the theory, not a drawback.

4 What's so bad about esotericism?

Although neither Williams nor Stocker provide good reasons for believing DEFECT, it may seem plausible. Isn't there something strange in the suggestion that a particular moral theory require that no-one believe it? This certainly seems to violate what Rawls calls the 'publicity condition' for a moral theory. Doesn't it seem right that if a moral theory is correct, it should be possible for everyone, or at least most people, to act as it prescribes and to believe that it is correct? Perhaps this is at least contingently true, but it is hard to see how it could be a necessary feature of the correct moral theory. Imagine that there are two deities, Bart, who is good, and Lisa, who is bad.[4] Imagine, further, that the correct moral theory is the following version of divine command theory:

> BARTISM An act is wrong iff it is forbidden by Bart, otherwise it is permissible.

Many people believe BARTISM and act on it. Many other people believe a false moral theory, LISANITY, which has the same structure as BARTISM, but which centers on the commands of Lisa. Both Lisa and Bart regularly appear to the people and issue their very different commands. There is nothing in the story so far to suggest that BARTISM could not be the correct moral theory. Suppose now that the people are getting better and better. In fact, most people now believe BARTISM and very few believe LISANITY. This annoys the hell out of Lisa, who desperately wants people to do what She says, so She works the following piece of trickery on the minds of the people. Every time Lisa appears to the people, they believe they are seeing Bart, and vice versa. Lisa, who, though evil is also more powerful than Bart, also fixes Bart so that He is not aware of the people's reversed perceptions. Now most, if not all, people who believe in BARTISM will actually fail to act as it prescribes. Conversely, those who believe LISANITY will usually do what BARTISM requires. Has this exercise of evil power by Lisa rendered the previously true BARTISM false? This would be a very strange conclusion. If BARTISM was true before, it is still true now, it's just that now it's better if people believe LISANITY instead.[5]

It will be easier to see both the appeal and the failing of DEFECT, if we pause briefly to consider the role of moral theories, or at least one central aspect of their role. Both moral realists and anti-realists (of various kinds) agree that moral theories are action-guiding in the following sense: they provide reasons for acting. If my moral theory contains a prohibition on coveting my neighbor's ass, I have a reason not to covet my neighbor's ass (I'm not sure whether coveting is a kind of action, but bear with me). But if, according to my moral theory, I shouldn't even believe my moral theory, how is it supposed to supply me with reasons? And if it can't supply me with reasons, how can it be a moral theory? The obvious answer to this is to point out that reasons don't have to be embodied in consciously held beliefs, or even unconscious beliefs, in order to apply. The smoker who doesn't believe that smoking is bad for her has the same reason to quit as the better-informed (or less self-deceived) smoker. At this point, the moral anti-realist will probably point out that the harmful effects of smoking are a matter of objective fact, whereas moral theories inhabit (according to him) an entirely different realm. The reasons supplied by moral theories are more like the reason I have for benefiting someone I care deeply about than the reason I have for quitting smoking. If I care deeply about Smith and you don't, I have a reason for benefiting Smith that simply doesn't apply to you. But this example can be modified to illustrate how moral theories can provide reasons for acting to those who don't accept them, even given moral anti-realism. Suppose I care deeply about Smith and want her to be happy, above all else. However, I also know, from bitter past experience, that when I care deeply about someone, I become irrational, possessive, violent, and obsessive. In fact, everyone for whom I have cared deeply has suffered terribly as a result. Given that I really do want Smith to be happy, I judge that it would be better if I could get myself not to care about her at all. Perhaps I succeed in this endeavor, and no longer care about Smith. As a result, she is a lot happier than she would have been. My emotional commitment to Smith provided the reason for me to change my feelings, and continues to provide reasons for my behavior, even though such reasons are now inaccessible to me. This suggests that the assumption that moral anti-realists must be committed to DEFECT stems from an impoverished view of how reasons for behavior can operate.

Now consider how a moral anti-realist might view my example. Given the kind of being Bart is, and the kind of person I am, BARTISM is my chosen theory. My acceptance and advocacy of BARTISM express something deeply rooted in my character. But what if Lisa were tricking me in the manner described above? Even though I embrace BARTISM, I judge that, were Lisa to be tricking me, it would be better, according to my chosen theory, if I were to embrace LISANITY instead. Perhaps I am told that LISA will begin Her trickery tomorrow (the trickery will, of course, include erasing my memory of being told this). There is a rigorous course of drug and behavioristic treatment, that I can undergo today. This treatment has a 95 percent chance of changing my character in such a way that I will embrace LISANITY. Given that I currently embrace BARTISM, I have a very good reason to submit myself to the treatment. The reason is supplied by BARTISM itself. I might regard it as regrettable that Lisa's power has driven me to this, but I don't consider BARTISM any less appropriate as a moral theory because of it. If the treatment is successful, and I come to embrace LISANITY (and therefore act as BARTISM requires), there is a very clear sense in which BARTISM is still providing me with reasons for acting, even though I would then believe otherwise.

There are good reasons, then, for believing both that FALSE is false and that DEFECT is false. Neither does the truth (or acceptability) of utilitarianism require that most people not believe it, nor would it matter if it did.

5 Sophisticated consequentialism

Elsewhere[6] I have explored and defended a utilitarian approach to commitments to people and to moral principles that expands on a seminal paper of Peter Railton's. Railton's concern is with close personal commitments, for example to one's spouse, but the approach can be applied pretty straightforwardly to commitments of friendship, or even to commitments to moral principles. Railton (1988) argues that a good moral agent will have a 'standing commitment to leading an objectively consequentialist life... *Objective consequentialism* is the view that the criterion of the rightness of an act or course of action is whether it in fact would most promote the good of those acts available to the agent' (p. 114). You can espouse values which can affect decision-making in a non-consequentialist way, just so long as you are committed to removing those values which tend to produce bad results. This doesn't mean that you cannot be committed to non-consequentialist values, even though you would attempt to remove them if you discovered that they were reducing overall utility (or some broader conception of good). You should probably be committed to removing, say, racial prejudice from your value system, but could be committed to a moral aversion to chemical and biological warfare, even though on some occasions such an aversion could result in a decision which was wrong from an objective consequentialist point of view. You may also, of course, have commitments that don't have any kind of moral character, such as personal commitments to friends and loved ones. Railton calls this view 'sophisticated consequentialism'.

Consider an example involving a commitment to a friend. John receives a phone call from a friend, Ned, suggesting that they meet for dinner. Ned has encountered several setbacks recently and is somewhat depressed. He always enjoys John's company, and could really do with cheering up. John had been planning on doing something that would have produced more overall good than having dinner with Ned, but not by a huge amount. He had been planning on doing a turn as a standup comic at an open mike night. He is a moderately funny comedian, and would have provided a little more total pleasure for a group of random strangers than he will for Ned, if he has dinner with him. Suppose John opts to have dinner with Ned. According to the criterion of right action of a traditional maximizing utilitarian, he acts wrongly. He could be a sophisticated consequentialist who has both a standing commitment to leading an objectively consequentialist life, and a non-consequentialist commitment to his friends. If he had been able on this occasion to perform the objectively right action, he would have been less committed to his friends. If he had been less committed to his friends, perhaps he would have done less good in the long run.

In my example, it is not clear whether John's commitment to Ned overrides his commitment to act for the best on this occasion, or whether he simply doesn't employ consequentialist considerations, or moral considerations at all. Railton's account of sophisticated consequentialism allows for both possibilities. Consider the following passage:

> ... individuals may be more likely to act rightly if they possess certain enduring motivational patterns, character traits, or prima-facie commitments to rules in addition to whatever commitment they have to act for the best. Because such individuals would not consider consequences in all cases, they would miss a number of opportunities to maximize the good. (Ibid., p. 120)

Railton is suggesting that a good sophisticated consequentialist will sometimes act directly on the promptings of certain commitments or character traits, without consulting consequentialism. This makes room for spontaneous or affectionate behavior. But Railton is not solely concerned with motivations that are either non-moral or not opposed to moral motivations. He is not just arguing for the place of 'moral holidays' in the life of a good consequentialist agent:

> Surely part of the attraction of these indirect consequentialisms is the idea that one should have certain traits of character, or commitments to persons and principles, that are sturdy enough that one would at least sometimes refuse to forsake them even when this refusal is known to conflict with making some gain – perhaps small – in total utility. (Ibid., pp. 118 and 120)

To return to the example of John, it is consistent with the description of John as a sophisticated consequentialist that he knows that he could do more good by ignoring his commitment of friendship to Ned. Perhaps he knows this, but doesn't consciously entertain the belief. A consequentialist can, in any case, allow for the possibility of conscious conflict between commitments, or other motivations that are justified on consequentialist grounds, and the belief that the right action is the action that produces the best results. Let me illustrate this with another story of John and Ned:

John and Ned are on vacation together in an exotic location, say Alabama. While at a bar in Tuscaloosa, John and Ned get to discussing military history, in particular the relative skills of various civil war generals. The discussion, though friendly, becomes a trifle heated, and loud, when it turns to a comparison of Sherman and Lee. John is of the opinion that Lee was a better tactician than Sherman. Ned vigorously disagrees. Both raise their voices to the point where other people in the bar can hear what they are saying. Shortly thereafter the police arrive and arrest Ned. It turns out that there is a local ordinance in Tuscaloosa banning the public praising of Sherman (or Grant). The violation is deemed to be particularly egregious when the praise comes in the form of a comparison with Lee in which Lee comes off worse. The penalty for Ned, apparently, is a week in jail, during which time he will be subjected to the constant strains of Lynyrd Skynyrd, ZZ Top, Hank Williams, and Ted Nugent on the sound system, and a diet of grits and chitlins. He can avoid this fate, if he, or a friend, pays a $200 fine, in cash (Tuscaloosa doesn't trust credit cards or checks, especially not from out-of-towners). Neither Ned nor John has any cash with him, so Ned is hauled off to the pokey, begging John as he goes to bring the cash to release him. John feels bad for his friend, and partly responsible for his plight. If John hadn't begun the discussion of the relative merits of Sherman and Lee, Ned would not have inadvertently violated the ordinance. So, John sets off to find an ATM.

On his way to the ATM, John meets a pastor (fill in your favorite religious denomination) with a distressed expression. He runs the local orphanage, he explains (the state of Alabama has long since ceased to support unwanted children, once they leave the confines of their mothers' bodies). The shipment of food for the next week's meals has arrived, but half the food is spoiled. They have no money to replace the spoiled food, so the orphans will be especially hungry this week, unless some kind stranger could donate the requisite money, which totals \$200. John would like to help, but he has only \$200 in his account and no provision for an overdraft. So, if he gives the \$200 to the pastor for the orphans, Ned will have to endure the privations of the Tuscaloosa jail for seven days.

Suppose that John chooses to help Ned. I think there is little doubt that we would not blame him for failing to give the money to the pastor. Indeed it would probably be psychologically extremely difficult for him to turn his back on his friend in this way. However, it also seems clear that giving the money to the pastor would produce more net utility (if it's not clear to you, simply increase the number of hungry orphans until it is). We may well feel that there would be something wrong with John if he could leave Ned to his fate without any soul searching. We think that, as a matter of psychological fact, it would be difficult for someone with a morally appropriate commitment to his friends to override it in such circumstances, but it would nonetheless be right for them to do so. We may even go further and think that, if John is able to turn his back on Ned in this situation, even with substantial regret, he can't be a true friend. So, if John stands by Ned in this case, we might both judge that he has acted wrongly, and judge that this reflects well on his overall character. Just how difficult it is for John to fail Ned may, and indeed should, vary according to the value of the alternatives. If, for example, the food for the orphans would make the difference between life and death for them, it should not be overly difficult for John to leave Ned in jail. In fact, if John clung to his commitment to Ned in the face of the certain death of many orphans (or even one), this commitment would be morally perverse. Nonetheless, even in such a case, regret at failing Ned in this instance would be appropriate. If John overrode his commitment to Ned without any regret or remorse, we would take that as a sign of a defective character, even though we realized that he had done the objectively right thing. The fact that John himself realizes that he has done the right thing does not diminish the appropriateness of regret or remorse on his part.

John can have a standing commitment to leading an objectively consequentialist life and have a moral commitment to his friends, even though the objectively right thing to do may, on occasion, involve abandoning his friends. John may even, in a calm hour, reflect on his commitment to his friends and realize that there may be situations in which this will make it difficult, or even impossible, for him to do the right thing. Yet he may judge that the costs of trying to change his attitude to friendship and to his friends will outweigh the benefits.

6 What about self-deception?

Does the sophisticated consequentialist find herself engaging in self-deception? What are we to say of the version of the example in which John refuses to abandon Ned, because of his commitment to friendship, even though he is aware that he will do more good by helping the orphans? If his choice to help Ned is motivated by a moral commitment to friendship, must he not believe that he is doing the morally right thing? But in that case, how can he at the same time believe that the morally right thing is what does most good, and that helping the orphans on this occasion would do most good? Must he not deceive himself into believing that helping his friend on this occasion is the morally right thing to do?

One possible reply to this charge of self-deception is to claim that John doesn't even consider the consequences of abandoning Ned. What it is to have a commitment to a friend is, at least in part, to be disposed to choose a course of action that doesn't involve abandoning that friend, without considering the consequences of this. The sort of person who has a commitment to a friend is the sort of person for whom the question of the consequences of such behavior doesn't arise.

This reply may be acceptable for a number of cases, and perhaps for more serious moral commitments, such as the commitment to not killing innocent people, but I think it is clear that it won't do as a general answer to the charge of self-deception. It is particularly implausible for the commitment to one's friends, as the second version of John's choice, involving death, as opposed to mere hunger, for the orphans demonstrates. It is obvious that a commitment to one's friends that never involved considering the consequences of breaking such a commitment would not be part of a good consequentialist character. Perhaps a good friend does not *usually* consider the consequences of acting against friendship, but there must be possible occasions that would trigger such conscious consideration. The reply also won't apply to all applications of a more serious moral commitment. Suppose that John refuses to kill an innocent person on an occasion when he could do more good by doing so. Even if he doesn't consider the consequences of killing the innocent person at the time of making his decision, he may well reflect on his choice later. He may realize that he did the wrong thing. It is reasonable to suppose that he will at least consider the consequences if another choice involving killing an innocent person should arise. More important, though, is the possibility of conflicting commitments. An admirable moral agent may have a commitment to her friends, to not killing innocent people, to saving the lives of innocent people, to increasing the level of welfare of suffering people, to keeping her promises, and so on. Given the variety of different commitments that one may possess, and the obvious possibilities for conflicts between them, it is hardly plausible to maintain that having a commitment to φ-ing involves being disposed not to consider the consequences of not φ-ing. Some commitments may be stronger than others. An admirable moral agent will be more likely to consider the consequences of abandoning a friend than to consider the consequences of killing an innocent person. To adapt an example of Elizabeth Anscombe's, a judge may be so strongly committed to not procuring the judicial execution of innocent people that she never actually considers the consequences of doing this in any particular case (Anscombe, 1958). Some people may have some commitments which never lead to a conscious conflict with the commitment to produce the best results, but it seems likely that most of the commitments which a consequentialist would endorse may sometimes lead to such a conscious conflict.

Despite the possibility that John's commitment to his friends will lead him to do something that he knows does not have the best results of all his available alternatives, I do not think that the charge of self-deception is justified. Consider John's commitment. Does this include the belief that abandoning a friend is always wrong, or even the belief that it is usually wrong? It is not clear that John's commitment needs to include any beliefs about what is right or wrong. It may include the belief that abandoning friends is bad, either in itself or because of its consequences, but it is not even clear that this is needed. John may have many moral beliefs about friendship, but these need not be part of his commitment to his friends.

John has a deep commitment to friends. If he fails a friend, he feels bad. Forming and maintaining friendships is one of the many projects around which he builds his life. John also has a deep desire to watch *The Simpsons*. If he misses out on an opportunity to watch an episode of *The Simpsons*, he feels bad. Watching *The Simpsons* is one of the many projects around which he builds his life. John's commitment to watching *The Simpsons* is not a moral commitment. Is his commitment to his friends and to the value of friendship a moral commitment? Part of the answer to this lies in the etiology of the commitment. John was probably taught that it was morally wrong to abandon one's friends. More importantly, perhaps John universalizes this commitment and tries to get other people to share it. If he hears of someone who abandons his friend, he feels moral disapproval. John's disapproval is not just of John abandoning his friends, but of anybody doing that. On the other hand, John can have a deep commitment to watching *The Simpsons* but not care in the least whether anybody else watches them. He may not even be inclined to spread his passion for what is undoubtedly one of the two finest products of western civilization.

It is clear that a sophisticated consequentialist needn't engage in self-deception, even when she knowingly follows a commitment at the expense of producing the best outcome. One might also ask what would be so bad about self-deception anyway. I suspect that the answer is 'not much', but I don't have space to go into that here. Nevertheless, isn't there something strange about the state of mind of someone who acknowledges that she is morally required, on consequentialist grounds, to do x, but admits that she is not going to do x? At least, isn't it strange to describe such a person as having a standing commitment to leading an objectively consequentialist life? However, such a commitment involves the disposition to attempt to change character traits that are overall harmful, not those that merely prevent one from maximizing utility on some occasions. At the very least, though, there seems to be a tension between the belief that x is morally required and a commitment to doing something other than x (such as standing by a friend). The tension may be diminished somewhat by rejecting the maximizing requirement in consequentialism. If John does not, in some cases, fail his friends, he has not done the morally best thing, but he hasn't failed a moral requirement. Such a scalar approach to morality, which has ample independent motivation,[7] can be combined with the approach of this chapter to give a more satisfying account of the utilitarian approach to personal commitments to people and to moral rules, than the maximizing sophisticated consequentialist approach. We should not, however, expect a moral theory to remove *all* the tension between our moral beliefs and commitments. Such tension is a fact of the moral life, not a problem for an account of morality. It is part of the richness of our moral lives that an admirable character involves commitments that conflict. A good life, even the best life, may involve often doing what is less than best.

Notes

1. I will speak interchangeably in this chapter of consequentialism and of utilitarianism, as it is the form of consequentialism I espouse. Nothing turns on the distinction for the purposes of my arguments.
2. Although Hooker calls his theory 'Rule-Consequentialism', rather than 'Rule-Utilitarianism', the differences aren't relevant to the present discussion.
3. For more on this, see Norcross (1997a).
4. See what I just did? You were expecting Lisa to be the good one, weren't you?
5. Although I talk of the 'truth' of a moral theory, the example could be recast to apply to moral anti-realist approaches.
6. Norcross (1997a).
7. See, for example, Norcross (2006a, 2006b, and 1997b).

References

G. E. M. Anscombe (1958) 'Modern Moral Philosophy', *Philosophy* 33 (124), January.

B. Hooker (2000) *Ideal Code, Real World. A Rule-Consequentialist Theory of Morality* (Oxford: Oxford University Press).

A. Norcross (1997a) 'Consequentialism and Commitment', *Pacific Philosophical Quarterly* 78, 380–403.

—— (1997b) 'Good and Bad Actions', *The Philosophical Review*, 106, 1–34.

—— (2006a) 'Reasons without Demands: Rethinking Rightness', in James Dreier (ed.), *Blackwell Contemporary Debates in Moral Theory* (Malden and Oxford: Blackwell), 38–54.

—— (2006b) 'Scalar Act-Utilitarianism', in Henry R. West (ed.), *Blackwell Guide to Mill's* Utilitarianism (Malden and Oxford: Blackwell), 217–34.

P. Railton (1988) 'Alienation, Consequentialism, and the Demands of Morality', *Philosophy and Public Affairs* 13 (2) (Spring 1984), reprinted in Samuel Scheffler (ed.), *Consequentialism and Its Critics* (Oxford: Oxford University Press, 1988), 93–133.

H.Sidgwick (1981) *The Methods of Ethics*, 7th edn (Indianapolis: Hackett).

M. Stocker (1990) *Plural and Conflicting Values* (Oxford: Oxford University Press).

B. Williams (1973) 'A Critique of Utilitarianism', in J. J. C. Smart and B. Williams (eds), *Utilitarianism: For & Against* (Cambridge: Cambridge University Press).

—— (1981) 'Persons, Character, and Morality', in his *Moral Luck: Philosophical Papers 1973–1980* (Cambridge: Cambridge University Press), 1–19.

10

Can a Christian Be a Friend? God, Friendship and Love of Neighbor

John Lippitt

> God is friendship.
>
> Aelred of Rievaulx

> [T]he praise of erotic love and friendship belongs to paganism ... Christianity has misgivings about erotic love and friendship simply because preferential love ... is actually another form of self-love.
>
> Søren Kierkegaard

Christian thought and friendship have had a sometimes stormy relationship. In the first part of this essay, I shall draw on St Augustine, Kierkegaard and C. S. Lewis to outline some key reasons for suspicion of friendship within the Christian tradition. I shall briefly discuss Kierkegaard's distinction between love of the neighbor and 'preferential' loves such as friendship, his worry that friendship is exclusionary and often a form of disguised self-love, and the related claim that the category of the neighbor is required in order to recognize genuine alterity. We shall see that Kierkegaard's concern about friendship's exclusionary nature is echoed in Lewis's remarks about the 'pride' of friendship. Moreover, his worry about friendship as disguised self-love is itself an echo of some of Augustine's comments in the *Confessions*. But while Kierkegaard is not the unequivocal enemy of friendship that he has often been portrayed as being (see, most famously, Adorno [1940]), neither is he as close a friend of it as he might have been. His insufficiently critical inheritance of the classical view of the friend as a 'second self' leads to a failure to see the true potential of friendship within the Christian life. In the second part of the essay, to illuminate this claim, I shall first discuss friendship's inspiration for, and potential as a bridge towards, love of neighbor. This enables us to understand the importance of mutuality within friendship in a more positive light than Kierkegaard seems to. Finally, I move on to consider how friendship might be informed and enhanced by *agapic* neighbor-love.

1 Some Christian anxieties about friendship

In *Works of Love,* Kierkegaard makes much of a distinction between love of the neighbor and what he calls 'preferential' love, such as 'erotic' or romantic love [*Elskov*] and friendship. Though he describes erotic love as 'undeniably life's most beautiful happiness' and friendship as 'the greatest temporal good' (Kierkegaard 1995, p. 267/SKS 9 266),[1] he is troubled by the hidden threats to love of God and neighbor that such 'natural' loves harbor, and that eulogies to such loves from 'the poet' overlook. (Kierkegaard considers erotic love and friendship to be 'natural' in the sense that human beings naturally incline towards such loves, whereas neighbor-love needs to be commanded 'You *shall* love your neighbour as yourself' [Matthew 22:39; Mark 12:31; Luke 10:27–28]), and such a command 'did not arise in any human being's heart' (Kierkegaard [1995, p. 24/SKS 9 32]. He regularly contrasts Christianity's view of love with that found in 'the poet' – the spokesman for preferential love.) Consider for instance the following passage:

> Just as self-love selfishly embraces this one and only *self* that makes it self-love, so also erotic love's passionate preference selfishly encircles this one and only beloved, and friendship's passionate preference encircles this one and only friend. For this reason the beloved and the friend are called, remarkably and profoundly, to be sure, the *other self,* the *other I* – since the neighbor is the *other you,* or quite precisely, the *third party* of equality. The *other self,* the *other I.* But where does self-love reside? It resides in the *I,* in the *self.* Would not self-love then also start loving the *other I,* the *other self*? One really does not need to be any great judge of human nature in order with the help of this clue to make discoveries about erotic love and friendship that are alarming to others and humiliating to oneself. The fire that is in self-love is spontaneous combustion; the *I* ignites itself by itself. But in erotic love and friendship, in the poetic sense, there is also spontaneous combustion. (Ibid., pp. 53–4/SKS 9 60)

A central claim here, with respect to friendship, is that love of the friend is exclusionary – unlike love of the neighbor, which recognizes the 'common watermark' of our humanity (ibid., p. 89/SKS 9 94). Moreover, Kierkegaard claims that I see in my friend some reflection of myself (compare the image of the friend as 'second self' in Aristotle, Cicero and others), such that love for my friend is a kind of disguised self-love. The reference to the neighbor as the 'first you' hints at the need to relate to the other as a genuine other, not just as some sort of reflection of myself (cf. Ferreira 2001, pp. 8 and 52). Only the neighbor is 'what thinkers call "the other", that by which the selfishness in self-love is to be tested' (Kierkegaard 1995, p. 21/SKS 9 29). The 'selfish' variety of self-love involves seeing the other simply as some kind of extension of myself, failing to respect their genuine alterity.

A related theme emerges in C. S. Lewis's discussion of friendship in *The Four Loves*. At one point Lewis (1960) wonders whether friendship, insofar as it is 'almost wholly free from jealousy', might be 'a natural love which is Love itself' (p. 77). But he ultimately answers this question in the negative. Amongst his worries is the *cliquishness* of friendship. The shared enthusiasm Lewis sees as central to friendship ('What! You too? I thought that no one but myself...') easily degenerates into a *coterie* or 'mutual admiration society', such that misguided, uncharitable or downright perverse enthusiasms are protected against criticism from those outside the group (ibid., pp. 78–80). Relatedly, he notes that 'we all know the perilous charm of a shared hatred or grievance', and in a terribly 'Oxbridge' reference, notes ironically: 'It is difficult not to hail as a Friend the only other man in College who really sees the faults of the Sub-Warden' (ibid., p. 79). Insofar as friendship involves shared enthusiasms,[2] for Lewis, there is something necessary about deafness to outside opinions. (Why should those who share an enthusiasm for, say, medieval theology trouble themselves greatly about the views of those who find its debates of no interest?) But what worries Lewis is when this 'partial indifference or deafness to outside opinion' leads to 'wholesale indifference or deafness' and thus 'corporate pride' (ibid., pp. 81 and 83). The 'pride' of friendship can be manifested in highbrow or vulgar ways, but in one way or another, it is about exclusion: 'Everyone who is not in the circle must be shown that he is not in it' (ibid., p. 85).

The overall point is this. The 'pride of friendship' is 'almost inseparable from Friendly love' (ibid., p. 86). Both Kierkegaard and Lewis see that friendship must exclude, insofar as it is preferential. Yet what Lewis shows, perhaps more clearly than does Kierkegaard, is the way in which the slope is slippery: 'From the innocent and necessary act of excluding to the spirit of exclusiveness is an easy step; and thence to the degrading pleasure of exclusiveness' (ibid.). At the bottom of this slope, '[t]he common vision which first brought us together may fade quite away. We shall be a coterie that exists for the sake of being a coterie; a little self-elected (and therefore absurd) aristocracy, basking in the moonshine of our collective self-approval' (ibid.)[3]

On the back of such worries, Lewis speculates that this is perhaps why scripture rarely presents the relationship between God and man as one of friendship, preferring images of *storge* (the representation of God as father) and *eros* (Christ as the bridegroom of the church) (ibid., pp. 78, 87–8).[4]

In these remarks, and in Kierkegaard's focus on friendship as disguised selfishness, there is more than an echo of St Augustine. In book 4 of the *Confessions,* Augustine reflects on the devastation of his younger self at the loss of an unnamed friend. He found himself unable to enjoy any of their previous shared activities and haunts: 'Everything that was not what my friend had been was dull and distasteful' (Augustine 1961, IV.7). The older Augustine reflects ruefully on his earlier foolishness thus: 'What madness, to love a man as something more than human!' (ibid.) He compares his grief to having poured out his soul 'like water upon sand, loving a man who was mortal as though he were never to die' (ibid., IV.8). Moreover, Augustine anticipates Lewis's worry about how one might be prevented from seeing the limitations of one's world-view by likeminded friends: 'My greatest comfort and relief was in the solace of other friends who shared my love of the huge fable which I loved instead of you, my God' (ibid.).

Note here that Augustine does not deny that the goods of friendship are genuine goods. But the illusion in which he had lived had at least three aspects. First, his misery is explained by the fact that he lived as one 'whose soul is tethered by the love of things that cannot last and then is agonized to lose them' (ibid., IV.6). Second, as his address to God demonstrates, this amounts to loving the creature more than the Creator. (Hence his remark that 'though they cling together, no friends are true friends unless you, my God, bind them fast to one another through that love which is sown in our hearts by the Holy Ghost' [ibid., IV.4].) But third, there is the point of which Kierkegaard's concerns might be seen as an echo: contrary to what he believed at the time, Augustine now claims that the creature he had loved most was not the lost friend, but *himself*: 'my own wretched life was dearer to me than the friend I had lost' (ibid., IV.6).[5] In other words, what presents itself as love of the friend may actually be disguised selfishness or improper love of self.

2 Resurrecting friendship

2.1 Friendship and mutuality – a problem?

A significant part of what troubles Kierkegaard about friendship and other forms of preferential love is their dependence upon mutuality or reciprocity. In a notorious passage of *Works of Love,* he claims:

> The merely human view of love can never go beyond mutuality: the lover is the beloved, and the beloved is the lover. Christianity teaches that such a love has not yet found its true object – God. The love-relationship requires threeness: the lover, the beloved, the love – but the love is God. Therefore, to love another person is to help that person to love God, and to be loved is to be helped. (Kierkegaard 1995, pp. 120–1/SKS 9 124)

Unsurprisingly, this has been controversial. Kierkegaard makes it sound as if human beings are of only instrumental value. God 'becomes the sole object of love, so that it is not the husband who is the wife's beloved, but it is God, and it is the wife who is helped by the husband to love God, and conversely, and so on' (ibid., p. 121/SKS 9 124). Unlike 'merely human' love, which can 'never go beyond mutuality' Christianity teaches that the true object of love is God. So to love another person – either *qua* friend or romantic beloved – 'is to help that person to love God, and to be loved is to be helped [to love God]' (ibid., p. 121/SKS 9 124). Hence the charge of some commentators, such as Peter George (1998), that Kierkegaard articulates an entirely solipsistic, inward-looking ethic which misses the point about what constitutes genuinely social human interactions. Should we be as dismissive of mutuality as Kierkegaard seems to be here?

Elsewhere I have argued that there is insufficient warrant for Kierkegaard's judgment that *because* I see in the friend some reflection of myself, friendship is disguised (improper) self-love.[6] This charge perhaps stems from an insufficiently critical inheritance, both within Kierkegaard and the wider Christian tradition, of the classical view of the friend as a 'second self'.[7] Yet I have also explored the significance for 'preferential' love of the idea that the friend or beloved should be first and foremost the neighbor, arguing that Kierkegaard's view of such loves is not as dismissive as such passages might make it appear.[8] Here I want to explore some background to Kierkegaard's approach amongst his precursors within the Christian tradition, both to get a sense of where such apparently dismissive ideas might have come from and to suggest how one might speak up for friendship from within that tradition.

At first blush, Kierkegaard's position above sounds like Augustine's relatively early distinction between use (*usus*) and enjoyment (*fruitio*). In his earliest Christian works, Augustine argues that only God is the proper object of 'enjoyment' (that is, only God is to be sought for his own sake). All others are to be sought for the sake of someone else: God. Moreover, only that which can genuinely be 'enjoyed' can bring about our happiness (this quest for happiness being that which motivates all human action). To 'enjoy' God, then, is to love God for his own sake: other things are to be 'used' in order to reach that which we can love for its own sake. The world is thus the means by which we reach God, and thus attain our happiness. The implication here seems to be as in Kierkegaard: our selves, friends, beloveds and neighbors are ultimately to be loved only for the sake of God. Does this not diminish the value of both friendship and love of the neighbor in a problematic way?

Commentators have noted that a subtle shift took place in Augustine's thought in writing his major work *On Christian Doctrine*. The language of 'use' and 'enjoyment' came to be replaced by talk of the love commandments in terms of 'Love of a thing which can be enjoyed [God] and of something which can enjoy that thing with us [the neighbor]' (White 1992, p. 200). In other words, a subtle shift from a view in which love of God is stressed at the *expense* of love of man – such that love of God and man are in tension – to a view in which, within a theological framework, love of man came to be valued more fundamentally than before.

Nevertheless, love of God remains indisputably primary. As in the Kierkegaard passage cited earlier, loving my neighbor as myself involves for Augustine wishing, helping and inspiring him to love God above all else. Compare here also Augustine's letter to the widow Proba in which he says that loving our neighbors as ourselves involves 'as far as we are able ... lead[ing] them to a similar love of God. And so we love God for his own sake and ourselves and our neighbours for His sake' (Augustine, Epistle 130.7.14; cited in White 1992, p. 201). So can we really love our friends for their own sake? Apparently not. Rather, what we love is God in our friends and our friends in God.[9] Augustine's anxiety in all this seems to be to avoid the position discussed above in the *Confessions*, of falling into the trap of loving creatures more than the Creator. So does love of God above all else mean that we are debarred from loving our friends as individuals?

Many within the Christian tradition have aimed to show how loving God thus is compatible with loving our friends as individuals, for their own sakes. Robert M. Adams makes a case I find compelling, and moreover one that trades on the above idea of loving God in our friends and our friends in God. Adams (1993) argues that unless we love someone for their own sake, we cannot genuinely be said to *love* (as opposed to *value*) them (p. 112). Yet he also argues that Augustine's anxiety above is ill-founded, as such genuine love for creatures can be a reflection of trusting love for God. The argument rests on an analogy between our relationship to God and that of small children's relationships to their mothers. Compare two children, one who is 'clingy', always keeping his mother in sight, and pestering her for attention, and another who is relatively secure in his independence. Adams suggests that, other things being equal, it is the latter kind of child who is likely to have the healthier relationship to his mother: 'The more independent children are apt to be those that feel more secure in their mothers' love and care, and they are therefore able to turn their attention with less anxiety to other things. This sense of security is, in part, a manifestation of their love for their mothers' (ibid., p. 122). The point here is that 'the strength of a loving personal relationship can be reflected in attention to things other than the loved person' (ibid.). The same applies in the adult world: security in a love-relationship can free us to take an interest in things outside that relationship; interest that would not be possible if all one's energies were focused on anxieties about this relationship.

So how does this apply to the relation between love for God and love for creatures?

> If one both loves God and trusts in God's love, this will issue in an inner peace or sense of security. And this ... will free one to take a lively interest in God's creatures for their own sake – to enjoy his gifts with un-self-conscious gratitude and to love one's neighbor. (Ibid., p. 123)

The recognition of there being something *intrinsically valuable, qua* creatures, about natural human loves edges us back towards seeing something of value in that mutuality which seems central to friendship. And perhaps, despite himself, we can already find a version of this thought – the intrinsic value of friendship-love – in Augustine. We can tackle this by considering the following question. If we are to love everyone, including our enemies,[10] what room does this leave for the particular love of friends? White argues that there is such a role, for Augustine, since love of neighbor in virtue of our common humanity is not the 'complete fulfilment of the Christian duty to love' (White 1992, p. 202): particular, 'special' loves have an important role too. Thus Augustine tried to secure for friendship an important place within the 'range' of love of neighbor (ibid., p. 203). The ideal is that each should love all others 'in God'. But this is impossible in this life. In a letter to Proba, Augustine seems to use the term *amicitia* to describe unrestricted love of neighbor:

> Friendship must not be restricted within narrow limits. It should embrace all people to whom love and affection are owed, although it will be stronger towards some, less so to others and it should extend as far as our enemies for whom we are commanded to pray. And so there is no one to whom we do not owe affection on account of the fellowship of our shared nature, even if our love is not mutual. But it is right that we should particularly love those who love us in return with a holy and chaste love. (Augustine, Epistle 130.13, cited in White 1992, pp. 203–4)

This passage makes some interesting claims. First, as well as recognizing the importance of a love of particular others, it seems at least to imply that friendship is also in a sense *the inspiration for love of neighbor.* The model seems to be that one aims to extend *amicitia* as far as one's finite, sinful and thus imperfect nature allows. White puts it like this: 'All that can be hoped for now [i.e. in the present life] is that a Christian should love a few men reciprocally, in an intense friendship founded on love of God, and extend his love as far as possible to others, including enemies, non-Christians, etc.' (White 1992, p. 203; cf. O'Donovan, 2006/1980, pp. 122–3).

Second, the second sentence in particular seems to hint at an idea later developed by John Henry Newman, amongst others, namely that the particular love of friendship has the potential to act as a bridge towards love of neighbor. Newman (1868) implies that it is in the arena of 'preferential' loves such as friendship that the virtues (such as patience and hope) needed for charitable love of neighbor are forged:

> by trying to love our relations and friends, by submitting to their wishes though contrary to our own, by bearing with their infirmities, by overcoming their occasional waywardness with kindness, by dwelling on their excellences and trying to copy them, thus it is that we form in our hearts that root of charity which, though, small at first, may, like the mustard seed, at last even over-shadow the earth. (p. 55)

It is easier, more 'natural', to love one's friend than any old neighbor – and certainly than the neighbor who is an enemy. But just as the second love commandment ('You shall love your neighbor as yourself') implies that we can work outwards from our natural love of ourselves to love of others, so Newman here echoes Augustine in his suggestion that we can work outwards from our natural love of our friends to love of our neighbors.[11] Compare also Lewis (1960), who claims that friendship is not 'a reward for our discrimination and good taste in finding one another out', but rather 'the instrument by which God reveals to each the beauties of all the others. They are no greater than the beauties of a thousand other men; by Friendship God opens our eyes to them' (pp. 89–90). At least one dimension of Newman's point is supported by some recent empirical evidence to the effect that it is through their friendships that small children first become genuinely concerned about the 'otherness' of another person.[12]

But here is an important point: love of friends has mutuality or reciprocity at its core. So perhaps the Christian tradition can understand mutuality within friendship in a more positive light than Kierkegaard seemed to above. According to O'Donovan (2006/1980), there are at least two senses in which love is reciprocal, for Augustine: he is committed to both a strong and a weak thesis on the reciprocity of love. The strong thesis is that neighbor-love depends upon a consciousness of being loved: 'no man can discover what it is to love unless he first experiences what it is to be loved' (O'Donovan 2006/1980, p. 126), and we can discover this through our friendships. The weaker thesis is that neighbor-love includes a desire to be loved in return, even when this desire is hopeless. O'Donovan suggests that for Augustine *the target of such love is friendship*, and that he has 'no knowledge' of a love 'which has no interest at all in establishing friendship' (ibid., p. 127). But this is not just a necessary evil stemming from human weakness:

> Augustine's belief that the ideal love is mutual, thereby conforming to the ideal friendship as described by ancient writers, is in fact based on the idea that it is the Holy Spirit, sent by God, which inspires true love in man and which forms the bond between men *as it does between the Father and Son within the Trinity*. (White 1992, p. 204, my emphasis)

In other words, in describing the internal dynamics of the Trinity, Augustine is willing to talk of friendship. For instance, he describes the Trinity's essential characteristics as unity, likeness and equality

(Augustine 1948, 7.6.12). White notes that these were traditionally regarded as characteristic of ideal friendship. But there is more than this. Being aware of the unity of the Trinity can inspire intimate human relationships, 'for by imitating the Trinity and clinging to God we are granted unity with one another and with God in the Holy Spirit' (White 1992, pp. 210–11). Thus Augustine combines scriptural insights with key elements of a classical view of friendship in such a way that the former clarifies the theocentric worldview inspired by the latter. Relatedly, a number of recent commentators, such as Darlene Fozard Weaver (2002), note that contemporary Catholic accounts of love 'still tend to construe love as mutuality', valorize it as such, 'and often draw upon Trinitarian accounts of God [i.e. that God is persons in relation]' in doing so (p. 6).[13]

That said, for Augustine, only in heaven can human relationships be perfect. Here his famous distinction between the city of man and the city of God becomes important. The latter involves 'a perfectly ordered and perfectly harmonious fellowship in the enjoyment of God and a mutual fellowship in God' (Augustine 1963, 19.13). The target at which the classical ideal of friendship aims is achievable only in this context. Nevertheless, Augustine uses language that recalls such accounts of friendship in the way he describes the heavenly community (White 1992, p. 205). So Augustine's disappointment in human friendships, referred to earlier, is importantly qualified by his eschatology. The friendships of this life, imperfect and prone to disappointment as they might be, are 'a foreshadowing of the true unity and intimacy to come' (ibid., p. 206). The significant point is that Augustine continues to use the language of friendship in this eschatological context.

The tradition of so doing is enhanced by a figure on whom Augustine, and especially the *Confessions*, was an enormous influence: Aelred of Rievaulx. Aelred's *Spiritual Friendship* is a conscious rewriting of Cicero's *De Amicitia* for a Christian audience.[14] Yet Aelred's praise of friendship is more liberal than Augustine's and certainly more generous than Kierkegaard's. Like Augustine, he claims that for all the limitations of this world, friendship, at its best, is a form of love which comes closest to the love of saints in heaven.[15] Yet he also adds that friendship, while natural in origin, is divinely sanctioned: 'nature itself impressed upon the human soul a desire for friendship, then experience increased that desire, and finally the sanction of the law confirmed it' (Aelred 1977, 1: 51). Moreover, it is for Aelred 'the practical expression of love between humans as it ought to be' (Roby 1977, p. 24).

In summary, then, we can find in the Christian tradition more effusive praise for friendship than the remarks from Kierkegaard, Lewis and Augustine in Section 1 might suggest. Friendship has been presented as being the relationship that inspires, and builds a bridge towards, love of neighbor. And Christians can see the mutuality of friendship – the source of one of Kierkegaard's major worries about it – in a different light if they note its importance in the dynamics of the Trinity.

Yet my task here is not only to salvage friendship from some criticisms within the Christian tradition. I also want to ask in what ways a focus on *agapic* love of neighbor might positively inform our understanding of friendship, taking us beyond the classical ideal that has been so dominant in the philosophy of friendship.

2.2 How can love of the neighbor inform friendship?

One preliminary point worth mentioning here is that if we take seriously the idea that everyone is my neighbor then this immediately includes a group who receive rather short shrift in much writing on the philosophy of friendship: women. Richard White (2001) is amongst those to note the centrality of traditionally 'male' qualities like autonomy, self-mastery and self-reliance in most classical accounts of friendship (pp. 15–16), and the male assumptions that lie behind accounts of friendship found in both Aristotle and Cicero.[16] (We shall return to the significance of this point in our discussion of White below.) Nor is this restricted to the classical world. Sandra Lynch notes Montaigne's dismissal of women's capacity for 'sovereign' friendship ('the ordinary capacity of women is inadequate for that communion and fellowship which is the nurse of this sacred bond; nor does their soul seem firm enough to endure the strain of so tight and durable a knot' [Montaigne 1965, p. 138]), and the wider tendency to dismiss or ignore female friendship (Lynch 2005, pp. 75–6).

Second, love of neighbor aims to extend beyond our friends those elements of the ideal of friendship that we might, with a nod towards Hegel, call 'recognition'. It is a commonplace that such friendship involves caring about the friend's well-being, valued as an end in itself. Richard White (2001) aims to specify what this amounts to in terms of four features: equality, reciprocity, solidarity and alterity. Though this is not White's own intention, I suggest that his account enables us to see something of the way that *agapic* love of neighbor can positively inform friendship.[17]

White (2001) comments with approval on Aristotle's view that those far apart in virtue, age or education (and, we could add, wealth [Aristotle 1998, 1159b]) face particular difficulties in being friends. But love of neighbor insists on the equality of *all* human beings as creatures of God, as we saw Kierkegaard note in his focus on the 'common watermark' of our humanity. So even if it would typically be too much of a stretch to describe the relationship between prisoner and prison guard, billionaire and pauper, as one of friendship, *agapic* ethics insists that these differences do not detract from what each owes to each other, such that our common humanity overrides the differences between us. A friendship with *agape* at its heart thus provides some assurances about changes in various kinds of 'status' that Aristotle sees as a threat to friendship.

What of reciprocity? We have already noted Kierkegaard's deep suspicion about mutuality or reciprocity, which he (like Lewis) seems to treat in terms of either mutual admiration societies or as the kind of mutual back-scratching that threatens to overlook the participants' duties towards those neighbors outside the charmed circle. However, we drew above on Augustine to suggest the possibility of a more positive view within the Christian tradition. White notes the centrality of reciprocity to friendship, and we can draw on this further to emphasize its prospects in relation to love of neighbor. White (2001) claims: 'Some forms of love do not require reciprocity – romantic love or parental love, for instance – but for two people to be friends *they must both like each other and be open and available to each other*' (p. 27, my emphasis). Leaving aside this controversial claim about romantic love, how might the emphasized idea also apply to love of neighbor? While natural *liking* for the neighbor clearly cannot be stipulated as a requirement – precisely because we are commanded to love *qua* neighbors those we do *not* naturally like, even our 'enemies' – there is an obligation, in *agapic* ethics, to look beyond our natural loves for the best in those to whom we are not 'preferentially' attracted. The second requirement, to be 'open and available' to each other, applies in this sphere in a more straightforward sense. The parable of the Good Samaritan, for instance, of which Kierkegaard makes much, highlights the requirement to put ourselves out for those from whom we are ethnically, politically and religiously distinct, rather than restricting the scope of our obligations to our nearest and dearest. We can recognize this as reciprocal in at least Augustine's senses discussed above. Thus, while the way that both equality and reciprocity operate is different in love of neighbor from how it is in friendship *per se* – that all human beings are of equal value does not imply they should necessarily be treated identically (such that my love for a stranger does not have to be identical to my love for my friend) – a form of both is operational in both spheres.

White's third and fourth criteria of friendship, solidarity and alterity, exist in dialectical tension. By solidarity, he means 'a basic sharing of values and perspectives and a similar sense of what is important and what is worth doing' (White 2001, p. 27). For all the differences between individuals and cultures, we might think of the 'shared horizon of concern ... that relates people to each other to begin with' (ibid.) as being part of what Kierkegaard's talk of the 'common watermark' of humanity is an attempt to get at. So love of neighbor aims to extend something of the common ground Aristotle thought to unite all Athenian citizens beyond the boundaries of Athens to the whole of humanity. But the real pay-off of considering White's view comes in considering alterity – the recognition of the friend as separate to and different from ourselves – as essential to friendship, contrary to Kierkegaard's remarks in Section 1. White claims:

> Perhaps with other forms of love, and especially romantic love, the goal is some kind of merging with the other person in the bliss of mutual abandonment. But this is not the case with friendship, *in which the specific difference of the other person's individual history and thinking about the world remains absolutely important.* (Ibid., p. 28, my emphasis)

Pace Kierkegaard, this seems intuitively right about friendship.[18] Yet commentators have noted how the emphasis in classical and later philosophical accounts of friendship on likeness between friends (even when cashed out in terms of likeness *in virtue*) has tended to underplay the crucial importance of such alterity. (White [2001] makes this charge explicitly against Aristotle, but the charge can be made more broadly.[19]) Indeed, one reason Kierkegaard tends to lump erotic love and friendship together is precisely the prevalence in discussions of friendship to over-emphasize likeness and unity between friends to such an extent that one is often put in mind, by some of the eulogies to friendship, of romantic love.[20]

An attempt to address this has been made by Dean Cocking and Jeanette Kennett (1998) in their 'drawing' view of friendship, which focuses on the way in which it is characteristic of close friendship that we are responsive both to our friends' interests and worldview, and to their way of seeing us.[21] An important implication of this is that a friendship in which there are important *differences* between the friends has a value that a friendship of perfect unity, harmony and likeness would lack. When added to the tendency for alterity to be overlooked in accounts of friendship, this starts to show how a recognition of the 'otherness' that *agape* registers might add something important to a friendship that lacked it. How so? First, a preliminary. It is essential to Kierkegaard's account of neighbor-love in *Works of Love* that we love the actual 'people we see', and as noted his warnings against reducing the other to 'another me' are stark. Kierkegaard (1995) insists on the duty to love people 'as they are' (p. 166/SKS 9 167); 'to love precisely the person one sees' (ibid., p. 173/SKS 9 173). What is at stake here is as follows:

> *in loving the actual individual person it is important that one does not substitute an imaginary idea of how we think or could wish that this person should be.* The one who does this does not love the person he sees but again something unseen, his own idea or something similar. (Ibid., p. 164/SKS 9 164, emphasis in original)

Some of the most obvious manifestations of this are in romantic infatuation, but it is a problem that can haunt friendship too. Not only in Aristotelian utility-friendships, but also when we focus only on what we have in common with the friend. The worry is that in such cases what we are loving is what Jamie Ferreira (2001) calls 'the self-generated image of the other person', which is 'not the same as loving the actual other person at all' (p. 109). In other words, we fail to relate to the friend as a genuine other, overlooking the fact that they cannot legitimately be reduced to our preconceived idea of them. As we saw in Section 1, Kierkegaard argues that we need the category of the neighbor to prevent this from happening. However, he tends to speak out so forcefully against friendship that many have got the impression that the target of his criticism is friendship *per se*, rather than what I think is his real point, which is to be critical of friendship that does not have *agapic* neighbor-love at its heart. Another way of putting this point is to say that Kierkegaard thinks that neighbor-love is the best insurance policy against the genuine good of friendship becoming degraded into a kind of disguised narcissism or 'selfish' self-love.

So what, more precisely, does *agapic* love of neighbor bring to the table? We can link the drawing view of friendship to the Christian view of love, in that the latter offers a version of the former's insight on a perhaps deeper level. The Christian realizes his vulnerability and dependence. And yet, Christianity teaches, he is loved. In sheer gratitude for this, he loves others, following the command to love his neighbors as himself. This recognition challenges the classical view of friendship insofar as it ditches what White (2001) calls 'the underlying ideals of self-sufficiency and sovereign self-containment' predominant in such views (p. 32). For both Aristotle and Cicero, flourishing requires self-sufficiency, and so there is a serious question as to whether the flourishing person needs friends.[22] An even stronger insistence on self-sufficiency is found in Seneca. In response to Aristotle and Cicero's question, he insists that the wise man can do without friends, since the 'Supreme Good calls for no practical aids from outside; it is developed at home, and arises entirely within itself' (Seneca 1991a, p.122). Just as, if he lose a hand or eye 'he will be satisfied with what is left', so he 'endures the loss of a friend with equanimity',[23] and like the sculptor who can replace one lost statue with another, so a lost friend is similarly replaceable (ibid., p. 120). Friendship is desirable but not necessary. The wise man desires friends 'if only for the purpose of practicing friendship, in order that his noble qualities may not lie dormant' (ibid.). Our attachment to friends is based not on need but on excess: I make friends in order 'to have someone for whom I may die, whom I may follow into exile, against whose death I may stake my own life' (ibid., p. 121).

So we can see that both Kierkegaard and Seneca are troubled by 'selfish need' (Seneca 1991a, p. 123) in friendship. But aren't there genuine needs that can't be dismissed merely as 'selfish', and don't we underplay these at our peril? As we have seen in our discussion above, the Christian tradition in general shows a far greater willingness to admit our mutual vulnerability and interdependence. In this sense, I suggest that it fits better with contemporary views of friendship. White (2001) notes that the commitment to another person signified by friendship involves 'adopting a more tentative relationship to one's own ideas and commitments' than is emphasized in the classical tradition (p. 37). Friends typically help us to clarify or deepen our ideas and thoughts, but will also typically 'force us to rethink some things that we may have taken for granted' (ibid.). This is perhaps not an aspect of friendship Kierkegaard would deny, but neither is it something he emphasizes. Moreover, insofar as friendship is about mutual recognition, one's self 'is not developed in isolation but in our ongoing relationships with other people, especially with our friends who know us best. Thus the duties of friendship, such as availability, caring, and nurturing, are duties that we owe to someone else insofar as we are committed to that person' (ibid., p. 40). The contrast with Seneca could hardly be starker.

In summary, we have seen in this section that a focus on neighbor-love challenges some of the features of classical friendship (such as the ideal of self-sufficiency) but also that it preserves some of its key goods (such as caring about others for their own sake, as ends in themselves). Yet it does this while aiming to expand the scope of the application of such goods. Perhaps most important of all is the recognition of the friend's alterity. We noted that this has tended to be downplayed in classical accounts, but it is crucial insofar as in the best friendships, it is a deep ethical respect for the other's alterity that is infused in and expressed by the profound trust I give to my friend and receive in turn.[24] I suggest that this is a feature of friendship that is likely to be enhanced by the recognition that one's friend is, first and foremost, one's neighbor.

Notes

1. In quoting from Kierkegaard, as well as citing the English translation given in the References, I also give the equivalent page numbers of the new Danish edition, cited as SKS (*Søren Kierkegaards Skrifter* (1997–), Vols 1–28 and K1–28, edited by Niels Jørgen Cappelørn et al. (Copenhagen: Gads Forlag)). *Works of Love* is volume 9, hence 'SKS 9'.
2. Common to both classical and early Christian accounts of friendship is the idea of what David Konstan (1997) describes as 'loyalty within a community with a shared vision of life' (p. 52).
3. See also Lewis's (1965) further remarks on this in his oration 'The Inner Ring'.
4. Lewis perhaps exaggerates this point. For a valuable account of Christian love in which *philia* plays a far more central role, see Vacek (1994).
5. As Peter Brown (2000) puts it, the young Augustine 'was an imperialist in his friendships. To be a friend of Augustine's, meant only too often becoming a part of Augustine himself' (p. 52).
6. See Lippitt (2007) and (2013, chapter 2).
7. See for instance Augustine (1961), IV.6. On the prevalence of this theme in the Church Fathers, see White (1992), passim.
8. See Lippitt (2013), especially chapter 4.
9. Cf. Augustine (1961), IV.9.
10. This view that the neighbor is everyone, including our enemies, has become so standard in Christian thought – Kierkegaard, for instance, takes it pretty much for granted – that it is possible to overlook the fact that it was not always interpreted thus. Oliver O'Donovan (2006/1980) claims that this view is stated for the first time in St. Jerome, and subsequently became for Augustine 'a firm rule of interpretation' (p. 121).
11. Augustine treats this as part of our spiritual convalescence from original sin: see O'Donovan (2006/1980), p. 126.
12. See Layard and Dunn (2006, p. 36) and Dunn (2004).
13. Again, Vacek (1994) is a good example. This is also perhaps why, in his discussion of Kierkegaard and the Catholic tradition, Jack Mulder (2010) devotes a full chapter to the 'order of love' (chapter 3). Are the specific obligations we have to our families and friends such that we have an obligation to prioritize them over the neighbor who is a stranger? The Catholic tradition in particular has often claimed that our nearest and dearest have a greater claim on us than strangers. As we have seen, Kierkegaard is suspicious about

such 'preferential' loves, and though much valuable work has been done to defend Kierkegaard against his harshest critics on this point (see e.g. Ferreira [2001]), an uncomfortable suspicion remains that in such defenses, troubling elements of Kierkegaard's account are glossed over. What I find most interesting about Mulder's treatment of this topic is his claim that the real issue at stake is not preference but *nature* (p. 96); not between preferential and non-preferential loves so much as how deeply defective (or otherwise) is 'natural' love. Hence, in a brief discussion of Aristotle on friendship and self-love, Mulder argues that for Kierkegaard, given his Lutheran heritage, even an Aristotelian 'perfect' friendship would count as sinful and not 'real' love (pp. 74 and 85). This is the position, Mulder thinks, which needs Aquinas and the Thomist tradition as a corrective. Drawing on the idea that grace does not destroy nature but perfects it, Mulder sides with Aquinas in arguing that 'the natural affection we have for those who are closest to us by way of blood-relationships or other such ties is reasonable and is not nullified by Christian charity' (p. 81). Yet the two figures are not poles apart. Kierkegaard agrees with Aquinas that we ought to love God more than ourselves. Both seem to hold some version of the view that all love is rooted in love of God (p. 80). And both, Mulder argues, view love of neighbor as arising out of this love for God (p. 95). For my own part, I do think that Kierkegaard's worries about preferential loves and the more egregious aspects of taking charity to 'begin at home' sometimes blind him to this possibility, and that there is much to be said for the greater trust Aquinas seems to have in our natural affinities.

14. As well as the influence of Cicero, which hardly any reader of *Spiritual Friendship* even remotely familiar with *De Amicitia* could miss, Douglass Roby notes the enormous influence of Augustine on Aelred. At the time of his death, the works Aelred had in his private oratory were a Psalter, John's gospel and the *Confessions*. Roby (1977) describes *Spiritual Friendship* as having 'a thoroughly Augustinian structure, built on the foundation provided by Cicero' (p. 31). Roby further notes that of the four short versions of the text in existence by the end of the fourteenth century, one was actually attributed to St Augustine (ibid., p. 39).
15. Compare also our opening epigram, 'God is friendship' (Aelred 1977, pp. 65–66), almost certainly inspired by Trinitarian thinking.
16. White notes both Aristotle's and Cicero's insistence that a good friend would refrain from burdening his friends with his own misfortunes and pains. Here, for instance, is Aristotle on the subject: 'people with manly natures take care not to make their friends fellow sufferers with them; and unless his insensitivity to pain is extreme, he does not tolerate letting them feel pain; and as a rule he does not welcome companions in lamenting, since he is not himself given to lamentation. Yet women and womanish men are glad to have people lament among with them, and they love them as friends and as sharers in their sorrow. But it is clear that one ought to imitate the better man in everything.' (Aristotle 1998, 1171b).
17. I also borrow the use of 'recognition' as a kind of banner headline for what follows from White.
18. Again, I here bracket off the question of whether or not White's remark is adequate as a judgment on romantic love. I strongly suspect not, but I shall not argue that case here.

19. See for instance Lynch (2005), p. 82.
20. Thus Montaigne: 'our souls mingle and blend with each other so completely that they efface the seam that joined them, and cannot find it again' (Montaigne in Pakaluk 1991, p. 192).
21. For a more detailed account of the 'drawing' view of friendship and its relation to Kierkegaard, see Lippitt (2007) and (2013, chapter 2).
22. Aristotle (1998), IX.9. On Cicero (1991), compare VIII.30 with XIV.51, where he somewhat grudgingly acknowledges that it 'may not be quite right for friends never to have any needs at all' (such as for advice or help from each other).
23. Compare also the epistle 'On Grief for Lost Friends', which Seneca opens thus: 'I am grieved to hear that your friend Flaccus is dead, but I would not have you sorrow more than is fitting. That you should not mourn at all I shall hardly dare to insist; and yet I know that it is the better way.' (Seneca 1991b, p. 125). Towards the end of this epistle, Seneca compares the loss of a friend with the loss of a tunic. His prospects for a job at the university counselling service seem limited.
24. I owe this way of putting things to discussion with John Davenport.

References

R. M. Adams (1993) 'The Problem of Total Devotion', in Neera Kapur Badhwar (ed.), *Friendship: A Philosophical Reader* (Ithaca: Cornell University Press), 108–32.

T. W. Adorno (1940) 'On Kierkegaard's Doctrine of Love', *Studies in Philosophy and Social Science* 8, 413–29, reprinted in Daniel W. Conway (ed.) (2002) *Søren Kierkegaard: Critical Assessments of Leading Philosophers*, vol. II (London and New York: Routledge).

Aelred of Rievaulx (1977) *Spiritual Friendship*, trans. Mary Eugenia Laker (Kalamazoo: Cistercian Publications).

Aristotle (1998) *Nicomachean Ethics Books VIII and IX*, translated with a commentary by Michael Pakaluk (Oxford: Clarendon).

Augustine (1948) 'On the Trinity', in Whitney J. Oates (ed.), *Basic Writings of Saint Augustine* (New York: Random House).

—— (1961) *Confessions*, trans. R. S. Pine-Coffin (Harmondsworth: Penguin).

—— (1963). *City of God*, trans. Henry Bettenson (Harmondsworth: Penguin).

P. Brown (2000/1967) *Augustine of Hippo* (London: Faber & Faber).

Cicero (1991) 'On Friendship' (*De Amicitia*), in M. Pakaluk (ed.), *Other Selves: Philosophers on Friendship* (Indianapolis: Hackett).

D. Cocking and J. Kennett (1998) 'Friendship and the Self', *Ethics* 108, 502–27.

J. Dunn (2004) *Children's Friendships: The Beginnings of Intimacy* (Oxford: Blackwell).

M. J. Ferreira (2001) *Love's Grateful Striving: A Commentary on Kierkegaard's Works of Love* (Oxford: Oxford University Press).

P. George (1998) 'Something Anti-Social about *Works of Love*', in George Pattison and Steven Shakespeare (eds), *Kierkegaard: The Self in Society*. (Basingstoke: Macmillan), 170–82.

S. Kierkegaard (1995) *Works of Love*, trans. H. V. and E. H. Hong (Princeton: Princeton University Press).

S. Kierkegaard (1997–) *Skrifter*, Vols 1–28 and K1–28, ed. Niels Jørgen Cappelørn et al. (Copenhagen: Gads Forlag).
D.Konstan (1997) *Friendship in the Classical World* (Cambridge: Cambridge University Press).
R. Layard and J. Dunn (2006) *A Good Childhood* (London: Penguin).
C. S. Lewis (1960) *The Four Loves* (New York: Harcourt, Brace).
—— (1965) *Screwtape Proposes a Toast and Other Pieces* (London: Fontana).
J. Lippitt (2007) 'Cracking the Mirror: On Kierkegaard's Concerns about Friendship', *International Journal for Philosophy of Religion* 61 (3), 131–50.
—— (2013) *Kierkegaard and the Problem of Self-Love* (Cambridge: Cambridge University Press).
S. Lynch (2005) *Philosophy and Friendship* (Edinburgh: Edinburgh University Press).
M. de Montaigne (1965) 'Of Friendship', in *The Complete Essays of Montaigne*, trans. Donald M. Frame (Stanford: Stanford University Press).
J. Mulder Jr. (2010) *Kierkegaard and the Catholic Tradition: Conflict and Dialogue* (Bloomington: Indiana University Press).
J. H. Newman (1868) *Parochial and Plain Sermons*, vol. 2, no. 5 (London: Rivingtons).
O. O'Donovan (2006/1980) *The Problem of Self-Love in St. Augustine* (Eugene: Wipf and Stock).
M. Pakaluk (ed.) (1991) *Other Selves: Philosophers on Friendship* (Indianapolis: Hackett).
D. Roby (1977) 'Introduction', in Aelred of Rievaulx (ed.), *Spiritual Friendship*, trans. Mary Eugenia Laker (Kalamazoo: Cistercian Publications).
Seneca (1991a) 'On Philosophy and Friendship', in M. Pakaluk (ed.), *Other Selves: Philosophers on Friendship* (Indianapolis: Hackett).
Seneca (1991b) 'On Grief for Lost Friends', in M. Pakaluk (ed.), *Other Selves: Philosophers on Friendship* (Indianapolis: Hackett).
E. J. Vacek (1994) *Love, Human and Divine: The Heart of Christian Ethics* (Washington DC: Georgetown University Press).
D. F. Weaver (2002) *Self-Love and Christian Ethics* (Cambridge: Cambridge University Press).
C. White (1992) *Christian Friendship in the Fourth Century* (Cambridge: Cambridge University Press).
R. White (2001) *Love's Philosophy* (Lanham: Rowman and Littlefield).

Part V

Friendship in a Good Life

11
The Goods of Friendship

Thomas Hurka

My topic is the value of friendship, but I will extend it to include all forms of love or close personal attachment, including familial love, such as between parents and children, and erotic love, between spouses or committed sexual partners. I take these all to involve the same principal elements, namely a desire to be with another person and get pleasure from her company and a desire for her happiness or for whatever else is good in her life, such as success in her career. We want to be with the people we care for and we want them to lead fulfilling lives, and we want these things more for them than we do for strangers. Of course the forms of love differ in important ways. Erotic love, for example, involves a desire to share sexual pleasure with a partner that is not found in familial love or non-sexual friendship. But this is just a specific form of the desires to be with a loved one and to give her pleasure. It does not make for something completely distinct from non-sexual friendship but for friendship with an added erotic element.

I will assume that friendship is indeed good, or does have value: that it is worth pursuing for its own sake and makes our lives more worth living. Other things equal, a life with close personal relationships is more desirable than one without. It is not that friendship is the only thing of value. Pleasure and happiness are good even when they do not result from a personal relationship. So is knowledge, or understanding the world around you; achievement, or successfully pursuing a challenging goal; and virtue, or being a morally good person. Nor is friendship an essential good, one without which a desirable life is impossible. If someone without significant personal attachments gets enough happiness from other sources, or achieves sufficiently important goals or is sufficiently virtuous, his life can be good overall and even as good as some lives that do contain such attachments. But without friendship it lacks something that would have made it better, and for most of us our personal relationships are among the best things we know.

Assuming that friendship is a good, there is a philosophical question of why it is good, or what kind of value it has. If it makes our lives more worth living, how exactly does it do so? In this chapter I will explore three views on this topic. The first view says that our personal relationships are a part of our lives where other, more generic goods are realized to a high degree. Friendship is not a distinct value, just a place where values that can be enjoyed elsewhere are especially easily found. The second view says that certain key features of our personal relationships make for distinctive forms of the more generic goods, with distinctive and additional value. Though not a completely free-standing good, friendship does make a separate contribution to value by generating special instances of value. And the final view says there are entirely distinct values in our personal relationships, containing goods not found in any form elsewhere. To participate in a friendship is to share in a kind of value that only friendship allows. These three views are not in competition with each other. They could all be true together, so friendship has value of three different kinds. But they make successively stronger claims about the distinctiveness of this value. Let me start with the first view.

1 Friendship and generic goods

This view says that friendship is good because it embodies other, more generic goods to a high degree, or is a part of our lives where goods that can be enjoyed outside of friendship are especially easily found. This was thought to be the whole truth about the value of personal relationships by the early twentieth-century moral philosopher Sir David Ross. He thought there are only three basic human goods – pleasure, knowledge, and virtue – and that all other goods are compounded out of these three. Thus aesthetic enjoyment, or the appreciation of art, is 'a blend of pleasure with insight into the nature of the object that inspires it', while mutual love or friendship is 'a blend of virtuous disposition of two minds towards each other, with the knowledge which each has of the character and disposition of the other, and with the pleasure which arises from such disposition and knowledge'.[1] Friendship may embody some of these goods to an especially high degree and therefore be especially valuable, but it does not involve any distinctive goods.

This first view certainly contains much truth and will be a large part of a complete account of the value of personal relationships. Love and friendship are, first, the source of powerful good feelings: the physical pleasures of sex, the delight of a good friend's company, your joy when she succeeds in her main pursuits, and perhaps most importantly, the standing happiness of knowing that someone you care for cares for you. Given the time you spend with a friend, you also understand her better than you do a stranger, so your relationship is an occasion for valuable knowledge, and it is also a site for valuable achievements. In a lasting relationship you pursue not just momentary but long-term goals, such as to raise a child or first save for and then decorate a house, and if there is extra value in cooperative activities, where you mesh your actions with another person's, those too are found to a high degree in friendship. Finally, and most centrally, your friends are the people toward whom you feel and act most virtuously. A key aspect of moral virtue is wanting other people's happiness and flourishing for its own sake, or overcoming your natural egoism and caring about another as much as you do about yourself. Most of us do this to only a limited degree with most other people, but much more with our children, partners, and friends, so with them we are most virtuous or morally at our best. Concern for another is good whoever its object, but we feel it most and best with friends.

To be sure, friendship also poses dangers. The more you care about a person, the more you will be pained if some tragedy befalls her; think of the anguish parents will feel if their young child dies. And in erotic love there is the hurt when the person you want rejects you. Love can also blind you rather than prompt knowledge, making you ignore a partner's obvious faults, and it can distract you from your most valuable projects – think of those who have wasted their talents because of an unwise infatuation. But despite these dangers, love and friendship are for most of us well worth seeking, offering more of goods like pleasure and virtue than they threaten harms, or a greater chance of enriching than of damaging our lives.

It may be objected that these goods are not ones *of* friendship but are merely caused by it, so the friendship is only instrumentally and not intrinsically good. And it is certainly true that the pleasure you get from spending time with a friend is an effect of your interaction with her, which is therefore good as a means. But I think the pleasure is internal to the friendship itself and helps make it what it is; surely if you got no pleasure from a person's company, your relationship with her would not be one of friendship. The same is certainly true of virtue. If you did not have any desire for her happiness you could not count as her friend, so your virtuous concern for her is part of your friendship rather than something resulting from it. It is not that all the goods I have listed are in this way essential to a relationship. There could be a deep friendship that did not involve much in the way of joint achievement, perhaps because the friends live far apart and communicate only by letter or email. There might also be a friendship without much mutual knowledge. But when these goods are present, they help make the relationship what it is and are therefore internal to it rather than mere effects, and that is certainly true of pleasure and virtue. That you enjoy being with another and want her good is not something caused by your friendship but part of its essence.

This first view will be part of any account of the value of friendship, but will it be the whole account, so the goods of friendship are always and only ones that could be found in other aspects of life? I think many will resist this conclusion and think friendship also offers distinctive goods, ones not found elsewhere. And the second and third views affirm different versions of possibility. But to approach them we need first to discuss another question about friendship, namely what its basis is, or what, when you love a person, you love her for.

2 Friendship and history

There is a kind of love that cares for all people equally – call it impersonal benevolence – but it is not our subject in this chapter. We are discussing relationships in which you care especially about a particular person, wanting more to be with her than with other people and caring more for her happiness. But what attaches your love to this specific person, or what do you love her in particular for?

Partly – though only partly, I will argue – you love her for qualities that other people could in principle share, such as her wit, generosity, and red hair. She is not the only witty or red-haired person in the world, but she does have those qualities – she is witty and has red hair – and you love her in part for that fact. But the qualities you love are of two kinds: some you admire, and some you just like.

You admire a quality if you think it is intrinsically good and would make anyone's life more laudable. Thus you may admire your partner's wit and generosity, and if you do, you do not think that is just a quirk in you. You think everyone should admire traits like those. But when you merely like a quality, you do not have that thought. If you like her red hair, for example, you do or should not think it is better than any other hair color or the one everyone should prefer. You just happen to like it yourself. Or if you especially enjoy her company, you need not think her style of socializing is the best possible. You can recognize that other reasonable people may prefer other styles of socializing and not enjoy her company most – but you just do.

Some philosophers have thought that a valuable friendship must be based primarily on qualities you admire or think of as good. More specifically, they have thought that a valuable friendship must be based on loving another person's moral character, or virtue. Aristotle, for example, thought that if you like someone because she is useful to you or fun company you do not really like her for herself and therefore are not really her friend; that is true only if you love her for her character.[2]

But this view is far too high-minded. What is wrong with just liking somebody or being attracted by her non-moral features? Aristotle seems to have assumed that if you like someone because she is fun company then you really like her only as a means to your fun, which is selfish rather than friendly. But this does not follow. Enjoying her company can lead you to want her happiness, success, and even moral virtue as ends in themselves, and in fact this often happens. You are attracted to someone first for partly selfish reasons, such as that she makes you laugh, but then come to care for her altruistically or for herself. What is valuable in love is the desires and feelings it involves once it has developed, and their value is largely independent of their origin. Beautiful flowers can blossom in ordinary dirt.

Though you love someone partly for qualities others could share, you do or should not love her only for those qualities. If you did, then if someone came along with the same qualities to a higher degree – someone wittier, more generous, and with redder hair – you would switch your love to her. Any reasons you had to love your present partner would apply even more to the new person. Or if your partner was about to die and scientists could replace her with a perfect molecular duplicate, you would not feel at all troubled by your loss. Everything you now had in your love you would have in her replacement. But surely you would not do or feel these things, and surely you should not; that would be emotionally unfaithful. In a truly valuable relationship you do not love another just for qualities she has that others could share; you also love her as an individual or for herself. But what exactly does that mean?

I do not think it can mean to love a person apart from all her qualities, if that even makes sense. It is to love her for qualities no one else could share, qualities that are unique to her and therefore separate her from everyone else. More specifically, it is to love her for historical qualities, involving her having participated with you in a shared past. The two of you have done things together and affected each other in many ways, and you can love her now for those historical facts: for how you first met in the park, for that chilly walk you took along the lake, for the concerts you enjoyed together. And later you can love her for how you together bought a house, raised children, and then matured and aged together.

These historical qualities are still qualities, or things true of your partner, and you can love her for having them. But they are also qualities that, once she has them, no one else can share. Someone else can be wittier or have redder hair, but once she met you in the park no one else can be the very person who did that then. Nor can any substitute, even a perfect molecular duplicate, be the same person you walked or heard that concert with. A shared history ties you to this person and only this person, and a love based on it therefore will not accept replacements. It will not trade up to greater wit or redder hair because it is loyal to the one person who did those things then.

Not just any history can play this role. It must be a history with a significant degree of interaction or mutual contact, and it must also be in some way a good history, one that involved concern for each other or in which you together did substantial good, either to each other or to others. (Think of that part of a couple's history that involved jointly raising a child for a good and happy life.) If your past with a person involved mutual hatred and hostility, that will or should not ground a positive attachment to her now. Likewise if your history was one of harming outsiders, as with former gang members who together terrorized a neighborhood. But if your past with another involved mutual benefits given from mutual love, that is another basis, alongside qualities like wit and red hair, for loving her especially now.[3]

This historical attachment is not something we feel only for people. I love my living-room furniture partly because it is a beautiful example of twentieth-century modernist design, but also because it is the furniture my father bought in the 1940s and that I grew up with. There may be more beautiful pieces in the world, even in the same style, but I want to keep living with these chairs and these bookcases. You can keep wearing a ratty sweater or driving a clunky car because you have done things and gone places with it for such a long time. The people we love are more complex than chairs or sweaters, and so is our history with them. But when we feel attached to them as individuals we love them in the same historical way as we can love material things, or for a similar role in our past.

A shared history is therefore an additional basis for love, alongside the qualities you admire or like in a friend. But it can also add to the qualities you like in her. Maybe you were first attracted by your partner's wit and generosity, but now also treasure her throaty laugh and fondness for snow. Did you think in the abstract about these qualities and decide, independently of who has them, that they are likeable? Or did you come to like them because they are hers? Surely the latter. You first liked her for some non-historical qualities such as her wit and generosity, then developed a history with her and loved her for her part in it, and later come to like others of her qualities because they are hers. You love the throaty laugh because it is the laugh of the person you did all those things with, though if she had had a tinkly giggle you would have loved that instead. A George and Ira Gershwin song relishes 'the way you wear your hat / the way you sip your tea'. But the singer did not first admire those ways of handling hats and cups and then notice his love using them; he first loved her and then loved them as things she did.

This second role of a shared history explains why love can survive the loss of the qualities that first inspired it. Maybe you first loved your partner for her smooth skin and slender waist, but now it is thirty years later and she has wrinkles and a thickening middle. Do you stop loving her? Not at all. You now love her wrinkles and bulges because they belong to the person you did significant things with. Having once loved her for her appearance, you now love her appearance for being hers.

3 Friendship and partiality

So a shared history adds to the bases of love, or the things you love a person for, in several ways. But it also allows our second view: that friendship is a partly distinctive good, whose features make for distinctive instances of the more generic goods Ross discussed.

Consider first virtue. A central aspect of it is wanting another person's good for its own sake, and this is something you do more with a friend than with a stranger. You want her happiness more intensely than you want a stranger's and are more pained by her troubles; in that way you are partial to her, or favor her interests over other people's. Some may condemn this partiality, saying you ought to care equally for all people, but this is not the view of everyday morality, nor, I think, what most of us believe. Imagine that your spouse is drowning in one lake and two strangers are drowning in another and you can only get to one lake. Surely you do not act wrongly if you save your spouse. On the contrary, if you decided to save the two because there are more of them, that would be wrong because it would violate a special duty you have to care for your partner. Or if you can comfort either your own child after a hurt or a stranger's child after a slightly worse hurt, you act wrongly if you comfort the other child. You have, most of us think, a stronger duty to promote the good of someone who is closer to you just because she is closer.

Nor is this the only duty that is stronger toward someone close. Alongside the positive duty to promote other people's good are negative duties not to hurt them, lie to them, break promises to them, and so on. And however wrong it is to do these things to a stranger, it is even more seriously wrong to do them to a friend or spouse. If you lie to her or break a promise to her, she can ask not only 'How could you do that?', but 'How could you do that *to me*?'

Let us concentrate, however, on the duty to promote a friend's good. What gives this duty its extra strength cannot be the qualities you admire or like in her, because others could have those to a higher degree: the two strangers in the other lake could each be wittier, more generous, and redder-haired than your spouse. It must instead be your shared history with her, or the things you have done together. And the way this history strengthens your duty to promote her good, I suggest, is by generating what philosophers call an agent-relative value. Though from a neutral standpoint your spouse's life is no more valuable than a stranger's – it is a human life, just like his – it is a life that has more value from your point of view, or relative to you, because of your shared history, and it should therefore matter more to you. More generally, the happiness or flourishing of someone close to you is a greater good relative to you than the equal happiness or flourishing of someone distant, and that gives you a stronger duty to promote it. You have in general a stronger duty to promote greater goods; thus, if you could either relieve one stranger's intense pain or another stranger's mild pain, you have a stronger duty to do the former. But then if your shared history with a friend makes her happiness a greater good relative to you than a stranger's, and you have a stronger duty to promote greater goods, it follows that you have a stronger duty to promote your friend's happiness than the stranger's. If you save your spouse from drowning rather than two people you do not know, you do what is positively right.

But as well as strengthening your duty to seek goods in your friend's life, your shared history with her also makes your wanting these goods a greater good, or a more valuable instance of virtue, in your life. It is an aspect of virtue that it is better and more virtuous to want or love greater rather than lesser goods and to hate greater evils. Thus, it is more virtuous to want another's immense happiness than to want to the same degree her slight happiness, or to feel compassion for her great suffering than to feel similar compassion for her mild suffering. The same attitude with the same intensity to a greater good or evil is a greater or better instance of virtue,[4] and that is also true of the attitudes characteristic of love. If your spouse's happiness is a greater good relative to you, then your wanting it to a given degree is better and more virtuous than your wanting a stranger's happiness to the same degree, and your being pained by her suffering is better than your being similarly pained by a stranger's. The history that gives your partner's happiness more value relative to you also makes your caring for her happiness more virtuous and therefore a greater good in your life.

This idea is different from Ross's. He thought friendship is especially valuable because in it you care more about another person's good than you normally do. You want a friend's happiness more intensely than a stranger's, and your doing so is more virtuous because it is more intense. While that is true, I am now suggesting that, differences in intensity aside, caring for a friend's good is also better because it concerns your friend. Wanting her happiness is more virtuous than wanting a stranger's even if the wants are equally strong, and it is better because it aims at what, relative to you, is a greater good. If your desire for a friend's happiness is stronger than for a stranger's, that means, on our current proposal, that it is better in two ways. It is better because it is more intense, but it is also better because it concerns your friend, or concerns someone whose happiness has more value relative to you.

And this means that your friendship makes for a distinctive form of the generic good of virtue. You are tied to this person by a shared history, and that now makes your concern for her more valuable than an otherwise similar concern for someone to whom you are not similarly tied. An essential feature of friendship, one not found in more distant relationships, makes for more value in your virtuous concern for a friend, or for a more valuable instance of a generic human good.

And what is true of virtue may also be true of other goods such as knowledge. Ross thought knowledge of a friend's personality is good because it has the features that make any knowledge valuable: it is integrated, explanatory, and leads to understanding rather than a mere grasp of unconnected facts.[5] But it is no better than a similarly integrated and explanatory knowledge of some other subject, and in particular, it is no better than a similarly integrated knowledge of a stranger's personality. Given your more extensive interaction with your friend, you are more likely to have this kind of knowledge of her, but if you somehow had it of a stranger, that would on Ross's view be every bit as good.

We may wonder, however, whether that is true. A psychiatrist may understand a patient's personality as well as she understands her spouse's, but is understanding her spouse's not more important relative to her and therefore a greater good in her life? Would it not be worse if she was mistaken about her spouse than about some patient? It may be said that correctly understanding her spouse will enable her to do many other good things for him, such as comfort him effectively when he is troubled. But understanding her patient will enable her to do the same for the patient, and if the patient's needs are greater it may enable her to benefit the patient more. It seems to me that her understanding her spouse is a greater good just because he is her spouse, or because their shared history makes her knowledge of him more valuable than an otherwise similar knowledge of someone else. I am not saying this kind of knowledge is the best or most important possible, because it is not. Given its immense breadth and explanatory power, Stephen Hawking's understanding of physics probably has more value than anyone's knowledge of even her closest intimate. But just as your shared history makes your wanting a loved one's happiness a somewhat better instance of virtue, so it can make your understanding her a somewhat better instance of knowledge.

This suggestion may connect with a more general claim about the value of knowledge. Arguing against the view that only pleasure is good, Robert Nozick asks us to imagine an 'experience machine' that by electrically stimulating your brain can give you the experience and therefore pleasure of anything you would like. Before plugging in you decide what experiences you would like to have – maybe that of being the first person to climb Mount Everest or that of seducing Brad Pitt – and then it is exactly as if you were doing those things. You get all the pleasure you would get from really doing them, and you believe you are really doing them, but in fact they are a machine-induced illusion.[6]

If pleasure were the only intrinsic good, then a life spent entirely on the experience machine would be as good as a life can be, but many of us do not think that – we think such a life would be seriously impoverished. And a central reason is that while on the machine you are isolated within your mind, lacking the contact with outside reality that normal life involves. One aspect of this contact is knowledge, or having true beliefs about reality, and it is partly its lacking such knowledge that is disturbing about life on the machine. But what specific lack of knowledge is most disturbing?

You need not lack knowledge of yourself while plugged in, since you have the same access to your inner mental states as you do in normal life. And though you may lack knowledge of how reality is apart from you, for example, knowledge of scientific laws, that does not seem as disturbing as the fact that you lack knowledge, and in fact have positively false beliefs, about where you are in the world, or about how you relate to your environment. You think you are halfway up a mountain or gazing into Brad Pitt's eyes when in fact you are motionless in a machine with electrodes in your brain. This suggests that alongside the value in integrated, explanatory knowledge that Ross discussed there is special or additional value in knowing how you relate to the world or how you are placed in your surroundings.

And it is not a great extension of this to say there is also special value in knowing your friends. They are an important part of your environment, in particular of your human environment, since they are the people you have interacted with most and will interact with most in the future. There can therefore be more value in knowing about your history with them than in knowing other historical facts, and that seems intuitively right. Is it not more important to remember your past with your spouse or best friend than to remember some stranger's past? There may similarly be more value in knowing facts about a friend that are independent of that history, such as her inborn personality. If it is in general better to know about your close environment, the shared history that makes her a key part of that environment may also make it better to know about her.

Something similar may hold for achievement. I have suggested that there is special value in cooperative achievements, where you organize not just your own activities in pursuit of a goal but another person's too, or work out with her what each of you will do. This too may have more value if it is done with someone you have a history with. Jointly designing a house or starting a business with a spouse or longtime friend may be a greater good than doing the same thing, even with the same degree of collaboration, with someone who outside this project plays little role in your life. Wider-ranging and longer-established ties may make for more value in specific cooperations now. The idea, again, is not that collaborative achievements with friends are the most valuable achievements possible. Even the solitary achievement of a very difficult goal, such as climbing Everest or making a major invention, can be more valuable than most shared projects of friends. But if there is some extra value in cooperative achievements with people you are close to, your history with those people will again make for a distinctively valuable form of a generic good.

Finally, the same may be true even of pleasure, so pleasure got from a friend's company is more valuable than the same intensity of pleasure from a stranger's, just because it is from your friend. Pleasures that connect to a shared history, in other words, can be better than ones that do not. But we need to be careful here. If your pleasure in a friend's company is in part pleasure that she is happy or in other ways flourishing, that is a form of virtue and more valuable as a virtue because its object is a state of your friend. So it is not relevant to the value of your pleasure just as pleasure, or apart from considerations of virtue. And it may be argued that the value of pleasure as pleasure, unlike that of virtue, knowledge, or achievement, depends only on its intensity and not at all on its origin or tie to a friendship. Then, setting aside these other values, the value of pleasure from a friend's company is no greater than that of an equally intense pleasure from some other source. I am not sure that this view is true, but I am also not sure it is false. Even if it is true, however, we have seen several ways in which love or friendship can make for distinctive versions of other generic goods: by making your virtuous concern for your friend, your understanding of her, and cooperative activities with her more valuable than otherwise similar instances of those goods that do not involve a friend.

This, then, is the second view I distinguished earlier: that an essential feature of friendship, its basis in a shared history, makes for distinctively valuable instances of more generic goods such as virtue and knowledge. But the third and more radical view is that friendship involves distinctive goods of its own. Let me end by considering that.

4 Friendship and reciprocity

The goods of friendship we have discussed so far have all been states of you, involving how you relate to your friend: your pleasure in being with her, your understanding of her personality, your achieving things with her, and your virtuously wanting her happiness. May there not be other goods in friendship that are not just states of you?

The most obvious possibility is that it is good not only to love someone but also to be loved by her: to have her want your company, understand you, and seek your happiness, all in part because of a history she has shared with you. The good here will still be located in your life, in that it will make your life more desirable. But what makes your life desirable will be a state of her, namely her loving you. It will be a good in your life not only that you care for her, but also that you are the object of her concern and affection.

Another person's love can have many good effects in your life. It can give you the pleasure of her company, as well as the standing happiness of knowing that you are loved. It can also lead to her helping you in your major projects. But in these cases her loving you is good as a means, or as something that promotes states of pleasure and happiness in you. And the possibility we are now considering is that her loving you is good for you in itself, or apart from any further effects. Does that sound right? Does her loving you by itself make your life better?

Precisely because of what it involves, this possibility is hard to assess. Ideally we want to consider a case where her loving you does not have good effects, for example, does not cause you pleasure. But there are only two ways this can happen: either she loves you and you do not know this, so you get no pleasure from her love, or you do know it and do not care. But in neither case do you have what can truly be called a friendship with her, so neither can help us decide whether, when there is a friendship, her love by itself makes your life better. And I have to say I am skeptical of this possibility. I do not see how something that is initially true just of her can make your life better, or be a benefit in your life. This is especially so when there is another way love can have distinctive value.

Imagine that you love another who loves you back. Your love involves pleasure, knowledge, and virtue that make your life better, and the same elements in her life make her life better. But the fact that your loves are reciprocated, or that each of you loves someone who loves you back, I now want to suggest, makes for a further value over and above those in your individual loves. The whole composed of each of your loves for the other is, because those loves are returned, a separate intrinsic good. The value in the relationship is not located just on its two sides, in what each wants and feels for the other. It also depends on the relationship's mutuality, or on the fact that the object of each love is a lover in return.

This idea involves what the early twentieth-century philosopher G. E. Moore called the 'principle of organic unities', according to which the value of a whole need not equal the sum of the values its parts would have on their own, because the relationships among the parts can have additional value.[7] This principle is illustrated by the idea of moral desert. Imagine that you could give some pleasure either to a virtuous person or to a vicious one. It would presumably be better to give it to the virtuous person since pleasure is something he deserves, whereas the vicious person deserves not pleasure but its opposite. But how exactly does desert make the virtuous person's getting the pleasure better? Moore would say it is because the combination of virtue and pleasure in the same person's life is good as a combination, or in addition to any values in the items it combines.[8] The first person's virtue is good, as is his pleasure, but there is a further good in the fact that the two are joined in one life. By contrast, if the vicious person got pleasure, his vice would be evil, his pleasure would be good, and there would be a further evil in the fact that the vice and pleasure are had by the same person. In each case, the value of the whole – either virtue plus pleasure or vice plus pleasure – does not equal the sum of the values its constituents would have on their own because there is a further value in the way they are combined.

This same idea can be applied to love or friendship. Your love for your friend has value on its own, because of the pleasure, knowledge, and virtue it involves, as does her love for you. But there can be a further value in the combination of your loves as a combination, or in the relationship of mutuality between them. Another Gershwin brothers' song speaks of 'loving one who loves you/And then taking that vow'; and vows aside, we can see the reciprocation it describes as a distinctive good found only in relationships of mutual love. This reciprocation will of course have many good effects: knowing you are loved is pleasing, and mutual lovers can more easily know and cooperate with each other. In addition, another's virtuously caring for you can heighten your concern for her: that she wants your happiness makes you want hers more. But I do not think reciprocated love is good only because of these effects; it is also good to some degree in itself. Imagine two situations involving the same four people. In the first *A* loves *B* who loves *C* who loves *D* who loves *A*, but no one's love is reciprocated. In the second *A* and *B* love each other, as do *C* and *D*. Even if the loves in these two situations are equally virtuous and the people in them equally happy – since the people in the first cannot get happiness from being loved, imagine that they get compensating happiness from some other source – is the second situation not better just because its loves are reciprocated? If so, there is value in reciprocation as such.

That there is this value seems to be another lesson of Nozick's experience machine. While on the machine, you lack contact not only with your physical surroundings but also with other people, in that you have no real relationships with them. You may imagine you are sharing mutual love with Brad Pitt and feel pleasure and have virtuous desires as part of that, but you are not actually relating to him and in particular are not loving someone who actually loves you back. If its lack of real and especially reciprocated relationships is another disturbing feature of life on the machine, that suggests that reciprocated love is another human good. There is, to be sure, room for debate about how great a good this is. Perhaps the lack of reciprocated love on the machine is, though disturbing, not as disturbing as the lack of knowledge and achievement. Maybe the situation with reciprocated love is somewhat better than the situation without, but not vastly better. If so, reciprocation is not as great a good as the pleasure, knowledge, and virtue in which the two situations are equal. Even so, it can be one good found in full-fledged friendships.

If we follow Moore's understanding of the principle of organic unities, we will see this good as located not in your life nor in your friend's but in the friendship as a whole, understood as a complex combining the two of you and your loves for each other. The good of mutual love is therefore not like the ones Ross discussed, which are located in the individuals who are parties to the friendship. It is a good found in the friendship itself, or in the reciprocation between its participants, and therefore is a good of a different type from the more individual goods discussed by Ross.

There are other possible organic unities in friendship. Consider the history that ties you to your friend, understood as a series of good interactions through time, interactions in which you successively benefit each other or an outsider from virtuous motives. Each one of these interactions has value because of the virtuous motives it involves, but it may be that there is additional value in the series as a whole, just because it is a unified series of good interactions between the same people. If this is so, then it is, other things equal, better to interact continuously with the same person than to have a series of distinct interactions, each as good in itself, with different people, or to have a lifelong attachment to one person than to have a series of distinct relationships, each in itself as intense, with different people. This again will not be a supreme value, or one that necessarily outweighs all others, so a life with, say, one marriage is necessarily better than any life with successive marriages. But it will be one additional good, of at least some weight, if your attachment to a given person lasts longer and thereby makes for a larger organic whole.

5 Conclusion

There may be yet further goods in friendship that involve organic unities, but rather than explore this possibility let me conclude by summarizing the three views I have discussed of the value of friendship. And remember that these views are not in conflict: it may be that all three are true, so personal relationships are good in three different ways.

The first view says friendship is good because it is a part of our lives where more generic goods, ones also possible outside friendship, are present or realized to a high degree. These goods include the many kinds of pleasure friendship can bring; the knowledge it involves of a friend's personality; your joint achievements with her; and your virtuous desire for her happiness, success, and overall flourishing. This first view may be the most important, accounting for the largest share of the value of friendship. And the most important good it cites may be virtue: the most valuable thing about friendship may be the way it takes you out of yourself and makes you care about another as much or almost as much as you care about yourself. Your friends are the people whose good you care about most and in relation to whom you are morally best or most virtuous.

The remaining two views say there are distinctive goods in friendship, ones not possible outside it. The second says your shared history with a friend makes for distinctive and better instances of the generic goods. Your virtuous concern for a friend has more value than your concern for a stranger not only because it is more intense, as the first view says, but also because it is concern for a friend, one whose involvement in your past makes her happiness, success, and so on greater goods relative to you than similar states of other people. Your caring for anyone is good, but for a friend especially so. Something similar may be true of knowledge, achievement, and perhaps even pleasure: knowing a friend's personality may be better than having similar knowledge of a stranger, and likewise for joint achievements with her and perhaps even, though more controversially, for pleasures derived from her company.

Finally, the third view says there are completely distinctive values in friendship, involving what, following Moore, I called organic unities. Thus mutual love, where the love of each is reciprocated by love from the other, may have additional value because it is mutual, or over and above the values of the individual loves that are its constituents. Now it is the relationship itself that has value, rather than what either friend brings to it, though the relationship only has this value because of what each brings. And there may be further organic unities in friendship, for example, in a long history of mutually loving interactions between the same people. All of which is just to say that love and friendship, though definitely and even incontrovertibly desirable, can be so in several different ways and on several different grounds.

Notes

1. Ross (1930, p. 141).
2. Aristotle, *Nicomachean Ethics*, Book VIII, chapter 3.
3. I defend this historical account of the basis of love in Hurka (1997). It is also defended in Kolodny (2003).
4. I defend this 'proportionality' view of virtue in Hurka (2001, chapter 3).
5. Ross (1930, pp. 147–8).
6. Nozick (1974, pp. 42–5).
7. Moore (1903, pp. 27–36). I discuss Moore's principle in Hurka (1998).
8. Moore (1903, pp. 214–16).

References

Aristotle (1980) *Nicomachean Ethics*, trans. David Ross (Oxford: Oxford University Press).

T. Hurka (1997) 'The Justification of National Partiality', in Robert McKim and Jeff McMahan (eds), *The Morality of Nationalism* (New York: Oxford University Press), 139–57.

—— (1998) 'Two Kinds of Organic Unity', *Journal of Ethics* 2, 283–304.

—— (2001) *Virtue, Vice, and Value* (New York: Oxford University Press).

N. Kolodny (2003) 'Love as Valuing a Relationship', *Philosophical Review* 112, 135–89.

G. E. Moore (1903) *Principia Ethica* (Cambridge: Cambridge University Press).

R. Nozick (1974) *Anarchy, State and Utopia* (New York: Basic Books).

W. D. Ross (1930) *The Right and the Good* (Oxford: Clarendon Press).

12
Friendship and Friends in the Stoic Theory of the Good Life

Anthony A. Long

This chapter is about how the Stoic philosophers of Greco-Roman antiquity investigated the notion of friendship and about what they understood by a truly *good* friend. To introduce the inquiry, I ask readers to set aside the modern use of stoicism as a name for uncomplaining endurance of life's sorrows and disappointments. We moderns do not associate stoicism with friendship, but that is because stoicism, in its modern usage, has largely lost touch with the original ideas of the philosophical school called Stoicism. Friendship actually was a central component of the ancient school's ethical theory, which, in turn, was the most influential component of a once mighty philosophical system. The ancient Stoics were the major intellectual force in the Greco-Roman world from about 300 BC to AD 200. The numerous books that they wrote have largely perished, but we are well informed about their doctrinal content, especially in the field of ethics.

In the first part of this study I present an overview of the Stoic theory of ideal friendship.[1] I next situate the theory within its cultural and philosophical context. After the elucidation of some technicalities, I turn to the Roman Stoic philosophers Seneca and Epictetus, who enable us to put some flesh on the bare bones of the theory. Finally, I offer an assessment of what we can learn about friendship from Stoic philosophy, making due allowance for its historical distance and its status as a theory about relationships between perfectly virtuous persons.

1

We often speak of a good friend, especially in cases where someone has been very helpful to us, saying: 'You have been a really good friend'. This expression shows that we typically look to our friends for help.

Stoic friends are unfailingly helpful to one another, but the goodness of Stoic friends signifies a much deeper quality than their readiness to assist each other when needed. Stoic friends are good because their character, values, and understanding of human nature are flawless, exemplary, completely admirable. In fact, you cannot strictly be a Stoic friend unless you are virtuous through and through.[2] Stoic friends would be expected to have the face-to-face knowledge of one another, shared experience, and common interests characteristic of any ordinary notion of friendship. But what makes Stoic friends loveable and capable of giving love is the excellence of their characters, nothing less and nothing more.

A natural first reaction to this idea is likely to be quite negative for several reasons. Most of us don't think of ourselves as moral paragons, and we don't look for, or typically find, that quality in our friends. Stoic insistence on moral excellence as *the* requirement of authentic friends seems to smell of elitism, pomposity, and sanctimony. Apart from that, we make friends for a range of reasons. If asked why so and so is our friend, we may mention how long we have known the person, the experiences we have gone through together, how we have helped one another, and so on. Actually, Stoic philosophers acknowledge that all normal human beings are innately sociable and that people whose character falls short of excellence can be strongly attached to one another. However, such attachments, in the strict Stoic view, are bound to lack the qualities necessary to friendship, properly speaking.

To be Stoic friends in this sense, persons 'treat their friends exactly as they treat themselves' (Diogenes Laertius 7.124/*SVF* 3.631, my translation). A Stoic friend is 'another I' or 'another self' (Diogenes Laertius 7.23 / *SVF* 1.71; cf. *SVF* 1.324). Stoic friends in this strict sense possess 'wisdom', which means that the love they show their friends is based upon knowing the exactly true value of things (Seneca, *Epistulae* 81, 10 / *SVF* 3.633). Stoic friendship involves 'agreement on everything human and divine, along with good will and affection' (Cicero, *De amicitia* 20). Stoic friendships are relationships of mutual help, but help in the sense of material benefit is not their basis; they are cultivated for their own sake and for the sake of the friend, not for the sake of anything useful by way of goods and services, which are simply incidental benefits from the friendship (Diogenes Laertius 7.124; Cicero, *De finibus* 3.70).

Some of these thoughts will certainly chime with our own. Sharing beliefs and values seems essential to any intimate and affectionate relationship. Other thoughts are much more alien and questionable. Should our friends be so like us that we regard them as second selves?

Wouldn't that be boring? Many of us are likely to think that some difference between friends is essential to friendship, so that our interest is engaged, enabling us to learn from our friends, coming to see things about ourselves that we would like to improve, and so forth.

Such critical responses to this outline of the Stoic theory would be quite in order if that theory were intended to describe the friendly relationships of everyday life and spontaneous feelings of affinity. In fact, the Stoic theory of friends and friendship was designed to characterize the features of an ideal partnership between persons, not as a description of actual experience, but to serve as a model for what friendships would be like if friends possessed wisdom. Stoic philosophers themselves did not lay claim to wisdom and even doubted whether it had ever been fully attained by any human being. However, we should not dismiss the theory for that reason as merely an academic exercise, but regard it, rather, as a template for assessing the friendly relationships of ordinary experience and seeing how well they measure up to the ideal standard.

In this light, we may see that critical responses such as those above are tinged with egoism. If we want our friends to be interesting and sources of self-improvement, are we loving our friends simply for their own sake rather than loving them, at least partially, for what we can get out of them? What does it mean to love a friend entirely for the friend's sake, and not at all for one's own sake? Is that psychologically feasible? If it is, or even if it is not, could this condition explain why the Stoics set the bar to authentic friendship so high in requiring that only persons of exemplary character can completely love one another for the other's sake and so be friends in the strict and proper sense?

Response to these questions will take us into the heart of Stoic philosophy. By way of background, we need first to reflect on the role of friendship in ancient Greek and Roman society, on how friendship had been treated a generation or two before the Stoics by Plato and Aristotle, and on how it was being treated by the Stoics' contemporary rivals, the Epicureans. Attention to these matters will help to show why the Stoics set the bar to authentic friendship so high.

2

The Greek for friendship is *philia* and the Latin word for it is *amicitia*. *Philia* may equally be rendered by love, and the Latin for love is *amor*. What one loves, in the usage of these words, can cover the entire spectrum of things we ourselves regard as loveable. Basic to the Greek verb *philein* is also the notion of 'regarding as one's own'. *Philoi*, translatable as friends, are one's own people, including one's family, the people one belongs to and who belong to oneself. Ties of affection are built into the very notion of what is one's own, most basically of course, oneself. To be dear to oneself, in this context, is not narcissism, but rather the recognition that nothing could be closer to anyone than oneself, or make a greater claim on one's regard and protection. Hence, to love (*philein*) the other as oneself or to treat the friend (*philos*) as a second self implies nothing less than the idea that the other person's identity is part and parcel of one's own.

We can now see why the most basic attitude such a notion of *philia* involves and requires is that of helping. If something belongs to us, we naturally cherish it, protect it, and try to look after it. This explains the intensity of Achilles' grief and remorse at the death of Patroclus in Homer's *Iliad*. Achilles had loved Patroclus in the strong emotional sense that any culture attaches to the notion of loving. But what most troubles Achilles is not, or not simply, the death of his beloved companion, but the recognition that he has failed to protect the life of the man who was his particular *philos*. In Sophocles' play, *Philoctetes*, we observe the anguish of someone who has been betrayed by his previous *philoi*. Philoctetes' fellow warriors have marooned him on a barren and unoccupied island, leaving him to fend for himself with a snake-bitten leg, because they could not stand the stench of his ailment on board ship. Philoctetes complains that his plight is a complete negation of the *philia* owed to him by his *philoi*. What devastates him is not primarily unrequited affection but concrete ill-treatment in place of the help required of one friend to another.

In its fundamental Greek sense, then, *philia* covers much more than spontaneous emotional bonding between individuals. Family members, who may not even like one another, are necessarily *philoi*. A son can inherit his father's *philoi*. Fellow citizens are one's *philoi*, since they are *ours*, our people, the people we belong to. In its most extended sense *philia* covers membership in societal groups of all kinds (Aristotle, *Nicomachean Ethics* 8, 1161b13). Philia is not a legal relationship such as marriage or parenthood, but it has a quasi-institutional aspect that is absent from our modern notion of friendship. This is especially evident in the Roman world where one's *amici* include clients and supporters, persons to whom one is tied purely by reciprocal benefit as well as those we today would regard as truly beloved friends with whom we have a strong emotional relationship.

The centrality to Greco-Roman society of these notions of friendship explains why the ancient philosophers, unlike their modern counterparts, treated friendship as a basic topic of ethics.[3] When scrutinized philosophically, moreover, friendship showed itself to be a far from intuitively clear and uncontroversial notion. The problems that philosophers could raise about it are briefly but trenchantly aired by Plato in his short dialogue *Lysis*.

Is utility the basis for friendship? Must the relation between friends be reciprocal? Do friends have to be good or virtuous people? What do people desire from friendship? Can a self-sufficient person want or need friends? How is friendship related to people's love of what is their own? As is typical of Plato's so-called Socratic dialogues, these questions of the *Lysis* do not receive much in the way of answers, let alone definite answers. The questions do, though, set the agenda for the philosophers who came after Plato, most notably Aristotle, and they have also, as I believe, strongly influenced the Stoics. If I am right about the Stoics' partial dependence on Aristotle, and more distantly on the questions raised in Plato's *Lysis*, that will enable us to supplement Stoic reasoning about friendship in ways that go beyond their directly attested ideas.

Aristotle has written on friendship more searchingly and influentially than any other philosopher. The points most germane to Stoic theory are his general account of friendship, his distinction between the types and grounds of friendship, and his discussion of whether the good man needs friends.[4]

Aristotle defines friendship as a relationship in which each party wants for the other what he thinks good, for the other's sake, not for his own sake, does his best to bring it about, and knows that such goodwill is reciprocated.[5] This definition specifies reciprocal affection and benefit as the essential constituents of any friendship. What the definition cleverly leaves open is the construal of benefit and the motivations of the putative friends. In Plato's *Lysis*, puzzles are generated by difficulties in determining the precise grounds for friendship. Are likes attracted to likes or to unlikes? Is the bad attracted to the good? Are friends attracted to what each of them lacks? The Platonic discussion proceeds on the presumption that friendship is a completely univocal notion. Aristotle, instead, provides a definition that is sufficiently broad to cover different kinds of goodness, each of which incorporates his reciprocal benefit condition. This refinement enables him to take account of different motivations for forming friendships and to differentiate between types of friendship. The differentiae he proposes are three in number – utility or material benefit, pleasure, and virtue.

A utility friendship's basis is the practical value one friend provides to another, for instance business services rendered and the payment the provider of the services earns. You may like your server at the checkout counter, she may like you, and you may wish each other well for each other's sake. This reciprocal affection and benefit are sufficient to make this encounter a kind of friendship, but one that goes no further in its basis than utility benefaction. In the case of a pleasure friendship, what each friend gives to the other is just that, pleasure. Such friends find one another appealing because they enjoy one another's company, irrespective of any material benefits they receive or of any firmly positive judgments concerning one another's characters. Mutual pleasure and enjoyment are what make these friends wish each other well in the contexts of their spending time together and keeping in touch. A pleasure friendship does not involve or depend on mutual services nor on admiration for each other's characters, which does not imply, of course, that two people could not be friends on the basis of utility *and* pleasure. Aristotle does not argue that utility and pleasure are mutually exclusive.

Friendship in the perfect and unqualified sense, for Aristotle, is a relationship in which the basis for the mutual affection, goodwill, and benefaction is each person's excellence of character.[6] He entirely anticipated the Stoics in holding that friendship, strictly speaking, is grounded neither in utility nor in pleasure. (For the Epicureans, all friendship originates in utility, but can then flower into a pleasurable relationship that is desirable, so the school claimed, for its own sake. That position could satisfy neither Aristotle nor the Stoics because it implies that egoism in the sense of one's own advantage is the foundation of every friendship.[7]) Aristotelian virtue friends are admirable persons who love one another and are good for one another entirely because of each other's virtues. In all likelihood such friends will be both useful and pleasurable to one another, but utility and pleasure are incidental to such friendships. Because the two friends are completely alike in their excellence of character, an Aristotelian virtue friend displays a form of self-love in loving his friend. This is not because he is narcissistic or self-centered, but because his own virtues are mirrored in the loveable virtues of the friend. In loving the friend because of the friend's virtues, an Aristotelian virtue friend cannot help but love himself too. According to Aristotle, virtue is the perfection of human nature, and this explains why a friend in the virtue sense is 'another self' (*allos autos, Nicomachean Ethics* 9, 1166a32).

The love Aristotelian virtue friends display towards one another involves the reciprocity condition – loving the other purely for the other's sake, and being loved in return purely for one's own sake. As such, the friendship is equally good for both persons. This is exactly the case for Stoic friendship, grounded, as we have seen it to be, in the friends' excellence of character. Like Aristotle (though without Aristotle's allowance of qualified friendships, based on utility or pleasure) the Stoics treat excellence of character as the necessary and sufficient condition for perfect friendship, with the corollary that only good persons can strictly be friends to one another. The Stoics too, as we have seen, take the friend to be 'another self'. Their notion of friendship resembles Aristotle's non-egoistic form of self-love since, according to Stoicism, both self-preservation and sociability are every normal person's instinctual drives.[8] What is best for a Stoic self is excellence of character. Hence Stoic best friends, in loving one another as second selves, are also loving and benefiting themselves. In one of our Stoic sources 'friendship with oneself' is given as the basis for being 'a friend to one's neighbors'.[9] Seneca (*Epistulae* 6, 7) expands this idea in a quotation from the Stoic philosopher Hecato: 'You ask what progress I have made? I have begun to be a friend to myself.' Seneca comments: 'He did indeed make great progress; he will never be alone. You can be sure that he is everyone's friend.' It is hardly news today that we need to care for ourselves if we are to establish successful relationships with other people.[10]

3

I now come to a big difference between Aristotle and the Stoics. This difference will cast fresh light on the Stoics' restriction of true friendship to relationships between morally excellent persons.

According to Aristotle, goodness comes in many forms: there are mental and moral goods, pertaining to one's soul; there are bodily goods to do with one's health, strength, and appearance; and there are external goods, which comprise everything else, animate and inanimate, that one has good reason to value – family, friends, property, reputation, national success, and so forth. Aristotle, regards goods of the first category as primary and the foundation for a good life, but that life, as he puts it 'needs the external goods as well; for it is impossible, or not easy, to do noble acts without the proper equipment. In many actions we use friends and riches and political power as instruments' (*Nicomachean Ethics* 1. 8, 1099a33–1099b2).

Unlike Aristotle, the Stoics have a monolithic theory of goodness. This theory is based on the claim that anything truly good should be beneficial in all circumstances, and anything truly bad should be always harmful. The only items that pass this demanding test in Stoic philosophy are virtue and vice, on the plausible assumption that such character states are unconditionally beneficial and harmful respectively.[11] Hence the referent of Stoic goodness is always and only a virtuous character, what Aristotle classifies as goodness of soul, and the referent of Stoic badness is always and only the opposite disposition. The Stoics do not deny the obvious fact that we are naturally disposed to prefer health and wealth to sickness and poverty. We could even say, on their behalf, that such things are quasi-good and quasi-bad. However, according to Stoic axiology, these things are not essentially good or bad, because people can misuse health and wealth, thus making them harmful and bad; contrariwise, virtuous people can make beneficial use of situations in which they find themselves sick or poor.

Rather than count health as a bodily good and wealth as an external good, as Aristotle does, the Stoics classify such things as 'preferred indifferents', and they classify their opposites as 'dispreferred indifferents'. These cumbrous expressions signify that health and wealth are things that we are naturally disposed to prefer to sickness and poverty and indeed should prefer, as long as such preferences are compatible with virtuous action. But such things are indifferent in the sense that they lack the unconditional beneficial value that is essential to happiness and to living a good life. We prefer to have them, but we can live perfectly well without them.[12]

The concept of preferred and dispreferred indifferents has been highly controversial ever since it was first propounded. Is it coherent or rather an instance of double talk? It is coherent if we make three assumptions: first, that health and wealth have an intrinsically positive value that their opposites lack, thereby giving us *prima facie* reasons to look after our health and our property and not to neglect these things; second, that anything truly good must be an essential and invariant constituent of happiness, whatever situation persons find themselves in; and third, that the only thing that satisfies this essentialist condition is virtue, i.e. excellence of character. The first assumption concerning our natural preferences is obviously sound. The second and third assumptions, on the other hand, highly controversial though they are, are central to Stoic philosophy and to its distinctiveness as ethical theory. Persons who are of excellent character satisfy the monolithic theory of goodness because virtue by its nature can never fail to benefit and do good. Such persons because of their character invariably benefit themselves and they also benefit others like them.[13] According to Stoicism, virtuous persons, by reason of their character, have all that they need, over and above basic subsistence, in order to flourish to the highest possible degree. These ideal persons, like everyone else, have natural preferences for what Aristotle calls bodily and external goods, and these preferences will normally enter into their conduct of daily life. But a preferred item is not a requirement of Stoic happiness, and so its absence cannot diminish the virtue that *is* unconditionally required.

Given this monolithic theory of goodness, we might well suppose that the Stoics would have no use for the concept of 'external goodness'. Since goodness is encapsulated by virtue and only by virtue, must it not be an entirely internal thing, the state of mind, constituting excellence of character? That account of virtue is incontrovertible because virtue is always internal to *a* mind, but virtue can in principle be instantiated in many minds, each of which would necessarily be external to the others. This explains why the Stoics after all have a use for the concept of external goods, a use that is both compatible with their monolithic theory of goodness and highly germane to their theory of friendship.

Some Stoic goods, we are told, pertain to the soul, while other goods are external.[14] Items of the first category are exactly what we would expect from the monolithic theory of goodness, 'virtues and virtuous actions'. The external category is what interests us here; for it is primarily occupied by friends, meaning virtuous people who are friends of virtuous people. It is easy to see why friends are classified as external. However close one's friends are, they remain literally as external to oneself as one's house and garden. The house and garden count as preferred indifferents, but what promotes friends to the status of external *goods*? The answer must be their virtue together with the further Stoic notion that virtue is unfailingly beneficial. The only thing outside virtuous persons that could be truly and unfailingly beneficial to them is the virtue of other virtuous persons because affectionate and mutual benefiting is the essence of friendship.[15] We can understand, then, why friendship and goodwill are also classified as 'relational goods', meaning character states that bring about one's beneficial and kindly relation to people who, as we have seen, will include oneself if one is a virtuous person.[16]

We should now ask how one virtuous friend benefits another. This is a telling question because virtuous persons are presumed to be completely self-sufficient, meaning that their excellent character gives them all that they need, in order to live the good life, over and above basic material necessities. In approaching the Stoic answers to the question, we should note that, besides placing friends in the category of external goods, the Stoics also place them in the category of 'productive' goods, saying that 'the friend and the benefits accruing from a friend are productive goods in as much as they produce happiness' (*eudaimonia*).[17] This cannot mean that happiness is causally dependent on friends. If that were the case, the virtuous person's unassailable self-sufficiency would be negated. A virtuous Stoic can in principle do without friends.[18] The necessary and sufficient producers of happiness are the virtues. Can we take the 'productive' contribution of friends to mean that friends in some way *facilitate* happiness? I shall suggest that this is on the right lines, but in what way it is on the right lines will require extensive discussion.

The Stoics classify the virtues as 'goods that are both constitutive and productive on the grounds that the virtues not only produce happiness but also complete it by being its very parts'.[19] The constitutive aspect of the virtues is central to Stoic ethics because of their doctrine that happiness consists entirely of a virtuous character.

As the terms 'productive' and 'constitutive' exemplify, the Stoics liked to use jargon to signify fine conceptual distinctions. What they seem to have in mind here looks like a version of the familiar distinction between means and ends. The Stoic end of life is happiness, constituted by virtue. This explains why the virtues are constitutive goods. Calling them productive goods as well looks a circular move, but it is not viciously circular if we take the virtues, as the Stoics did (Cicero, *De finibus* 3.24), to be analogous to skills that produce their goal by being performed, like dance. As to the friend's status as a productive good, this must have to do, for reasons we have already seen, with the friend's virtues and only his virtues. I underline this point in order to underscore the absence of material benefit from the Stoic notion of friendship. Virtuous Stoics do not need material benefits from their friends in order to complete their happiness.

But this analysis raises the following question. If the virtues, which are internal to the self, both produce and constitute happiness, why do the Stoics emphatically make the virtuous friend, who is external to the self, a productive good in his own right? How or why does the self-sufficing virtuous person want friends?

Aristotle devoted a chapter of the *Nicomachean Ethics* (9.9) to this very question. While he differed from the Stoics in assigning instrumental *goodness* to material benefits, subject to that qualification, his treatment of virtuous friends is very close to that of the Roman Stoic Seneca. Aristotle and Seneca do not think that neediness or helplessness has anything to do with virtue friendship, but they are equally insistent that their exemplary persons want to have friends. A fascinating balancing act is at work in both philosophers' views on how to reconcile self-sufficiency and friendship.

4

Aristotle situates his rejoinders to the self-sufficiency question by posing a seeming inconsistency between the virtuous and happy person's supply of goods and the notion of a friend as another self. The 'other self' idea, he proposes, would be plausible if a friend does for you what you cannot do for yourself (otherwise the friend would not be an *other* self), but if you are flourishing anyway and self-sufficient, won't a friend be superfluous?

Aristotle has a four-part reply. First, he concedes that a genuinely flourishing person will be adequately supplied with life's wherewithal. But he finds it 'strange' that such a person would be without friends because friends are thought to be the greatest of external goods. Second, Aristotle takes it that friendship is more concerned with benefiting than with being benefited, and that benefiting is especially characteristic of a virtuous person. In this case, he infers, a virtuous person will need friends in order to have people to benefit; otherwise his social virtues will be merely potential rather than actively exercised. Third, Aristotle argues, human nature is inherently and essentially sociable, so a flourishing and virtuous person will choose a sociable life and one spent with friends rather than strangers. Finally, with his fourth and most interesting response to the self-sufficiency challenge, Aristotle draws on his previous distinction between the three grounds for friendship – utility, pleasure, and virtue. A virtuous person will *have no need* for friends purely on the basis of a friend's utility or pleasure-giving qualities. However, the non-necessity of such friends does not entail the virtuous person's ability to be happy without any friends. On the contrary, virtuous people need virtuous friends in order to be fully aware of the goodness that is common to their own and their friends' existence. In this perfect form of friendship, a pair of virtuous friends illuminate each other's characters, and are thus of immense cognitive value to one another in exemplifying and revealing their cognate virtues.

We have already noted the Stoics' affinity to Aristotle in their assigning friends the status of external goods, their making mutual helpfulness a function of virtuous character, and the attribution of sociability to all normal human beings. They also developed ideas, according to Seneca, that recall this striking Aristotelian notion that the friend, in being another self, is an instructive mirror for the self.[20] Seneca is our fullest source for the Stoic philosophy of friendship. His most relevant work is his series of *Moral Letters to Lucilius*.[21]

Whether the correspondence was genuine or a literary ploy we shall never know for sure, but Seneca's expressions of love and concern for Lucilius ring true. The main theme of the Letters is how to achieve progress towards the Stoic ideal of wisdom. Seneca presents himself as devoted to this project both on his own account and as an adviser and helper for his younger friend Lucilius. Thus the Letters, with one proviso, may be read as a literary instance of Stoic friendship in action – the friend as a 'productive good' – with the more advanced Stoic exhorting and advising the other one.

The proviso is the fact that, in strict Stoic theory, as we have seen, you have to be someone of flawless character in order to qualify as a Stoic friend. Seneca is at pains to indicate his own shortcomings, and shortcomings pertain even more to his implied correspondent. We do not, then, have a pair of Stoic paragons writing to one another, but what the Stoics themselves called progressives, fallible persons doing their best to achieve a fully virtuous character. The merely progressive status of Seneca and Lucilius actually enhances the interest of the Letters. Many of them are literary attempts to approximate ideal Stoic friendship. The warm tone Seneca adopts towards Lucilius shows how mistaken it is to call Stoic friendship, as one scholar has done, 'austere',[22] or to say, as another scholar has done, that the Stoics had small interest in friendship.[23] Apart from registering deep affection and joy, Seneca also gives Lucilius detailed instructions concerning the theory of Stoic friendship in its strict sense. In what follows, I will be chiefly concerned with the theory, but I will preface that by translating much of one short letter (number 35), as an example of the correspondence's characteristic mixture of affection, jesting and admonition.

> When I ask you so insistently to get serious, I am doing my own business: I want a friend, and that can't happen to me unless you proceed to develop yourself, in the way you have begun. At present you love me, but you are not my friend. 'Hey', you say, 'Are these things different?' Yes, very different. One who is a friend loves, but one who loves is not automatically a friend. That's why friendship is always helpful, but love sometimes even does harm. If for no other reason, make progress, so you can learn how to love. And make haste, while you are making progress for me, lest another person benefit from your lessons. Actually I am already getting a profit from imagining the time when we shall be of one mind... but I also want to rejoice over the reality. Joy comes to us from those we love even when they are distant, but it is light and fleeting; the sight of

> them, their presence and conversation, has a pleasure that is alive, at least if you not only see the person you want to, but also see him in the condition you want him to be in. So bring yourself to me, an immense gift, and to put on speed realize that you are mortal and I am old. Hurry to me, but hurry to yourself first. Make progress, and above all take pains to be consistent with yourself.

This letter delineates the reciprocal benefits accruing to both parties from a virtuous or would-be virtuous friendship. Seneca gently taunts Lucilius for lacking what it takes to be an authentic Stoic friend – knowledge of how to love. You can love someone without being unfailingly beneficial, which is what Seneca hopes for from Lucilius. If Seneca's hope looks self-seeking or egoistic, we should notice that it is entirely related to his benefits to Lucilius, meaning his efforts to advance Lucilius's progress. Any of us will press a friend to come and visit us, but Seneca makes his wanting to see Lucilius conditional on Lucilius's progress, which he expresses by saying 'hurry to yourself first'. The 'self' Seneca urges Lucilius to hurry towards is Lucilius's improved character, a self that will approach the Stoic ideal of human nature at its best.[24] For Seneca and Lucilius really to benefit one another with the love required by Stoic friendship, they would need to be completely of one mind and moral character. That at present is only a distant prospect. In the letter prior to this one, Seneca had congratulated Lucilius on the latter's progress, calling Lucilius 'my handiwork' (*opus*), choosing a metaphor based on the way a farmer takes delight in the fruition of his orchard (*Epistulae* 34, 2). In this ensuing letter he assures Lucilius that his mentoring has not been entirely disinterested. He wants to profit from it by a friendship with Lucilius that the latter's progress can facilitate, and he jestingly wants to be sure that he, and not someone else, will reap that profit.

We need to be careful in how we interpret Seneca's talk of profit. He is not suggesting that he has befriended Lucilius in order to benefit from him. That would be seeking a friendship from utilitarian, self-interested motives. Seneca's friendly motivations are on behalf of Lucilius and for Lucilius's benefit. Still, friendship of any kind, however virtuously motivated, must be reciprocal to some extent. You can love someone who doesn't love you back, but you cannot be genuine friends with persons who do not make a significant return to you in care and affection. Seneca's hoped-for and so-called profit from Lucilius is reciprocal benefit from the younger man in return for the interest in him that Seneca has been taking and the instruction Seneca has been giving. As

Seneca states in another letter, 'It is a part of love and of friendship to return favours' (*Ep.* 81, 12).

Although Seneca and Lucilius are not friends according to strict Stoic theory, the way Seneca presents their relationship is instructive as a guide to that theory precisely because of the way the pair presently falls short. Seneca is trying to instruct Lucilius in the principles of the Stoic way of life. Lucilius's imperfect grasp of these principles is implicit in Seneca's observation that Lucilius does not yet know how to love. By trying to instruct Lucilius, Seneca pretends to play the role of a fully fledged Stoic friend. As we have seen, the Stoics counted friends as 'external' and 'productive' goods, meaning that each provides the other with the benefit of their own virtues. Stoic virtues consist in moral knowledge, knowledge of how to conduct oneself appropriately in all circumstances. Stoic friends benefit one another by sharing in one another's virtues, and since Stoic virtues are invariant in quality and value, and in the knowledge that they require, such friends benefit one another equally. At present Lucilius is the greater beneficiary. But Seneca, though more advanced in his understanding and practice of Stoicism, lacks the infallible knowledge of the Stoic wise man.

Why do the Stoics, in their theory of perfect friendship, lay such emphasis on knowledge in the special sense of infallible grasp of goodness? To respond to that question, I briefly digress from Seneca in order to outline a discourse from Epictetus (2.22). With the heading 'On friendship', It was delivered some fifty years after Seneca's death in the early years of the second century AD. I summarize the argument as follows.

1. True love requires complete devotion to whatever one loves.
2. A person can be completely devoted only to good things.
3. Therefore, true love requires knowledge of good things.
4. Wise persons know good things and can distinguish them from things that are bad or indifferent.
5. Non-wise persons lack that knowledge.
6. Therefore, only the wise are capable of true love.

The conclusion is startling: you have to be completely knowledgeable about authentic values in order to love truly.

The argument's first premise, 'True love requires complete devotion', is acceptable provided that one thinks of loving that is unqualified and unconditional. The second premise, 'A person can be devoted only to good things', is also acceptable as long as it means that one can be devoted only to things that one believes to be good, or to things that one likes a lot; for it would be absurd to be devoted to things that one finds bad, or dislikes, or regards as indifferent. The controversial premise is the third one, 'True love requires knowledge of good things'. By 'knowledge' Epictetus means objective certainty, and by 'good' he means 'whatever is always and unfailingly beneficial'. As we have already seen, the Stoics classified numerous things that people ordinarily find good (health, wealth, and so forth) as preferred indifferents, and they classified the opposites of such things not as 'bad' but as dispreferred indifferents. The Stoics reasoned that our natural preferences do not confer goodness or badness on these things. Such value judgments are applicable, instead, to the use made of the things, with the good or bad use dependent on people's judgments and intentions, not on the things themselves.[25] Hence the Stoic concluded that no preferred or dispreferred thing is essentially beneficial or harmful.

When we build these points into Epictetus's argument, we can begin to understand his startling conclusion that true love requires wisdom. If people are completely devoted to physical exercise or financial success or their family's prestige, it would be irrational for them not to judge such things to be desirable goals and to deem success in pursuing them to be good and contributory to happiness. But if such things (though preferable) are indifferent to happiness and excellence, given the posited connections between love, goodness, and knowledge, they cannot be objects of true love.

Epictetus elaborates his connection between true love and wisdom by imagining someone who admits lack of wisdom but who also claims to love his child. He has a discussion with this person and finds that the person's lack of wisdom consists in the instability of his value judgments and emotions:

> Do you think that you can be the friend of someone if you hold incorrect opinions about him?
>
> No.
>
> What if your opinion about him is subject to change. Can your relations be warm?
>
> No.
>
> And if you alternate praise with criticism?
>
> Not then either.

As the dialogue continues, Epictetus confronts his respondent with situations in which quarrels develop between father and son over an inheritance or a girlfriend or an award for public service. The point of this discussion is to show that true love is only possible between people who understand and endorse the indifference of all these contested things, and who situate goodness in one another's excellence of character. Stoic wisdom, the argument runs, is essential to true love; for without it people's friendships are bound to be unstable and unable to benefit one another in the virtuous ways that only true friends, persons who have such a character, can actually do.

Epictetus's exposition will probably strike many readers as throwing cold water over our most intimate relationships. Must we see our friends or be seen by them as moral perfectionists if our friendship is to flourish or even get off the ground? The strict Stoic answer is affirmative, but it must immediately be tempered by the recognition that Stoicism is a perfectionist philosophy. Strictly speaking, all people, including Stoic philosophers, are ignoramuses according to the infallible standard of Stoic wisdom. In setting the bar to perfect friendship beyond realistic attainment, Stoicism challenges our everyday complacency. Seneca, however, even when speaking of this unattainable point, offers many thoughts that are applicable to imperfect friendships. This will be especially clear if we review his responses to Aristotle's question about why the self-sufficient and virtuous man wants to have friends.

In Letter 9, specifically on this topic, Seneca explains a Stoic distinction, hard to render in English, between 'lacking' (*egere*) on the one hand, and 'requiring' (*opus esse*), on the other hand. Wise persons, thanks to their virtuous character, cannot *lack* anything relevant to happiness. Even if they are maimed or suffering from other disadvantages, they are not needy or incapable of living well. Still, for living a normal daily life they *require* adequately functioning limbs and sense organs. Such persons can, if circumstances dictate, do without friends and still maintain happiness; but they do not wish or choose to be alone. They *require* friends in order, as Seneca, in his typically extreme way, puts the point, 'to have someone to die for or whom I may follow into exile'. In this perspective, friendship is desirable, not for one's own utility or pleasure or making up for what one lacks, but as the means of exercising the moral virtues, just as Aristotle had previously argued.

In a later Letter (109), Seneca gives a more searching response to the self-sufficiency question. If friendship is a relationship of mutual benefit, how can wise persons, who are replete with all that is good in their individual characters, benefit one another?

In the first place, he says, they do so by activating one another's virtues, motivating one another, giving each other opportunities for honorable action. They prod one another and learn from each other. Secondly, by cheering each other on, they are a source of joy and confidence. 'One wise person will help another, not only with his own strength, but also with the strength of the one he is helping'. Here we can observe the deficiency that Seneca was still finding in Lucilius's character. Seneca now imagines someone objecting that the two wise people do not really help one another; rather each helps himself. I quote Seneca's retort in full:

> The wise man cannot maintain his mental disposition unless he has access to friends like himself with whom to share his virtues. Furthermore, you should note that there is mutual friendship between all the virtues. Therefore help is provided by one who loves the virtues of a person like himself and who in return supplies his own virtues to be loved. Things that are alike give pleasure, especially when they are honourable and their recipients know how to be mutual in approving them. Besides, the only person who has the expertise to motivate a wise man is another wise man, just as only a human being can rationally motivate another human being. Therefore, just as reason is needed to motivate reason, so perfect reason is needed to motivate perfect reason. (*Epistulae* 109, 9–11)

Here, if I am not mistaken, we have Seneca's version of the Aristotelian mirror notion of friendship: you love your friend's good qualities, and your friend gives you in return the reflection of your own virtues.

5

The Stoic theory of friendship, like Aristotle's virtue friendship, is an ideal. It is not intended to cover the affectionate relationships that ordinary people engage in from day to day. But the ideal nature of this friendship, with its exclusive focus on virtuous character, enables the theory to serve as a touchstone for the quality of imperfect relationships by getting us to ask such questions as the following. Do our friends really deserve our regard for them, and do we really deserve their regard? What do we owe our friends, and are we genuinely of help to them and they to us? Do we and our friends have enough in common to constitute a relationship that is so mutually helpful, lasting, and intimate that we can share everything with our friend? De we really and fully love our friends for their sake rather than our own sake? We may well be disinclined to ask such questions because they seem too rationalistic and peremptory to suit the spontaneity we moderns associate with the formation and continuation of friendships. However, the answers to such questions could forestall the disappointments and ill will that sometimes bring modern friendships to conclusions of mutual recrimination.

We may still find Stoic friendship disturbingly remote from our own experience in the little interest that it explicitly takes in a friend's personality and uniqueness, and in the circumstances under which friends come to care for one another. Aristotle, with his emphasis on virtuous character rather than personality, has been criticized on these lines, and the Stoics seem liable to the same criticism, perhaps even more strongly. Seneca states that the Stoic wise man will never lack friends because it is always in his power to replace the friends he has lost (*Epistulae* 9, 5). Instead of lengthily mourning deceased friends, Seneca recommends us to love them 'greedily' while we have them and rejoice in remembering them thereafter (*Epistulae* 63). Both statements, even in their full context, are rather chilling to a modern sensibility.

By way of explanation, we need to fill them out. Grief is never an acceptable emotion for a Stoic because it is presumed to involve the mistaken belief that one has suffered a real harm as distinct from losing a 'preferred' indifferent.[26] As to forming new friends, Seneca presents that as the proper application of an ideally loving nature. Truly good persons want many friends, in order to extend their capacity to love. Seneca characterizes anyone who has *only* one friend to lose as deficient in affection.

Such observations on the desirability of making and replacing friendships remind us that the Stoics were fashioning their views within a world where friendship in the general sense of reliable and mutual benefit was expected and even essential for the conduct of daily life in all its forms. Ancient friends, as I remarked earlier, strongly depended on one another's affection, loyalty, reciprocity, and practical help. The Stoics completely endorsed these attributes of friendship, but they challenged their conventionally utilitarian basis by treating virtuous character as the essential foundation for a truly loving friendship.

In this proceeding, they can be seen to have canvassed what Jennifer Whiting (1991) calls 'impersonal friends'. Whiting bases her argument on Aristotle's virtue friendship, but it applies equally well, or perhaps even better, to the Stoics. Character friends, as Whiting calls them, value themselves as persons of a certain sort, namely as virtuous, and valuing someone for the sake of the person's virtuous character entails valuing that same character in the case of anyone of that sort anywhere.

In this way, Whiting argues, we can envision a 'pool of impersonal friends', people the virtuous person *could* love not because of who they are in particular but 'as persons of a certain sort'. In fact, of course, the virtuous person's actual friendships will depend on contingencies of time, place, and interest – whom she meets and how she gets along with whom she meets – but what she primarily values in her actual friends could have been satisfied by the similar merits of others.

'Impersonal friends' sounds like an oxymoron, but it does not mean that such friends do not value one another *as individual persons*. To the contrary, it means that they value one another for individually embodying the virtues of character. That the Stoics envisioned impersonal friends in Whiting's sense should be clear from my earlier remarks, but it is also made quite explicit in the following testimonies:

> If a single wise person anywhere at all extends his finger prudently, all wise persons throughout the world are benefited. This is their friendship's function; this is what wise persons' virtues, with their shared benefits, are for.[27]

and

> All virtuous persons benefit one another, but they are not in all circumstances friends and well-wishers ... of one another because of not being acquainted or not living in the same place. But their disposition to one another is always friendly and well-wishing.[28]

In other words, according to Stoicism, any virtuous person could potentially become the friend of any other virtuous person because all virtuous persons share the same wise and benevolent character.[29] These traits transcend their particular qualities as the unique individuals that they are. As in friendship of any kind, however, to become actual friends even these Stoic paragons need to get to know one another and have the same location. Do they also need to be drawn to one another as personalities? That condition, so basic to our modern idea of friends, is not specified. What the Stoics offer us instead is the mutual attractiveness that fully virtuous people have for one another.

Notes

1. For complementary accounts, see Graver (2007, chapter 8), and Reydams-Schils (2005, chapter 2).

2. Stobaeus (2.108, 15/*SVF* 3.630) summarizes the Stoic theory as follows: 'Friendship is confined to the wise because they alone are of one mind (*homonoia*) concerning the things pertaining to life: being of one mind is knowledge of goods that are shared. This is because authentic, not simply nominal, friendship is impossible without trust and reliance... True love is only possible between virtuous people.' Similarly Diogenes Laertius (7.124/*SVF* 3.631).
3. See Lynch (2005) and Nehamas (2010).
4. For detailed discussion, see Cooper (1999, chapter 13).
5. I am giving a composite definition based on *Rhetoric* 2.4 and *Nicomachean Ethics* 8.2.
6. See *Nicomachean Ethics* 8.3.
7. The Epicurean school at Athens was founded a few years before the Stoic school in the last years of the third century BC. For the next few centuries the two schools competed for followers, holding opposite positions on such primary questions as the intrinsic value of pleasure and virtue, and the natural appropriateness of community life.
8. As reflected in the Stoic concept of *oikeiosis*: see Cicero, *De finibus* 3.16–7 and 62–3 with discussion by Long (1996/2001, chapter 7).
9. Stobaeus (2.9, 27 / *SVF* 3.98). See Banateanu (2001, pp. 70–2).
10. See for instance Fromm (1956); Ricoeur (1992, pp. 180–8); and Kwan, Bond, and Singelis (1997).
11. The Stoics defined virtue as 'a consistent character, choiceworthy for its own sake and not from fear or hope of anything external' (Diogenes Laertius 7.89). The primary Stoic virtues are prudence, courage, justice, and moderation. For the details, see Long and Sedley (1987, chapter 60).
12. For the Stoic sources and discussion, see Long and Sedley (1987, chapter 58).
13. For the extension of virtue's benefits to other virtuous persons, see Bett (1997, p. 89).
14. Stobaeus (2.70/*SVF* 3.97); Diogenes Laertius (7.95/*SVF* 3.97a); Sextus Empiricus, *Adversus mathematicos* (11.46/*SVF* 3.96).
15. In Stoicism, because pleasure is indifferent to happiness, it is not specified as a consequence of the friendship between virtuous people, as it is in Aristotle. See Fraisse (1974, pp. 359–61).
16. Stobaeus (2.73, 16–19 / *SVF* 3.112). See Banateanu (2001, p. 78); and Reydams-Schils (2005, p. 69).
17. Diogenes Laertius (7.96/*SVF* 3.107). Cicero, *De finibus* (3.55/*SVF* 3.108), classifies the friend as the only good that is simply productive.
18. See Seneca, *Epistulae* 9, 5–9.
19. Diogenes Laertius ibid. The Greek word that I render by 'constitutive' is *telikos*. Literally translated, this word means 'ultimate' in the teleological sense of fulfilling an end.
20. *Magna Moralia* 1213a10–26.
21. Seneca's observations on friendship are well treated by Reydams-Schils (2005, chapter 2).
22. See Lesses (1993).
23. Konstan (1997, p. 113).
24. For a full treatment of Seneca on the self, see Long (2006, chapter 17).

25. See Long (1996/2001, pp. 28–9), for the Stoic notion that goodness does not reside in 'things' but in the kind of use people make of things or the way people respond to things.
26. Epictetus counsels verbal sympathy, and even sharing someone's groans, but refraining from 'groaning within oneself' (*Encheiridion* 16). Here we may see a difference from Aristotle, who acknowledges 'grieving with' one's friend as a characteristic of friendship; see *Nicomachean Ethics* 9, 1166a7; *Eudemian Ethics* 7, 1240a36–9, *Rhet*oric 2.4, 1381a3–5. However, Aristotle emphatically recommends people not to burden friends with their own suffering, *Nicomachean Ethics* 9, 1171b4–10.
27. Plutarch, *De communibus notitiis* (1068F / *SVF* 3.627).
28. Stobaeus (2.101, 24/*SVF* 3.626). According to Cicero, *De natura deorum* (1.121/*SVF* 3.635), the Stoics held that the wise are friends even without knowing one another, but that extreme claim conflicts with the second testimony cited above, which is a much more reliable source.
29. Underlying these striking statements is the Stoic doctrine that all virtuous persons form a community constituted by the perfection of reason in which they share along with the gods. See Banateanu (2001, chapters 7–8); Reydams-Schils (2005, pp. 70–82); and Vogt (2008). This world-wide community is completely utopian, owing to the absence of any actually wise persons, but the ideal that it represents can serve as a model in the way that I have argued here in the case of Stoic friendship. The cosmic scope of Stoic social theorizing is a marked divergence from Aristotle's understanding of the tiny Greek city-state as the paradigm human society.

References

A. Banateanu (2001) *La théorie stoicienne de l' amitié* (Fribourg: CERF).

R. Bett (1997) Sextus Empiricus*: Against the Ethicists* (Oxford: Oxford University Press).

J. M. Cooper (1999) *Reason and Emotion. Essays on Ancient Moral Psychology and Ethical Theory* (Princeton: Princeton University Press).

J. C. Fraisse (1974) *Philia: La notion d'amitié dans la philosophie antique* (Paris: Vrin).

E. Fromm (1956) *The Art of Loving* (New York: Harper and Row).

M. R. Graver (2007) *Stoicism and Emotion* (Chicago: University of Chicago Press).

B. Helm (2009) 'Friendship', *Stanford Encyclopedia of Philosophy* (online).

D. Konstan (1997) *Friendship in the Ancient World* (Cambridge: Cambridge University Press).

V. S. Y. Kwan, M. H. Bond and T. M. Singelis (1997) 'Pancultural Explanations for Life Satisfaction: Adding Relationship Harmony to Self-Esteem', *Journal of Personality and Social Psychology* 73 (5), 1038–951.

G. Lesses (1993) 'Austere Friends: The Stoics and Friendship', *Apeiron* 26 (1), 67–75.

A. A. Long and D. N. Sedley (1987) *The Hellenistic Philosophers* (Cambridge: Cambridge University Press).

A. A. Long (1996/2001) *Stoic Studies* (Cambridge/Berkeley: University of California Press).
A. A. Long (2006) *From Epicurus to Epictetus. Studies in Hellenistic and Roman Philosophy* (Oxford: Oxford University Press).
S. Lynch (2005) *Philosophy and Friendship* (Edinburgh: Edinburgh University Press).
A. Nehamas (2010) 'Aristotelian *Philia,* Modern Friendship', *Oxford Studies in Ancient Philosophy* 39, 213–48.
G. Reydams-Schils (2005) *The Roman Stoics: Self, Responsibility, Affection* (Chicago: Chicago University Press).
P. Ricoeur (1992) *Oneself as Another* (Chicago: University of Chicago Press).
SVF = *Stoicorum Veterum Fragmenta,* ed. H. von Arnim, 3 vols (Leipzig 1903–5). This is the standard collection of the original Greek and Latin texts that preserve the doctrines of the early Stoic philosophers.
K. M. Vogt (2008) *Law, Reason, and the Cosmic City. Political Philosophy in the Early Stoa* (Oxford: Oxford University Press).
J. Whiting (1991) 'Impersonal Friends', *The Monist* 74 (3), 3–29.

13
Aesthetics and the Art of Friendship

Sheila Lintott

> What is so pleasant as these jets of affection which make a young world for me again? What so delicious as a just and firm encounter of two, in thought and feeling? How beautiful, on their approach to this beating heart, the steps and forms of the gifted and the true?
>
> Ralph Waldo Emerson, 'Friendship'

In the spirit of exploring fresh perspectives, I offer this investigation into the aesthetic aspects of personal relationships with a focus on friendship.[1] Glossing the aesthetic aspects of friendship, as we too often do, impoverishes our understanding of the value and meaning of friendships, relationships which give shape and content to our lives, which animate our lives or, as Nancy Sherman (1993) puts it, relationships which structure the good life. The friendships we forge and those we forgo, the loves we cultivate and those we lose, these varying and variable relations broaden (or impoverish) our experiences, intensify (or diminish) our feelings, and help (or hinder) our self understanding and self creation. I wish to explore here how friendships are aesthetic expressions and impressions in and of our lives, as form and color are aesthetic expressions and impressions in and of paintings. I do so by pursuing an analogy between art and friendship as well as by investigating some of the aesthetic aspects of friendship: how cultivating and enjoying friendship invites creative and relatively free expressions of self, the ways aesthetic taste factors into with whom we are friends, and the manner in which friendships can help to harmoniously round out a life.

1 Friendship: freedom and openness

Ralph Waldo Emerson (1991) explains that with a friend, 'I may think aloud...I may drop even those undermost garments of dissimulation, courtesy, and second thought, which men never put off, and may deal with him with the simplicity and wholeness with which one chemical atom meets another' (p. 225). Friendship, along these lines, is sometimes compared to a home, to a place where one is comfortable and can be her true self, a place where she can shed the various masks she dons throughout her day. We need not put on airs for our good friends, at least not typically, and we feel confident that they know and like us for who we are, blemishes and all. We might say that there is a good degree of interpersonal freedom found in friendship which allows for greater creative expressions of self, greater both quantitatively and qualitatively. Friendship is a site rich in potential for the sort of creative activity that is most commonly associated with art appreciation and art making.

Compared to most other social interactions, friends are relatively free in the company of one another. There is little by way of a social script for friends to follow. As Alexander Nehamas points out, friendship is difficult to represent pictorially because there are no necessary or typical activities associated with it, unlike the relationships we foster with parents, lovers, and co-workers. Friends, he tells us, can be doing anything together, from fighting with one another to embracing in a tender hug. This makes it difficult to read friendship off any single moment:

> We can't tell whether two people are friends simply by looking at them on a particular occasion any more than we can do so in painting, because there is no clear path that leads from a discrete interaction between two people to their friendship. Even dying for me – that staple of our mythology of friendship – does not necessarily show that you are my friend. (Nehamas 2010, p. 269)

A less eloquent way of expressing this observation is to say that there seem to be relatively few clichés to fall into in friendships, whereas the feeling that one is behaving in a common, at worst, even cliché manner can be uncomfortably common among lovers and within families.

So, there is a degree of freedom in friendship that is not common in other social interactions, even other intimate relations. This freedom, of course, demands as much as it affords: we are supposed to be sincere, honest, and 'real' with our friends. This freedom is enacted both in moments of receptivity and in moments of expressivity. Friendship demands sincere curiosity and an attitude of openness, lest our encounters with friends be reduced to utilitarian exchanges or narcissistic co-existence. Consider Yi-Fu Tuan's characterization of a good person: 'One kind of definition of a good person, or a moral person, is that that person does not impose his or her fantasy on another. That is, he's willing to acknowledge the reality of other individuals, or even of the tree or the rock. So to be able to stand and listen' (Yi-Fu Tuan, quoted in Saito 1998, p. 135). Admittedly, the ability to 'stand and listen' is not a sufficient condition for being a moral person, but it seems to be a necessary one.[2] Likewise, when friends 'stand and listen' to one another, they act out of friendship and are being good people in Tuan's sense.

The openness required in friendship is similar to that required in art appreciation. Yuriko Saito applies Tuan's conception of a good person to the aesthetic realm and argues that as art and nature appreciators, provided we wish to engage in genuine appreciation, we must attend to the object of appreciation on its own terms. Following Dewey, she maintains that 'art...both challenges and entices us to overcome (at least to a certain extent) the confines of our own perspective by inviting us to visit an often unfamiliar world created by the artist' (Saito 1998, p. 136). To visit that unfamiliar world, one needs to be able to see past one's own agenda and obsessions. Jerome Stolnitz (1960), for example, describes the aesthetic attitude as one that is disinterested and sympathetic. In other words, when appreciating something or someone aesthetically, one should not be preoccupied with, but rather distanced from her own interests or expectations, yet simultaneously, one should also be deeply attentive to the object of appreciation.

When we truly appreciate something or someone's aesthetic features, we do so, as Saito (1998) puts it, on its own terms, not on ours. Arnold Berleant (2005) comments on the power of the aesthetic when it is engaged in openly: 'From the central place accorded perceptual awareness, aesthetic experience is, at least in principle, unconstrained by preconceptions...' and 'those who can set aside the preconceptions of aesthetic distance...may discover that the fullest and most intense experiences of art and natural beauty reveal an intimate absorption in the wonder and vulnerability of the aesthetic' (p. 152). Likewise, one who cares for one's friend and wishes to understand her is invested in her world; she strives to refrain from projecting her own agenda and expectations on her friend. Of course, this is an ideal and, moreover, one which some individuals are better able to approximate than others. My contention is that like Tuan's good person, a good friend, all things being equal, can set one's agenda aside, allowing a friend's needs or desires to trump her own. The balance of this other-regarding behavior fluctuates in friendship as the lives that surround a friendship fluctuate as well. In moments of openness with friends, we are also free to create ourselves with our friends and are expected to help and allow them to create themselves. In this mutual freedom we find wonder and vulnerability; comparing the attitudes and approaches of good friends with those of good aesthetic appreciators discloses a parity that is remarkable.

2 Friendship: from freedom to creativity

We do not generally apply means-ends thinking within friendships. Elizabeth Telfer (1970–1) warns against trying to take such pragmatic shortcuts in the process of forming friendships, shortcuts that she argues are counter-productive; if one aims explicitly at an end, such as accumulating friendships, one thereby curtails the free expression and freedom to explore found in the forming and maintaining of friendships:

> Too much dwelling on the values of friendship has its own dangers. It may lead people to concentrate on looking for friendships rather than friends ... it may well be that this attitude ... is also self-defeating: in other words, that we attain the valuable relationship of friendship only when we cease to think about it and concentrate on the friend himself. (p. 241)

In this warning we hear echoes of familiar sentiments about creating art. Artists are often told 'to stop thinking; stop evaluating; just do what feels right'. Andy Warhol (1975), for example, says:

> When I have to think about it, I know the picture is wrong. And sizing is a form of thinking and coloring is too. My instinct about painting says, 'If you don't think about it, it's right'. As soon as you have to decide and choose, it's wrong. And the more you decide about, the more wrong it gets. (p. 149)

Telfer's warning is also comparable to the distinction Collingwood draws between the creation of art and that of craft. Craft, he maintains, always involves a predetermined end that the craftsperson aims to achieve, whereas with art, there is not necessarily a goal or set end: 'the poet extemporizing his verses, the sculptor playing with his clay ... the artist has no idea what the experience is which demands expression until he has expressed it. What he wants to say is not present to him as an end towards which means have to be devised; it becomes clear to him only as the poem takes shape in his mind, or the clay in his fingers' (Collingwood 1958, p. 29). For Collingwood, art-making is more about process than product. Comparably, a friend is less focused on the goal of making or maintaining a friendship than on the way in which the friendship itself motivates and inspires. In a similar vein, Michael Stocker (1993) argues against purely teleological characterizations of acts of friendship, explaining that, 'when one acts out of friendship, friendship is not, as such, a goal, but rather it plays both a sensitivity and a sine qua non role' (p. 253).

According to Charles Thomas Taylor (2006), 'friendship is essentially subjective, not objective; a habit, not a methodology; and an art, not a science' (p. 92). In other words, friendships and their respective codes are created by the subjects involved in them while in the process of creating them. As we have discussed in the previous section, freedom plays a key role in friendship and Laurence Thomas offers a way to understand the freedom in friendship that helps illuminate some of the creative activity inherent in friendship. Thomas puts social interactions on a continuum from those that are maximally structured to those that are minimally structured, where maximally structured social interactions are highly governed by social roles, rules, and conventions, and in minimally structured social interactions, factors such as roles, rules, and conventions are less relevant. Thomas (1993) maintains that most social relationships are structured to a high degree, with the notable exceptions of friendship and love:

> Friendships and romantic loves are characteristically and paradigmatically minimally structured interpersonal relationships. Even matters of etiquette and protocol are often put aside. We would not know quite what to make of two such individuals who, for instance, insisted upon addressing each other formally or holding each other to the minutest detail of etiquette when they are alone together, save that this was a precious form of amusement between the two of them. Deep friendships and romantic love are the only two forms of interpersonal relationships in which the two parties interact immensely and frequently, but yet, aside from the rules of morality, the nature of that interaction is not defined by this or that set of social rules. (p. 51)

This freedom from rules and expectations is reminiscent of the freedom that can be felt in artistic creation. The aesthetic notion of genius is another point of comparison that highlights the freedom and creativity in both art and friendship. Perhaps a good friend is a sort of interpersonal genius. Kant (1987), for example, conceives of artistic genius as follows: '*Genius* is the talent (natural endowment) that gives the rule to art' (p. 174). The genius doesn't follow any rules, but rather makes her own rules in the process of creating. The absence of rules, however, is not to be likened to an absence of the property of being exemplary:

> Genius is a *talent* for producing something for which no determinate rule can be given, not a predisposition consisting of a skill for something that can be learned by following some rule or other; hence the foremost property of genius must be *originality*... Since nonsense too can be original, the products of genius must also be models, i.e., they must be *exemplary*; hence, though they do not themselves arise through imitation, still they must serve others for this, i.e., as a standard or a rule by which to judge. (Kant 1987, p. 175)

An excellent friendship is not excellent because it is like other excellent friendships. Montaigne (1991) describes his peerless friendship with La Boétie in such a fashion: 'This friendship has had no ideal to follow other than itself; no comparison but with itself.' (p. 10). An excellent friendship is excellent in and of itself and on its own terms, but it may also serve as an ideal, as a model which other friendships, in their more formative stages, might follow. Perhaps it's an exaggeration to say that there are no rules in art or friendship, but those that exist are more rules of thumb or guidelines than strict and specific codes of conduct and creation. A good friend, like a good artist, is able to succeed in original and context sensitive ways within the loose bounds of convention (Berleant 2005, p. 155). For example, in my friendship with my dearest friends, although I admittedly behave in some conventional ways, the vast majority of our interactions feel improvised on the spot.

3 Friendship: escape from alienation

The bonding or feeling of camaraderie with another is reminiscent of a kind of pleasure one might derive from the aesthetic experience of art. Lewis's (1960) description of finding another self in friendship is potent: 'It is when two such persons discover one another, when whether with immense difficulties and semi-articulate fumblings or with what would seem to us an amazing and elliptical speed, they share their vision – it is then that Friendship is born, and instantly they stand together in an immense solitude' (p. 65). Compare this with Tolstoy's (1996) description of the communion, indeed the spiritual union, found in the apprehension of great art:

> The receiver of a true artistic impression is so unified to the artist that he feels as if the work were his own and not someone else's – as if what it expresses were just what he had long been wishing to express. A real work of art destroys, in the consciousness of the receiver, the separation between himself and the artist... In this freeing of our personality from its separation and isolation, in this uniting of it with others, lies the chief characteristic and the great attractive force of art. (pp. 139–40)

Friendship is an obvious example of one way we seek to escape alienation and loneliness. But in addition to finding companionship, in friendship we can experience an awareness of self with other that is similarly enjoyed via art appreciation. As Arnold Berleant (2005) claims, 'in both art and love we may have a sense of being in place, of a dissolution of barriers and boundaries, of communion. And in both an intimate connection can develop. Such connectedness, such continuity, such engagement lie at the very centre of the aesthetic' (p. 156). Like art, friendship destroys or at least momentarily obscures the awareness of a division between self and others: when with a friend, we can become aware that we are in the presence of, as Aristotle put it, 'another self' (*Nicomachean Ethics*, 1166a32). Even in silence with a friend, we can feel a sense of communion. In fact, even when alone, provided one knows she has a true friend somewhere, she may not feel lonely.

Another way humans find relief from alienation is in play. To some, including me, play is an essential element in a good life. For example, Martha Nussbaum (1999) includes play, which she characterizes as 'being able to laugh, to play, to enjoy recreational activities' in her list of activities that together are definitive of a *human* life (p. 42). Focusing on the role of play and playfulness in friendship also helps point up similarities between the value and the creation of friendship and of art. The concept of play is extremely important in many theories of aesthetics; the so-called play-theory was once a leading theory of art which we can find evidence of at least as early as Plato, and also in Schiller, Kant, Hegel, and Spencer. What is play but an activity that is enjoyable for its own sake and perhaps for the sake of some other end? The end in play, for example, winning a game, is not everything (although admittedly it's not nothing either); it's worth playing even if you lose. According to play-theories of art, the artist adopts a playful attitude in the process of creating art. Playfulness opens up possibility; self-consciousness and norms constrain it. As Warhol advises artists: 'Don't think about making art, just get it done. Let everyone else decide whether it's good or bad, whether they love it or hate it. While they're deciding, make even more art' (Warhol quoted in Makos 2002, p. 112). And although to some, play connotes something trivial, a life without play would hardly resemble a human life, and definitely not a desirably human life. As Lewis (1960) says, 'Friendship is unnecessary, like philosophy, like art… It has no survival value; rather it is one of those things which give value to survival' (p. 71). And as Aristotle says, 'no one would choose to live life without friends even if he had all other goods' (*Nicomachean Ethics* 1155a5).

The playfulness one is likely to feel in the company of friends has potential beyond its mere enjoyment. This playfulness allows one to see beyond the given, to envision alternatives to the status quo. When we feel safe and free, we can be playful. Among friends playfulness should flourish. The social and political importance of playfulness is also underscored by María Lugones in her inspiring essay, 'Playfulness, "World"-Travelling, and Loving Perceptions' in which she explores the importance of playfulness in a human life. She says, playfulness is 'in part, an openness to being a fool, which is a combination of not worrying about competence, not being self-important, not taking norms as sacred, and finding ambiguity and double edges a source of wisdom and delight' (Lugones 1987, p. 17). Friendship, like art that engages our imagination, can help us see anew and feel less alone. Amy Mullin (2003) explores how feminist art does just that:

> The imagination involves our capacity to think in detailed ways about states of affairs with which we are not immediately acquainted. We can imagine the past and the future, and we can imagine as well states of affairs that may never or could never exist. Through our imaginations, we can explore both possibilities and impossibilities, and combine things not generally seen as coexisting. It is uncontroversial to maintain that artworks may imaginatively explore patterns, colors, shapes, the movement of bodies, and the interaction of a number of such elements. It should be uncontroversial, as well, to acknowledge that artworks may imaginatively explore moral and

> political ideas, and the emotional responses they engender. When artworks attempt to explore aspects of our moral and political lives, they may have both artistic and moral or political significance. (pp. 196–7)

Marilyn Friedman (1989) also articulates this power of friendship, one that I maintain it shares with (at least some) art: 'Friendship is more likely than many other close personal relationships to provide social support for people who are idiosyncratic, whose un-conventional values and deviant life-styles make them victims of intolerance from family members and others who are unwillingly related to them. In this regard, friendship has socially disruptive possibilities' (p. 286). Friendship and art are both potential sources of solace and inspiration, places where the disenfranchised can feel enfranchised.

4 Aesthetics: ties that bind

Let's now explore a truth that might be difficult to admit: we choose our friends partly for aesthetic reasons, that is, due to their personal appearance, their aesthetic likes and interests, and their projected persona. It seems that aesthetic similarities are one major factor in friendships, and social science research supports this conjecture. For example, in a recent set of four studies, psychologists found that people are most likely to behave in a friendly manner toward and congregate with those who seem, based on sensory perception, similar to them; and salient similarities include not only race and gender, but also factors such as hair color and length and the wearing of eyeglasses (Mackinnon, Gordon, and Wilson 2011). This initial self-sorting helps to further explain previously noted correlations between friends' levels of attractiveness (Cash and Derlega 1978). Finding someone's physical appearance welcoming and attractive because they seem like us is often the first step in social exchanges. Admiring or being captivated by another's appearance and projected persona can motivate further curiosity and instill a sense of comfort, which together might give way to active listening and self-disclosure – both key elements in friendship. In at least one sense, we are attracted to our friends in a manner akin to the way we are attracted to our lovers.

Attraction and similarities in appearance are not the only aesthetic factors at work in friendship. As C.S. Lewis (1960) explains, 'friendship arises out of mere Companionship when two or more of the companions discover that they have in common some insight or interest or even taste which the others do not share and which, till that moment, each believed to be his own unique treasure (or burden)' (p. 65). The shared element in question is sometimes a shared aesthetic taste, for example, a shared liking for something like steampunk, opera, folk art, pinot noir, or B-horror films. The realization that another shares your aesthetic interests and taste can help to solidify a nascent friendship. If David Hume (1998) is correct that 'we choose our favorite author as we do our friend, from conformity of humour and disposition' (p. 150), then it is not surprising that shared aesthetic tastes and interests are good indicators of potential for friendship.

Aesthetic attraction between individuals based on personal appearance and shared aesthetic tastes can lead to great friendships, but these aesthetic groundings of friendship are also potentially socially and politically problematic. Friendship, after all, is by its nature exclusionary and leads to preferential treatment. We think it perfectly natural for and indeed expect people to privilege their friends. The fact that people are most likely to befriend others like them raises important issues related to, for example, racism, sexism, homophobia, classism, and ableism.

Take social class as an example. Class is often associated with very specific aesthetic and artistic tastes: 'At its most basic, class is one way societies sort themselves out...Classes are groups of people of similar economic and social position; people who, for that reason, may share political attitudes, lifestyles, consumption patterns, cultural interests, and opportunities to get ahead' (Scott and Leonhardt 2005, p. 8). Artistic tastes tend to differ along class lines, although admittedly not without exception. David Novitz argues that there are clear political reasons for such artistic divisions. Again, it seems that people seek comfort; as Novitz (1989) explains: 'The dominant classes...find high art congenial. Art that raises disturbing political, moral, economic, or religious issues, that questions gender relations, or points a finger at the sexism, racism or economic injustices that abound in our society, is sometimes dismissed as mere propaganda, or, at best, as popular or as political art' (p. 224). And aesthetic class divisions are not only political; they are also economic, based on what people can afford. People who divide their time between different classes, perhaps working in a setting inhabited by people of high socioeconomic class relative to their own, are aware of subtle marks of fit or alienation; they are 'sensitive to the cultural significance of the cars people drive, the food they serve at parties, where they go on vacation – all the little clues that indicate social status' (Scott and Leonhardt 2005, pp. 64–5). These 'little clues' function to produce a predominance of class segregated friendships, which, with their close bonds and preferential treatment, tend to perpetuate the concentration of wealth and influence in the hands of a few.[3] Moreover, as Friedman (1989) points out, these relationships can be stifling, as 'besides excluding or suppressing outsiders, the practices and traditions of numerous communities are exploitative and oppressive toward many of their own members' (p. 281). Many people, for example many women, homosexuals, and persons of color, know the feeling of being alone in a crowd, of finding themselves nested in a community of 'friends' whose values and commitments one feels at odds with.

Whether we are aware of it or not, we are constantly interpreting the self-presentations of those with whom we have contact, and sometimes our interpretation moves from aesthetic apprehension to moral evaluation based on mere associations and without ample evidence for the moral assessment. In her excellent book *Staring: How We Look*, Rosemarie Garland-Thomson discusses ableism and the cultural construction of the disabled body. Garland-Thomson (2009) explores examples of ways in which we interpret persons based on their appearance, from perception to association and judgment:

> We are exquisitely sensitive to the nuances of meaning encoded in appearance variations and to the rituals of social encounter that tell us who we are in relation to others. Think of the hint implied in a wink, the moral equation of good posture and upstanding citizenship, the gendered connotations of sitting with one's legs spread apart. (p. 38)

These associations are dangerous because, although they are merely metaphorical in origin, they can become literal in use. Consider, Garland-Thomson urges us, the implications of the associations with bodily comportment and posture for a person with facial tics or who navigates the world in a wheel chair; a person with facial tics might be taken as winking or even as manic, and a person in a wheelchair, regardless of posture, is unlikely to be associated with the resolve and confidence of a standing person with excellent posture. She asserts that 'someone permanently seated in a wheelchair...confounds the usual interpretive web of social significances clustering around what we might call the postural arrangement of bodies' (Garland-Thomson 2009, p. 38).

The connections between cultural clues and friendship and between friendship and preferential treatment should concern us. And we should work to cross aesthetic and cultural boundaries in social interactions, to trouble cultural associations between appearance and moral virtues and vices, and to find some less obvious common ground on which to meet. Doing so is required for the sake of diversity and equality, but also for our own sakes – for we can learn so much from our friends, and this potential is severely diminished when our friends are all carbon copies of one another and ourselves. As Socrates asks in the *Lysis*, 'when something, anything at all, is like something else, how can it benefit or harm its like in a way that it could not benefit or harm itself?' (214e). Some commonalities must hold us together with our friends, but there is a wide variety of possible commonalities, perhaps a shared history or a shared commitment, and differences between the friends must exist in friendship so that the friends can learn from and about one another and about themselves. Among our friends, we should seek beauty as Francis Hutcheson (2004) conceives of it, 'Uniformity amidst Variety' (p. 28); something should tie us to each friend, but not the same thing in every case, and much variety should enter into the mix.

5 The ineffability of friendship and aesthetics

G.E. Moore thinks that the personal affection felt in friendships is directed at a person we assess in a positive aesthetic light, but he insists that the knowledge of the person's character and personality serves to enhance our apprehension and appreciation of them as an aesthetic object. In *Principia Ethica* he explains as follows:

> In the case of personal affection, the object itself is not *merely* beautiful...but is itself, in part at least, of great intrinsic value. All the constituents which we have found to be necessary to the most valuable aesthetic enjoyments, namely, appropriate emotion, cognition of truly beautiful qualities, and true belief, are all equally necessary here; but we have the additional fact that the object must be not only truly beautiful, but also truly good in a high degree. (Moore 1929, p. 203)

Moore continues, musing over how mental or subjective states are instantiated by appropriate physical expression and appearance:

> Wherever the [personal] affection is most valuable, the appreciation of mental qualities must form a large part of it, and...the presence of this part makes the whole far more valuable than it could have been without it. But it seems very doubtful whether this appreciation, by

> itself, can possess as much value as the whole in which it is combined with an appreciation of the appropriate *corporeal* expression of the mental qualities in question. (p. 203)

It's also worth noting that friends are not only attracted to one another's personal appearance and aesthetic tastes; friendships deepen as a result of a mutual understanding and appreciation of one another's person and persona. Contra Aristotle, we can form true friendships based not only on virtue; more so, we like our friends for who they are as people, for their character, which includes not only their virtues, but also their vices. The mixture of virtues and vices, habits and peeves, and likes and dislikes as they intermingle in a friend result in a distinctive and unique individual whom we love for being just as they are.

A personal example will help me explore this insight. My dearest friend, we'll call her 'P' because she is intensely private, is the most beautiful woman I have ever met.[4] When I say that P is beautiful, however, I don't only mean that she is physically beautiful (which she is, very much so; she is a woman whose presence literally causes men to walk into walls). P, however, is a beautiful person in every sense. She is beautiful *and* she looks beautiful. She is, as we sometimes say, beautiful on the *inside* as well as on the outside. She is a brilliant scientist, a caring mother, and an incredibly generous and fun and funny person. Of course, she is more than all of that and I cannot possibly connote here even half of the special features that make her so wonderful, both in herself and, to me even more so, in our friendship. However, neither is she nor our friendship flawless. Perfection is not beauty; perfection is boring, beauty is interesting. Kathleen Higgins (2000) argues that flawlessness is one of the contemporary 'false paradigms of beauty' that has 'obscured the fact that human beauty manifests an ideal of balance and health that is neither self-conscious nor a consequence of deliberate effort' (p. 87).

So, just as we don't want to reserve valuable friendships for moral saints alone, neither should we want to reserve valuable friendship for aesthetic saints alone. For example, P can be impatient, proud, and stubborn and we sometimes butt heads because we share these traits. Yet, this occasional friction also grounds a deep mutual respect and creates precisely the friendship we have. Without these 'flaws', she wouldn't be P and our friendship wouldn't be as it is; I wouldn't feel for her or our friendship just as I do. And I absolutely cherish her and our friendship. Indeed, I wouldn't be precisely who I am if she were flawless; our friendship, which has spanned most of my life, and all the virtues and vices that have been honed and dulled within it have helped to create me. Over many years, we have grown and learned with and through one another; for example, due to my close friendship with P I have gotten a sense of what life is like for the visually stunning and have learned, to my surprise, that is it a mixed blessing and curse.

Perhaps 'liking' as understood by Elizabeth Telfer best captures what I mean by being attracted to a friend's persona. Actually, Telfer's (1970–1) account is quite relevant here as she explicitly refers to the liking involved in friendship as a 'quasi-aesthetic attitude':

> Liking is a difficult phenomenon to analyze. Although it is a reason for seeking someone's company, it is not simply equivalent to enjoyment of his company, as might first seem, as we can for a time enjoy the company of people whom we do not basically like – indeed, certain kinds of unpleasant people have their own fascination. It seems rather to be a quasi-aesthetic attitude, roughly specifiable as 'finding a person to one's taste', and depends partly on such things as his physical appearance, mannerisms, voice and speech, and style of life; partly on his traits and character, moral or other.
>
> This account of liking suggests that before we can like someone we have to tot up items in his nature and strike a balance between the attractive and the unattractive aspects of it. But in reality our reaction, like a reaction to a picture, is to a whole personality seen as a unified thing. (p. 253)

The liking we feel for our friends, in other words, cannot be explained like a mathematical equation. It is neither logical nor purely ethical or prudential. It is also aesthetic. According to Richard Avramenko, the best interpretation of Nietzsche's views on the ground of friendship is that friendships are groundless, being based on taste as opposed to reason. Avramenko (2008) explains that 'taste, unlike rationalism, has no universal aspirations... Whereas reason is nonarbitrary, taste is completely arbitrary. Taste resides in the abode of the particular... Taste is dangerous, uncertain, unpredictable; intellect and reason are safe and, at bottom, aim at certainty and predictability' (p. 291).

For example, consider my friendship with Lissa (who is also beautiful and whose name I can disclose because she is not intensely private; note the diversity). Lissa is a relatively new friend of mine and I like her very much, actually I've come to love *and* like her. However, it is impossible for me to explain *fully* why I feel for and with her as I do, which is not to say that I can't explain much about the grounds of our friendship. Likewise, it is impossible to explain *fully* why I like Louise Bourgeois' sculptures as much as I do, which is not to say I have nothing to say about the aesthetic merits of her work. To say that I am friends with Lissa, for example, because we share philosophy, motherhood, and the joys and struggles of both is true, but this amounts to only a very partial and painfully incomplete explanation of our bond. We're also friends because she is funny and smart with a decidedly dark streak, and in her company I feel at ease. But still, this misses much – and much of what explains my friendship with Lissa is ineffable. As Montaigne (1991) explains, if asked why I love a friend 'I feel that this cannot be expressed, except by answering: Because it was he, because it was I' (p. 192).

On this way of understanding the grounds of friendship, the love in friendship is something like faith: if one can offer a rational explanation of its causes that fully explains the phenomenon, then the feeling is neither faith nor love. We can't say precisely why we are friends with someone – why we like and love him or her. If we could, it would be evidence against the friendship. As Nehamas (2010) puts it, in any attempt to explain why one loves a particular friend there remains 'that most important element that can be expressed but can't be described' (p. 277). This difficulty may also be evidenced in Plato's *Lysis*, in which, as Alyssa Hennig (2010) suggests, perhaps more is *shown* than is said about the nature of friendship.

6 Conclusion: friendship and taste

Laurence Thomas (1993) explains how the feelings in friendship are an interesting mixture of, as he puts it, 'a matter of choice, on the one hand, and things that happen to us on the other' (p. 52). For Telfer (1970–1), the liking and sense of bonding essential to friendship is rational: 'In the sense that they are necessarily based on beliefs about the nature of the friend: we *like* a person and we feel we *are like* him because of what we think he is *like*' (p. 226). However, she qualifies this claim to rationality, noting that 'even where we *can* give our reasons for liking someone or feeling a bond with him, we cannot further justify these reasons, or explain why they operate in one case and not in another apparently similar' (Telfer 1970–1, p. 226). The groundless ground of friendship also helps us explain why we cannot predict with certainty whether two of our friends will be able to become good friends to one another, just as it is possible to recommend a film to a good friend in complete confidence that she'll love it, only to learn that she hated it.

(P, for example, surprised me by not enjoying *Little Miss Sunshine* after I recommended it to her.)

That the ground of friendship is based on taste, and largely on aesthetic taste, might make such relationships seem somewhat bankrupt or corrupt. Yet although the social and political issues discussed previously are serious and should give us pause, they are not aesthetic issues per se. The mere fact that we are often motivated and affected by aesthetic factors is not something about which we should be ashamed, what's shameful is underestimating these aesthetic motivations and affections, ignoring them and therefore accepting as given whatever consequences follow from them. Nehamas (2004) is right when he tells us that:

> It is ignorance, sometimes willful, that prevents people from recognizing that aesthetic experience is neither marginal to life nor restricted to a few privileged arts. Aesthetic experience is, in fact, inextricably woven into the everyday, so that perhaps no experience is completely unaesthetic... Art and beauty can be found everywhere, and therefore so can interpretation, without which they slip unnoticed by while we sail on oblivious of the wax blocking our ears. (p. 30)

And he continues, noting that the problem isn't that aesthetic matters are intertwined with various other values and motivations, it is rather that we too often fail to consciously attend to and take seriously the aesthetic in everyday life: 'The issue is only whether we know – or whether it matters to us to learn – how to discern the beauty and engage in its interpretation' (Nehamas 2004, p. 30). Noticing the aesthetic influences and nuances in various aspects of our lives, including those within friendships, is a necessary first step in arriving at a full interpretation of the lives we lead.

We have seen that aesthetic taste is involved in various aspects of friendships and sometimes works against our egalitarian commitments. The aesthetic forces in our personal relationships are ubiquitous. We choose friends, whether we want to admit it or not, based at least in part on aesthetic concerns – their appearance, their apparent status, their tastes. We cherish our friends for their unique individuality, which is due in part to apprehension of their aesthetic features and preferences. We create ourselves through interactions with friends and as a result of the aesthetic activities we share with them: the conversations we enjoy, the music we listen to, the films we discuss. The freedom in friendship intersects, parallels, and mutually informs the freedom and playfulness that is often constitutive of aesthetic appreciation and art making. Our friendships round out our lives, creating, in the ideal, an organic unity. Indeed, my life wouldn't be my life as I know it, I wouldn't be the *I* I am, but for my friendships, for example, with P and Lissa.

Attention to the aesthetic aspects of friendship helps to articulate the value of all friendships, not only those between the closest or best of friends. Of course, the closer the friendships and deeper the affection, the greater the impact the friendship will have on the texture or one's life and the creation of self. Berleant (2005) points out that 'sometimes... a building casts its character over an entire neighbourhood. For buildings are not self-sufficient objects but are places for human activity, determining the patterns of movement toward, into, and out of them, as well as within them' (p. 153). Likewise, sometimes a friendship casts its character over an entire life. For friends are not self-contained objects, but human beings with whom a person interacts, engages, and, as Pindar and Nietzsche put it, with whom she can *become the person she is* (Nietzsche 1974, sec. 270). How graceful or awkward my various friends are, that one is soft-spoken and another brash, the nervous tics of one and the calm resolve of another, one's excellent taste and the idiosyncratic likes of another, my friends' variable attractiveness, wittiness, pessimism, and optimism, all of these things add to the texture and narrative of my life. These features help make my life mine. My friends, that is, are colors, lines, and patterns on the canvas of my life.

Notes

1. I would like to thank the students in my Fall 2011 seminar at Bucknell University entitled Philosophy of Friendship for their willingness to explore the topic of friendship with me from virtually every philosophical perspective imaginable. I learned a great deal from and with them. I am also grateful for the helpful feedback, conversation, and comments I received on earlier drafts of this chapter from Jim Anderson, Damian Caluori, Sue Ellen Henry, Sherri Irvin, Eric Johnson, Aaron Meskin, Keith Sansone, Ryan Sappington, Jim Wilcox, and Hannah Zachary.
2. I thank Damian Caluori for bringing this point to my attention.
3. Thanks to Sherri Irvin for helping me see this point.
4. Readers might think I am biased in this assessment; I am quite confident I am not. Nonetheless, an interesting inquiry into aesthetic partiality in friendship is worth making to complement already existing inquiries into moral and epistemic partiality in friendship (philosophers who have explored the topic of partiality in friendship include, S. Wolf, L. Blum, A. Jollimore, and S. Stroud). Space and time constraints prevent me from pursuing this topic

here, but I plan to do so elsewhere in the near future. For insightful discussions of the interplay between personal feelings for a person and ascriptions of aesthetic properties to that person see David Novitz (1991) and Glenn Parsons (2010).

References

Aristotle (1984) *Nicomachean Ethics*, in J. Barnes (ed.), *Complete Works of Aristotle*, vol. 2 (New York: Oxford University Press).

R. Avramenko (2008) 'Zarathustra and His Asinine Friends: Nietzsche and Taste as the Groundless Ground of Friendship', in Von Heyking and Avramenko (eds), *Friendship and Politics: Essays in Political Thought* (Indiana: University of Notre Dame Press).

N.K. Badhwar (ed.) (1993) *Friendship: A Philosophical Reader* (Ithaca: Cornell University Press).

A. Berleant (2005) *Aesthetics and the Environment: Variations on a Theme* (Burlington, VT: Ashgate).

T. F. Cash and V. J. Derlega (1978) 'The Matching Hypothesis: Physical Attractiveness among Same-Sexed Friends', *Personality and Social Psychology Bulletin* 4, 240–3.

R. G. Collingwood (1958) *The Principles of Art* (New York: Oxford University Press).

R. W. Emerson (1991) 'Friendship', in M. Pakaluk (ed.), *Other Selves: Philosophers on Friendship* (Indianapolis: Hackett Publishing Company).

M. Friedman (1989) 'Feminism and Modern Friendship: Dislocating the Community', *Ethics* 99, 275–90.

R. Garland-Thomson (2009) *Staring: How We Look* (New York: Oxford University Press).

A. Hennig (2010) 'What Really Happened in Plato's *Lysis*', *Otherwise: An Online Journal of Philosophy*, http://otherwisejournal.net/contents.html, date accessed 6 January 2012.

K. Higgins (2000) 'Beauty and Its Kitsch Competitors', in P. Brand (ed.), *Beauty Matters* (Bloomington: Indiana University Press).

D. Hume (1998) 'Of the Standard of Taste', in S. Copley and A. Edgar (eds), *David Hume: Selected Essays* (New York: Oxford University Press).

F. Hutcheson (2004) *An Inquiry into the Original of Our Ideas of Beauty and Virtue* (Indianapolis: Liberty Fund).

I. Kant (1987) *Critique of Judgment*, trans. W.S. Pluhar (Indianapolis: Hackett Publishing Company).

C. S. Lewis (1960) *The Four Loves* (New York: Harcourt).

M. Lugones (1987) 'Playfulness, "World"-Travelling, and Loving Perception', *Hypatia* 2 (2), 3–19.

S. Mackinnon, C. Jordon, and A. Wilson (2011) 'Birds of a Feather Sit Together: Physical Similarity Predicts Seating Choice', *Personality and Social Psychology Bulletin* 37, 879–92.

C. Makos (2002) *Andy Warhol* (New York: Charta Art Books).

M. Montaigne (1991) *On Friendship* (New York: Penguin).

G. E. Moore (1929) *Principia Ethica* (New York: Cambridge University Press).

A. Mullin (2003) 'Feminist Art and the Political Imagination', *Hypatia* 18 (4), 189–213.
A. Nehamas (2010) 'The Good of Friendship', *Proceedings of the Aristotelian Society*, 110 (3), 267–94.
—— (2004) 'Art, Interpretation, and the Rest of Life', *Proceedings and Addresses of the American Philosophical Association*, 78 (2), 25–42.
F. Nietzsche (1974) [1882] *The Gay Science*, trans. W. Kaufmann (Vintage: New York).
D. Novitz (1989) 'Ways of Artmaking: The High and the Popular in Art', *British Journal of Aesthetics* 29 (3), 213–29.
—— (1991) 'Love, Friendship, and the Aesthetics of Character', *American Philosophical Quarterly* 28(3), 207–16.
M. Nussbaum (1999) *Sex and Social Justice* (New York: Oxford University Press).
G. Parsons (2010) 'A Face Only a Mother Could Love? On Maternal Assessments of Infant Beauty', in S. Lintott (ed.), *Motherhood – Philosophy for Everyone: The Birth of Wisdom* (Malden, MA: Wiley-Blackwell).
Plato (2006) *'Lysis'*, in C. D. C. Reeve (ed.), *Plato on Love* (Indianapolis: Hackett Publishing).
Y. Saito (1998) 'Appreciating Nature on Its Own Terms', *Environmental Ethics* 20 (2), 135–49.
J. Scott and D. Leonhardt (2005) 'Shadowy Lines That Still Divide', in B. Kelly (ed.), *Class Matters* (New York: Times Books).
N. Sherman (1993) 'Aristotle on the Shared Life', in N.K. Badhwar (ed.), *Friendship: A Philosophical Reader* (Ithaca: Cornell University Press).
M. Stocker (1993) 'Values and Purposes: The Limits of Teleology and the Ends of Friendship', in N. K. Badhwar (ed.), *Friendship: A Philosophical Reader* (Ithaca: Cornell University Press), 245–63.
J. Stolnitz (1960) *Aesthetics and Philosophy of Art Criticism* (New York: Houghton Mifflin).
C. Taylor (2006) *Symbiosism* (New York: Hamilton Books).
E. Telfer (1970–1) 'Friendship', *Proceedings of the Aristotelian Society* 71, 223–41.
L. Thomas (1993) 'Friendship and Other Loves', in N. K. Badhwar (ed.), *Friendship: A Philosophical Reader* (Ithaca: Cornell University Press).
L. Tolstoy (1996) *What Is Art?* (Indianapolis: Hackett Publishing).
A. Warhol (1975) *The Philosophy of Andy Warhol (From A to B and Back Again)* (New York: Harcourt Brace Jovanovich).

Index